Bank Insolvency Law in Developing Economies

The subject of bank stability has been under a great amount of political and legislative scrutiny since the mid-2007 to late-2009 global financial crisis. However, these efforts have centred on developed economies. Little coverage is given to strategies adopted by many developing economies. While there is a global discourse on the subject of insolvency generally, there is ample scope to contribute to the growing body of work on the narrow subject of bank insolvencies. This book provides a unique perspective on an emerging theme in at least two respects. First is the focus on selected developing economies and selected developed economies in the EMEA region alongside cross-border developments, with the objective of deciphering the regulatory approach to bank insolvencies. The second is the analytical consideration of methods that may be implemented to preclude or resolve bank insolvencies in developing economies. This book explores the nexus between developing economies and their banking institutions. Developing economies are acutely dependent on their banks for the functioning of their cash-based economies. Recent events, however, suggest a weakness in the long-term viability of some of their banks and a mixed-bag regulatory approach to redress this weakness. This book evaluates the effectiveness of regulatory frameworks in selected developing economies that are designed to prevent or resolve the insolvency of banks. At a time of global economic uncertainty, this book will prove to be a valuable resource to the discourse on the viability of banks, businesses, and economies in developing States.

Kayode Akintola is Assistant Professor in corporate insolvency law, School of Law, University of Sheffield, UK and Barrister, Gray's Inn, Supreme Court of Nigeria.

Folashade Adeyemo is Assistant Professor in banking law at the School of Law, University of Reading, UK, and Barrister and Solicitor, Supreme Court of Nigeria.

Routledge Research in Finance and Banking Law

Banking Regulation in Africa
The Case of Nigeria and Other Emerging Economies
Folashade Adeyemo

Crypto-Finance, Law and Regulation
Governing an Emerging Ecosystem
Joseph Lee

Regulation and Governance of Mutual Funds
United Kingdom and United States of America Perspectives on Investor Protection
Mohammed Khair Alshaleel

Regulation of Debt Collection in Europe
Understanding Informal Debt Collection Practices
Cătălin-Gabriel Stănescu

The Regulation of Megabanks
Global Systemically Important Banks and their Legal Frameworks
Katarzyna M. Parchimowicz

Regulating Open Banking
Comparative Analysis of the EU, the UK and Taiwan
Chang-Hsien Tsai and Kuan-Jung Peng

Bank Insolvency Law in Developing Economies
Edited by Kayode Akintola and Folashade Adeyemo

For more information about this series, please visit: www.routledge.com/Routledge-Research-in-Finance-and-Banking-Law/book-series/FINANCIALLAW

Bank Insolvency Law in Developing Economies

Edited by Kayode Akintola
and Folashade Adeyemo

Routledge
Taylor & Francis Group
LONDON AND NEW YORK

First published 2023
by Routledge
4 Park Square, Milton Park, Abingdon, Oxon OX14 4RN

and by Routledge
605 Third Avenue, New York, NY 10158

Routledge is an imprint of the Taylor & Francis Group, an informa business

British Library Cataloguing-in-Publication Data
A catalogue record for this book is available from the British Library

ISBN: 978-0-367-71186-3 (hbk)
ISBN: 978-1-032-00397-9 (pbk)
ISBN: 978-1-003-17398-4 (ebk)

DOI: 10.4324/9781003173984

Typeset in Times New Roman
by Apex CoVantage, LLC

For PNA, TTA, IMSB, RAJ, and RAA

Contents

Contributors

Dr Folashade Adeyemo, University of Reading

Dr Kayode Akintola, University of Sheffield

Dr Saleh Al-Barashdi, Sultan Qaboos University Oman

Professor Andrew Campbell, University of Leeds

Dr Sofia Ellina, Lancaster University

Pedro Ferreirinha, University of Minho

Mr Kenneth N.O. Ghartey, University of Ghana

Dr Anthony Idigbe, Senior Advocate of Nigeria

Dr Joy Malala, University of Warwick

Dr Hamiisi Junior Nsubuga, Middlesex University London

Clara de Sousa Alves, Cerejeira Namora Marinho Falcão

Dr Horace Yeung, University of Leicester

Preface

This edited collection on the management of distressed banks in developing economies is an extremely important addition to both the academic and practical literature on a subject which has been seen as increasingly important since the global financial crisis (GFC) which commenced around 2007.

The Editors, Dr Kayode Akintola and Dr Folashade Adeyemo have gathered an impressive group of scholars from a number of countries who examine and discuss a wide range of issues relating to distressed banks and bank insolvency in a number of African jurisdictions as well as two jurisdictions in the Gulf Region.

As the Editors note 'the discourse on the subject in many developing countries, such as African States, has been decidedly limited. This, in part, is due to the fact that these jurisdictions were insulated from the GFC, given their lack of engagement in sophisticated transactions' Sub-Saharan African banks have not, however, managed to avoid distress and insolvency. For example more than 25 banks have been liquidated since 2009 by central banks in Uganda, Kenya, and Tanzania and banks in the Gulf Region have not been immune either.

In fact, there was not much in the way of academic literature or debate on the subject of bank distress and insolvency prior to the pioneering work of Dr Tobias Asser at the Legal Department of the International Monetary Fund in the early years of this century. But what we now see as bank insolvency and resolution procedures were largely developed by the Federal Deposit Insurance Corporation in the United States from its formation in 1933 during the Great Depression. Bank insolvency law was not the norm outside the United States and some jurisdictions had no legal rules for banks. Banks were simply subject to the general corporate insolvency law. For example, when insolvency law was reformed in the United Kingdom in the 1980s, the reforms were based on the Report of Sir Kenneth Cork. The Cork report did not even mention the word 'bank.' Accordingly it was not until after the GFC that the UK introduced a bank insolvency law. It could not be put off any longer and by 2009 it was generally agreed that banks are sufficiently different from other types of corporations to deserve special treatment.

The Editors make the point that 'Developing economies are acutely dependent on their banks for the functioning of their economies' and this is undoubtedly true. So having a legal and regulatory framework in place is vitally important to ensure that orderly and effective action can be taken quickly when there is distress in the banking sector.

This edited collection clearly demonstrates the exceptional issues faced by banks in developing countries and points out many of the difficulties faced.

The selection of certain sub – Saharan Africa (Ghana, Kenya, Nigeria, Tanzania, and Uganda) provides an excellent backdrop for this study. This book deserves to be a major reference point for everyone with an interest in the regulation of banks. Those of us who have only focused on developed countries will learn much from reading about the issues faced by countries such as Uganda, Kenya, and Tanzania.

This scholarly work deserves to find a wide audience from academia, government officials, central banks, commercial bankers, and lawyers in the financial sector.

The Editors should be congratulated for making this work a reality and for recognising the need for such a work at this time. All the contributors have produced Chapters which are both relevant at the present time and which are of very high quality.

Professor Andrew Campbell
Emeritus Professor of International Banking and Finance Law
School of Law
University of Leeds
June 2022

Acknowledgements

This book is an expanded version of thoughts that emerged from the Bank Insolvencies in Developing Economies (BIDE) Conference that was held in April 2019. In the months and immediate years that would follow, it seemed like the COVID-19 pandemic thrust us and the world around us into a black hole with a gravitational pull so strong that we could not conceive a way out. Yet, a number of colleagues and institutions continued to support this book and our professional aspirations with unrelenting force and willpower that it would be remiss of us to not acknowledge them here. We are immensely grateful to all delegates, speakers and sponsors of the BIDE conference. In particular, we owe a debt of gratitude to Lancaster University, University of Reading and Stephenson Harwood LLP. Many thanks also go out to Professor David Milman and Professor Andrew Campbell. As subject matter experts, their thoughts (and witticisms) often deepened our perceptions on critical issues relating to insolvency law, banking law and bank insolvency law in recent years. Thanks are also due to the anonymous referees who provided constructive comments on the original proposal for this edited collection. We would also like to extend our gratitude to our colleague at Routledge, Siobhan Poole, who provided expert professional guidance in progressing this book to completion.

The editors and contributors are recognised experts in their respective fields or avid scholars of the subject matter. Their task was to produce a clear and accurate discussion of the relevant rules and/principles. This book is therefore a product of years of learning on the subject, and we are grateful to the contributors for their time and dedication to the brief. The law is stated as it stood on 1 June 2022.

Kayode Akintola and Folashade Adeyemo

1 June 2022

Part I

Bank Insolvencies in Developing Economies

1 *Prologue* The Management of Distressed Banks in Developing Economies

An Overview

Kayode Akintola and Folashade Adeyemo

Introductory

If we accept that business or commercial activities are the primary drivers of economic growth,[1] banks as institutional providers of commercial capital are key facilitators of the desired economic growth and stability in society. Thus, bank regulation, stability and insolvency are not trivial subjects. This is particularly so, more than a decade after the global financial crisis (GFC) of 2007–2009. The importance of these interconnected subjects is self-evident in current literature, much of which reflects upon the position in developed countries on issues such as enhanced regulatory response to internal and macroeconomic risk, streamlined role of bank regulators or central banking authorities, the introduction of bespoke bank insolvency law as well as a shift in the focus of bank insolvency law.[2]

In this context, the discourse on the subject in many developing countries, such as African states, has been decidedly limited. This, in part, is due to the fact that these jurisdictions were insulated from the GFC, given their lack of engagement in sophisticated transactions such as subprime mortgages. Nevertheless, the state of banking law in these developing economies, particularly those that relate to their fiscal stability and resolution of insolvency events, is also critical and deserving of tailored consideration for several reasons.[3] First, and an obvious point, is that the economies of these nations are also acutely dependent on capital and other banking provision of banks. A second point is that due to the proliferation of cross-border commerce, banks, non-financial institutions, and the economies in other jurisdictions have pecuniary exposures in these developing states that could be protected by effective regulation of banking entities. A third point, and closely linked to the second, is that many developing states remain strategic economic partners for developed nations, more so in a post-Brexit and -pandemic world.

This book presents a nuanced discussion of issues that impair bank stability in selected developing countries. Critically, it examines the law's response to the downside of a banking enterprise in those jurisdictions – insolvency. In so doing, it analyses some critical questions, including: how can the law of these jurisdictions preclude and resolve bank insolvencies?[4]; when insolvency

DOI: 10.4324/9781003173984-2

does occur, as it often does – or could – with legal-commercial enterprises, what ought to be the priority of the law in this regard?; should the priority of the bank insolvency law in developing economies be stratified along the lines of peculiar-structural attributes of developing states?; what aspects of the regime of bank insolvency law in developed nations could be adopted by these developing states, bearing in mind limitations associated with legal transplantation?;[5] and given the inter-economic dependence of developed and developing states highlighted earlier, how could developing states be best aligned with international standards when dealing with cross-border bank insolvencies? Unless otherwise indicated, the discussion of banks in this book relates to the activities of clearing, commercial and merchant banks as opposed to those of investment banks.

Bank Insolvency Law: A Case for Developing Economies

Developing economies are acutely dependent on their banks for the functioning of their economies, which are conventionally cash-based. Recent events, however, suggest a weakness in the long-term viability of some of their banks and a mixed-bag regulatory approach to redress this weakness. Despite credible sentiment expressed in the aftermath of the GFC that, on average, many banks in Africa are well capitalised and liquid,[6] we examine recent cases of bank failures and the associated local context, including the legal framework, to evaluate aspects of bank insolvency law that should be introduced or streamlined. This book also presents the issue of bank insolvency law in these developing states as a continuum: the legal structure of a bank, its operational and managerial structure, and its stakeholder structure all inform the cause, priority and resolution of a bank's insolvency. This is worthy of cursory amplification. As we shall see in the next section of this chapter, the legal/commercial vehicle of a banking business might raise the question of whether its insolvency ought to be resolved according to the ordinary insolvency norms that apply to non-bank businesses that use a similar vehicle. Further, the peculiar ownership of banks in these developing nations, particularly banks with dominant foreign ownership, opens the question of whether bank resolution mechanisms such as bail-in, rather than bail outs, ought to be *de rigueur* in such insolvencies. In addition, where should the priority of bank insolvency law in these developing economies lie? Which of the spread of stakeholders dependent on banks should be accorded priority by the law in an insolvency scenario – creditors or shareholders? If creditors, should priority of protection go to financial or depositor creditors? Should bank insolvency law in these states, rather than prioritise private interests, give precedence to fiscal stability?

At a time of global economic uncertainty, this book will prove to be a valuable resource to the discourse on the viability of banks, businesses and economies in developing economies. It also draws attention to the significant impact that these states, functioning with well-calibrated bank insolvency laws that offer improved investor and systemic protections, could have on a post-Brexit and -pandemic world by way of enhanced trade partnerships.

Managing Distressed Banks and Their Stakeholders

We now briefly turn attention to the legal nature of banks, and how this nature impacts upon current and proposed treatment of bank-stakeholder interests in developing economies in an insolvency scenario. It is evident that many banks are structured as companies. This verity ought not be taken for granted for at least four reasons. The first is that, even in developed economies, the business of banking was not always carried out through the corporate vehicle. For example, in the United Kingdom (whose laws were and are still routinely transplanted into the legal framework of many developing economies in the African region), banks were routinely structured as partnerships until the statutory recognition of the joint stock company and the associated twin concepts of separate legal personality and limited liability.[7] One should, of course, appreciate that the use of an ordinary partnership (which lacks the risk minimising devices of separate legal personality and limited liability)[8] as a vehicle for a commercial enterprise with acute economic dependencies was not sustainable, if not imperceptive. It therefore accords with reason that many bank proprietors swiftly transferred their business to newly incorporated companies in order to limit their personal and pecuniary liability as soon as the joint stock company was introduced in that jurisdiction.[9] That said, much of commercial life, and the law's response to the use of companies to further commercial activities, is about allocation of loss: if the corporate vehicle minimises the risk involved in a commercial enterprise, it would normally do so by allocating that risk to other stakeholders connected to that enterprise. Indeed, while the separate legal personality of a company and the limited liability of its shareholders may be seen as enterprise promoting devices as they minimise commercial risk, it is also arguable that the company's commercial counterparts see them as risk redistributing devices as they (the counterparts) will have to bear some or all of that risk in an insolvency scenario. This brings us to the second reason for highlighting the innate connection between companies and banks.

A company is a network of interests or 'nexus for contracts.'[10] For example, a corporate firm like a bank will encompass the interests of shareholders, the company itself, corporate managers, suppliers, consumers, employees, the state, to name a few. It is often convenient to categorise these interests in three forms: managers, shareholders and creditors. The corporate construct is therefore acute in this context due to the trade-off engendered by separate legal personality and limited liability, as well as the fundamentally divergent nature of these interests. The law's base response to these issues is to manage the corporate construct through contractual rights accentuated by legal provisions. In the context of banks, this response will include banking regulations. For example, in the European Union, there are rules that require banks to set aside enough equity capital to cover unexpected losses and keep themselves solvent in a crisis.[11]

This translates to the third reason for underscoring the legal nature of banks. Many banks, particularly those of systemic importance,[12] would be structured as public companies. The public company structure accentuates the trade-off engendered by separate legal personality and limited liability concepts. This is so because there is no restriction on the transfer of shares of such companies in the sense that they could be offered to the public. Moreover, such companies are more suited to trade on a cross-border basis, which increases their risk profile. Thus, the classic agency problem (that is, the potential conflict of interest between shareholders and managers/directors, or shareholders and managers/directors as insiders on the one hand and creditors or other external corporate participants on the other) that much of corporate law seeks to redress is not trivial in the context of a public commercial enterprise. Indeed, directors, as trustees, typically owe a fiduciary duty to the company which shareholders may seek to enforce whenever a corporate decision threatens the survival of the company. The economic impacts of the GFC have caused some bank shareholders to pursue enforcement of this duty.[13] It is, however, plain that traditional corporate law, despite its heightened regulation of public companies relative to private companies (which are largely deregulated) might not be sufficient to address economic and other aspects of the agency problem in the context of banks. For example, in many European nations, the minimum capital requirement for a public company is 25,000 euros.[14] This level of capital requirement, and the rules that underpin the corporate use of capital,[15] is at odds with the pecuniary exposures of banks. To take a very basic example, the deposits held by many banks would far exceed this sum, thus highlighting the value of some of the bank capital adequacy standards mentioned earlier.[16]

Whether structured as a public or private company, some of the interests that make up a bank network are also deserving of bespoke attention. This leads us to the fourth reason for highlighting the underlying nature of banks: the peculiarity of bank creditors. While many modern company and bank insolvency frameworks are engineered to rescue the financially distressed company and/the whole or part of its underlying business,[17] insolvency law in its core seeks to rationalise the interests of creditors.[18] Credit gives insolvency meaning; for an enterprise is typically insolvent due to its inability to meet its credit obligations. When a company is insolvent, or in the zone/vicinity of insolvency (twilight period),[19] it is not unusual to find that the law would impose upon corporate managers or directors a duty to the company to have regard to the interests of the company's creditors.[20] A rationale for this rule being that, since the insolvency of an enterprise would notionally signify a paucity of assets that may be used to satisfy outstanding pecuniary obligations to creditors,[21] it behoves the managers of the enterprise to enact strategies that could minimise the detriment to creditors whenever insolvency is reasonably foreseeable or does occur. In pure banking contexts, this state of events suggests that bank regulations (for example those that require maintenance of adequate capital referred to earlier) are not, on their own, sufficient to deal with incidences of bank insolvencies. Indeed, custom-built bank insolvency laws of many countries, some of which are presented in this book, attest to this.

Of equal importance, however, is the fact that creditors of a bank would include other banks (for example, due to the use of a payment or clearing house system) and depositors. The knock-on effect of a bank's insolvency on its bank-creditors may, therefore, generate a systemic crisis and will not be trivial from a macro-economic standpoint. In relation to depositor-creditors, we ought to briefly deal with two scenarios where a bank is insolvent: (a) the depositor/customer holds a deposit balance in their account; and (b) the depositor/customer is expecting a deposit payment in their account by way of fund transfer from another party. In the first scenario, it is trite law that the relationship between a customer and the bank is contractual or personal, not proprietary. It is for this reason that monies deposited into a bank account may be utilised by the bank as it deems fit, albeit ringfenced by a promise by the bank to return the money on demand (or other set condition) by the customer. This makes a customer's deposit balance property of the bank.[22] A bank, without more (such as a specific instruction from a customer) does not hold the funds in the account on trust for the customer.[23] It follows, therefore, that in this first scenario a bank customer with deposits in their account has loaned money to the bank. Where the bank is insolvent, the customer, subject to a unique insolvency law treatment that will be highlighted in the next subheading, will be an unsecured creditor. Many unsecured creditors get nil or paltry returns in an insolvency scenario.[24] This is tied to the verity that insolvency typically signifies inadequate assets to offset liabilities noted earlier, and the treatment of unsecured creditors in insolvency which would, ordinarily, require them to share any available assets rateably (*pari passu*) *inter se* following the satisfaction of prior claims (such as secured claims and insolvency expenses) according to statutory order of priority in the relevant jurisdiction.[25] With these in mind, while average retail customers may not be sophisticated commercial players, they are rational enough to make a run on a bank at the first signal of financial instability. To this end, many jurisdictions endeavour to preclude this incidence by non-insolvency policies that insure or automatically protect deposit amounts in bank accounts.[26]

We now briefly turn to the second scenario where a bank depositor/customer is expecting a deposit payment in their account and its receiving bank enters an insolvency procedure. A few legal-cum-commercial questions arise in this scenario. Is the customer/payee a creditor of the receiving-insolvent bank to the extent of the sum expected in its account? The answer to this ought to be that the receiving-insolvent bank will be liable where it has unconditionally accepted the payee as its creditor or unconditionally accepted the transfer from the paying bank.[27] Thus, the fact that the payee's bank account has not been credited should not dislodge the existence of the payee's credit claim against the bank. In this scenario, it is also apposite to ask whether the payer is a creditor of the receiving-insolvent bank? The logical response to this ought to be 'no'. The payer, as illustrated in the first scenario earlier, does not own the monies in their bank account. At best, the payment instruction to their bank (the paying bank) triggers a personal claim against the paying bank to complete the instruction or restore the payer's position if payment is possible without fault on the part of the payer.[28] The payment instruction, in principle, simply involves adjustments of balances in the relevant bank account and clearing house systems the banks use to effect the payment. If the preceding analyses are correct, then one ought to also ask whether the paying bank is a creditor of the receiving bank? The answer to this could depend on how payment by fund transfer between bank accounts is effected in the relevant jurisdiction. Let us take a domestic payment in England as an example, where the common systems for effecting such payments are the Clearing House Automated Payment System (CHAPS) and Bankers Automated Clearing Services (BACS). In these systems, the Bank of England (BOE) serves as intermediary between the banks and performance of the payment instruction should result in a concomitant debit and credit of the paying and receiving banks' accounts at the BOE. Ordinarily, because CHAPS facilitates same day payment, one could speculate that the receiving insolvent bank's account with the BOE might not have been credited with the payment amount and that failure to make such payment due to insolvency should not give rise to a credit claim in favour of the paying bank although other credit claims may arise due to loss suffered as a result of the insolvency-triggered default. However, it would appear that the receiving bank's account is credited following settlement on the Real-Time Gross Settlement (RTGS) System with funds received by the receiving bank before crediting the payee on the same day.[29] Similarly, BACS payment facilitates actual payment or credit to the payee's account by the third clearing day, and first requires the receiving bank to have been paid by the payer's bank on the second clearing day. As such, in either case, where the insolvency of the receiving bank precludes performance, then two alternative credit claims ought to arise against it in ordinary commercial contexts: one from the paying bank whose account in the BOE has been debited for the payment amount; or one from the payee expecting the deposit payment since it is plausible that receipt in the receiving bank's BOE account leads to unconditional acceptance of the payee as its creditor in respect of the amount transferred. We have only presented these scenarios to illustrate nuanced questions of credit and rationalisation of the creditors' interests that arise in ordinary corporate insolvencies, and how they could be more acute in bank insolvencies.

These are key private law questions on contract/proprietary rights that sit alongside critical macro-economic questions of financial stability. Thus, still using the example of a payment in England, it is clear that one response to this quandary is that the payment rules enable the BOE to suspend a bank if it appears likely that an insolvency event will occur in relation to that bank.[30] Moreover, and in relation to bank insolvency law, since payment systems like CHAPS are 'designated systems' for the purpose of the Financial Markets and Insolvency (Settlement Finality) Regulations 1999[31] (which apply in the European Union through Directive 98/26/EC of the European Parliament), there are rules to reduce risks associated with participation in payment and securities settlement systems by minimising the disruption caused by insolvency proceedings brought against a participant in such a system. For example, a 'transfer order', which will instruct a bank-participant in the payment system to place at the disposal of a recipient an amount of money by means of a book entry on the accounts and which results in the assumption or discharge of a payment obligation, cannot, generally, be invalid under ordinary insolvency law.[32]

Bank Insolvency Law: Précis

In this section, we briefly introduce typical bank insolvency procedures or systems that will be amplified in subsequent chapters of this book in the context of developing economies. The systemic importance of banks to economies often gives some banks the tag: *too big to fail*.[33] Contemporary events, such as the GFC, have taught us that this label reflects desperation more than reality. For the reality is that, like any corporate entity, banks may not always enjoy the perpetual succession associated with separate legal personality due, in part, to liquidity problems.[34] Moreover, big scalps of the GFC redress the fallacy that some banks were 'too big to fail'; for it cannot be assumed that governments would always provide a bail-out – an orthodox resolution strategy for financially distressed but systemically important banks.[35] Our preceding discussion on the nature of banks *qua* corporate entities suggests that the insolvency of banks poses a legal quandary in terms of the objective of bank insolvency laws, *viz*:

- should the legal framework focus on the rationalisation of creditor interests by, for example, effecting an optimum and fair distribution of the distressed bank's assets (a traditional objective of ordinary insolvency law)?
- should the legal framework prioritise rescue or rehabilitation of the financially distressed bank (a modern objective of ordinary insolvency law)? or
- should the legal framework prioritise systemic and financial stability (an objective of bank resolution regimes, particularly where the insolvent entity is a systemically important bank)

A preliminary point to note, however, is that the first objective, which is creditor-centric, is hardly conducive to resolving bank insolvency outcomes due to the nature of dependencies on these institutions, including those that might not fit the label of systemically important/too big to fail. Nevertheless, as we shall see later, this is not to say that the critical 'allocation of loss'[36] will fall on creditors in bank insolvencies due to a safeguard that ensures *no creditor in a bank insolvency is worse off than they would be in ordinary insolvency proceedings*.

In many jurisdictions, alongside regulatory measures such as adequate capitalisation or recapitalisation, transparent balance sheets, bail-in measures and structural reforms (ring-fencing) sit a bank resolution regime which will manage the insolvency of banks. The bank resolution regime is largely driven by the Financial Stability Board's (FSB) international standards for resolution regimes for banks and other financial institutions.[37] The standards set out 12 key attributes that should be part of the resolution regimes of all jurisdictions, and are primarily aimed at systemically important banks or financial institutions in order to preclude severe systemic disruptions occasioned by bank failure,[38] although the resolution regime in countries like the UK, which also apply the FSB's international standards, have extended their resolution regime to cover all banks, building societies and certain investment firms.[39] In the context of a bank's insolvency, the nub of the resolution regime is three-fold:[40] (a) rescue or restoration of the insolvent bank; (b) orderly winding-up (or 'wind-down') of the whole or part of the bank; and (c) effective cross-border cooperation and coordination in cross-border insolvency contexts.[41] Thus, bank insolvency procedures in many jurisdictions include terminal procedures such as **liquidation**, which facilitates orderly and timely realisation of available assets, distribution to creditors like depositors and closure of the bank. It will also include rescue procedures such as **administration**.[42] This procedure is used to either effect a rescue of the bank or its business and restore it to viability, for example through a sale of the business. Being part of the wider bank resolution regime, it is important to note that these procedures: (a) are normally modified to ensure that relevant objectives of the resolution regime (e.g., protecting insured deposits) can be achieved despite the firm entering insolvency. Once such objectives are fully achieved, the procedures revert to ordinary liquidation or administration; and (b) once modified, might involve the exercise of the broad and non-exhaustive list of resolution powers in the international standards, including overriding rights of shareholders, use of asset management vehicles, use of bail-in within the resolution regime to recapitalise, imposition of a moratorium, and temporary stay on exercise of contractual termination rights like *ipso facto* clauses.[43]

Given the impact of insolvency on creditors, it is worth noting that the bank insolvency and resolution regime's treatment of creditors is propitious. There are at least two reasons for this assertion. First is that the bank resolution regime is designed to be used at an early stage before the bank is balance-sheet insolvent (though it may be cash-flow insolvent),[44] and before all equity has been fully wiped out. This could ring-fence assets that could be used to satisfy creditor claims, which is made possible by a commercial reality where liabilities do not exceed assets. The second is the safeguard alluded to earlier that, in modified bank insolvency or resolution procedures, creditor hierarchy should be respected (including maintaining the subordination of equity to debt in bank insolvency proceedings) and no creditor should be worse off than they would be in ordinary insolvency proceedings.[45] Given that a key cog of these international standards is flexibility, this safeguard may, however, be altered to achieve designated aims, such as protection of depositor-creditors who are generally unsecured creditors and should, ordinarily, rank as junior claimants in insolvency. An example of this flexibility is to be found in the UK's treatment of uninsured deposits. Deposit amounts not covered by the Financial Services Compensation Scheme are now treated as secondary preferential debts in a bank's insolvency ranking above the prescribed part fund for unsecured creditors, claims covered by a floating charge security and ordinary unsecured creditors.[46]

Bank Insolvency Law in Developing Economies: The Outline

This edited book culls together contributions from subject experts, including academics, legal practitioners and insolvency practitioners. The mix of subject experts ensures the perspectives set out in the book are nuanced and appeal to a broader audience. The contributors bring with them varied experiences, which are instrumental in achieving the main themes and issues raised. In this text, we focus on selected African, Middle Eastern and European countries. Segments of the book are also devoted to harmonisation issues in bank insolvency law by reviewing model frameworks on cross-border insolvency law. The selected economies and frameworks, though not exhaustive, provide a veritable account of typical legal and commercial issues encountered in these regions when bank insolvencies occur, and allow for further analysis of their regulatory responses. The core of this text consists of two parts, the contents of which we now briefly outline.

Part I of this book explores bank insolvencies and associated laws or policies in a selection of developing economies in Africa. As with any text, it would be difficult to cover all the countries in this region. Therefore, the contributions to this text have been selected from Nigeria, Uganda, Kenya, Tanzania and Ghana. The choice of these countries was informed by various factors. Crucially, these countries have been at the forefront of legislative change in the region, given that the GFC and global pandemic have precipitated overdue-but-necessary changes to the way business is conducted in a region that is conventionally wedded to legislative inertia. Some of these countries have had specific changes to their (or simply introduced) banking, company, and insolvency regulatory regimes, which should, of course, have a bearing on the stability of banks or resolution of their pecuniary challenges in the long term. The first contribution in this part, Chapter 2, examines Nigeria. It provides a rigorous scrutiny of the efficacy of asset management companies (AMCs), bridge banks and securitisation in resolving financially distressed banks in the country often caused by non-performing loans (NPLs). Nigeria has introduced copious legislations that affect the business, solvency and the insolvency of banks. For example, there is the Banks and Other Institutions Act (BOFIA) 2020. BOFIA 2020 departs from the previous regulatory approach adopted by BOFIA 1991, including the way banks were licenced,[47] the revocation of bank licences,[48] redefining the role of the Nigerian Deposit Insurance Corporation (NDIC) in the resolution of banks in distress,[49] the creation of resolution tools,[50] and establishing a bank sector fund which provides funds for the operation of bridge banks.[51] From a company law perspective, Nigeria has introduced the Companies and Allied Matters Act 2020 (CAMA) 2020, an overdue change from CAMA 1990. The new Act introduced new measures designed to fast-track the process of registration and regulation of corporate vehicles, and to condense the compliance requirements for small and medium enterprises (SMEs) – a constituency that ordinarily brings much of the banking business in that jurisdiction. This piece of legislation also introduces governance controls that will impact the stability of banks *qua* public companies. These include the requirement of disclosure of multiple directorships and the introduction of a minimum requirement of three independent Directors on the board.[52] It also introduces an extensive insolvency regime, which includes Company Voluntary Arrangements and Administration as rescue/restructuring tools in insolvency;[53] these tools may operate in bank insolvencies following the attainment of resolution objectives in bespoke bank insolvency procedures. We ought also to point out the introduction of the Secured Transactions in Moveable Assets Act (STMA) 2017, which streamlines the process of creating, attaching and perfecting security interests in Moveable assets. This piece of legislation enables banks and businesses, particularly SMEs, to unlock the value of varied moveable assets in debt finance transactions. This is also critical to the viability of the banking business in the jurisdiction given the role of banks as the largest providers of debt capital.

The next contribution in Part I, Chapter 3, focuses on the East African Community (EAC). It analyses the collapse of banks and financial institutions in three African countries, namely, Uganda, Kenya and Tanzania. This chapter provides a historical analysis of the business and regulation of banking and its evolution in these member states, pre- and post-GFC. The chapter provides a structured analysis of the causes of bank insolvency, including NPLs, poor governance controls, and perceived abuse of the privileges of separate legal personality and limited liability in the context of foreign ownership of local banks. The chapter also examines effective legal responses to these issues, and makes a case for a regional cross-border banking resolution framework in the EAC as a measure that would combat bank insolvencies and harmonise the resolution tools in the region.

Part 1, Chapter 4, of the book contains a contribution on bank insolvency law in Ghana. In the case of Ghana, the Banks, and Specialised Deposit Taking Institutions Act (BSDIA) was enacted in 2016. This Act significantly improved the regulation and scrutiny of banks, one of the failings of the previous legislation, the Banking Act 2004. BSDIA 2016 operates in a similar way to the position adopted by Nigeria under BOFIA 1991 in relation to the issuance of directives or soft law to regulate banks in the system. In relation to resolution measures, this chapter juxtaposes causes of bank distress in the country and a rigorous scrutiny of formal options for resolving bank insolvency that may be found under the BSDIA 2016, including early intervention mechanisms, official administration, and liquidation.

The final contribution in Part 1 of this book is Chapter 5, which contains an exclusive and rigorous examination of the position in Kenya. It provides a useful accompaniment to Chapter 2 due to Kenya's proactive legislative response to bank stability and general insolvency law in the region. This chapter considers the role of insolvency law in safeguarding the financial stability of banks. The chapter examines the 'paradigm shift'[54] in the priority of international and local bank insolvency regimes. The chapter argues that effective balancing of the competing interests of creditors, depositors, and the public trust is necessary for addressing bank failures. The chapter also contextualises the role of the Kenyan Deposit Insurance Act 2012 in light of significant bank failures in the country since the 1980s.

Part II of this collection considers bank insolvency law using paradigms from the Middle East, Europe and Model Law. It therefore consists of three contributions to the subject. This part opens with Chapter 6, which examines the value of the relatively nascent institutional models of the Dubai International Financial Centre (DIFC) and the Qatar Financial Centre (QFC) to financial stability in the United Arab Emirates, Qatar and neighbouring regions. This is approached in three ways. The first is a comparison of the common law regulatory underpinnings of the centres with UK law in order to ascertain the degree of protection afforded to market participants, particularly on the occurrence of an event of default such as insolvency. The second is a robust examination of the centres' rules and regulations in order to underscore a perceived regulatory gap between the two systems. The third is an appraisal of the DIFC and QFC's approach to transplanting insolvency law to deal with the pecuniary problems of financially distressed bank participants. In this regard, the point is made that the region is yet to adopt bespoke bank insolvency law regimes and, to that extent, there is a case to be made for a sophisticated general insolvency regime and a competent application of such regime to bank insolvencies.

Chapter 7 is the following contribution in Part II of this text. This chapter focuses on Cyprus. Cyprus is a useful exemplar of a European system with experience of the direct systemic shocks associated with bank insolvency, which drove a raft of regulatory responses to redress the system. The Chapter critically examines the high incidence of NPLs in Cyprus as one of the root causes of the Cypriot banking crisis of 2013. Thus, we are in this chapter introduced to Cyprus as the country with the second highest number of NPLs in Europe, as well as how bank resolution tools in the EU Bank Recovery and Resolution Directive, such as bail in, could resolve NPLs-associated bank insolvency for the benefit of a range of stakeholders.

Chapter 8 is the final contribution in Part II of the text. The chapter explores bank insolvencies and the UNCITRAL Model Law. The thrust of this chapter is the global/multi-jurisdictional disruption that could be engendered by the insolvency of banks that operate on a cross-border basis, thus necessitating effective cross-border controls and cooperation in the resolution of such insolvencies. While admitting the hackneyed-but-critical point that the systemic importance of banks justify a special regime for bank insolvency, it makes the case that, in cross-border bank insolvencies, there is scope to enhance outcomes through tailored application of controls and cross-jurisdictional cooperation to be found in the principles of the UNCITRAL Model Law on Cross-Border Insolvency – operating alongside other international standards such as the FSB's principles discussed earlier.

Further Thoughts

This book is designed to explore the nexus between developing economies, their banking institutions, and bank insolvency frameworks. The book, through the carefully selected contributions, evaluates the regulatory frameworks in place to prevent or resolve insolvency. The selection of economies in this text is timely, as these economies have been at the forefront of legislative change and have also initiated change in terms of their commercial regimes. The issue of bank insolvency law in the context of developing economies is a sparsely covered subject. Thus, the diverse contributions help to provide a more holistic overview, and should serve as a panacea for further reforms on the law in those regions and reflections on best banking and governance practices. In that regard, readers of this text are treated to an analytical mix of views that are based on empirical, comparative, socio-legal, doctrinal, inter-disciplinary and commercial perspectives. Readers are therefore enjoined to enjoy this text at their own risk; after all, the business of banking is all about risk taking!

Notes

1 A point that is often captured using Gross Domestic Product (GDP) as a metric of economic growth in a time period.

2 For a general overview, readers may consult: J Black, 'Paradoxes and Failures: New Governance' Techniques and the Financial Crisis' (2012) 75(6) Mod Law Rev 1037–63; A Lui, *Financial Stability and Prudential Regulation: A Comparative Approach to the UK, US, Canada, Australia and Germany* (Routledge, 2016); B Wessels and M Haentjens, 'Three Paradigm Shifts in Recent Bank Insolvency Law' (2016) 31 J Int Bus Law Rev 396–400; R Lastra, *International Financial and Monetary Law* (OUP, 2017); G Moss, B Wessels and M Haentjens, *EU Banking and Insurance Insolvency* (OUP, 2017); U Volz, P Morgan, and N Yoshino, *Routledge Handbook of Banking and Finance in Asia* (Routledge, 2018); D Arner and others, *Research Handbook on Asian Financial Law* (Edward Elgar, 2020); D Singh, *European Cross Border Banking and Banking Supervision* (OUP, 2020).

3 For a recent overview of bank regulation in Africa, see F Adeyemo, *Banking Regulation in Africa: The Case of Nigeria and Other Emerging Economies* (Routledge, 2021).

4 For a general discussion of the role of the law in preventing banks from failing and in resolving bank failures when they do occur, see A Campbell and P Cartwright, *Banks in Crisis: The Legal Response* (Ashgate, 2002).

5 For an overview of legal transplants, see A Watson, *Legal Transplants: An Approach to Comparative Law* (2nd edn, UGA Press, 1993).

6 See T Beck and others, *Financing Africa: Through the Crisis and Beyond* (The World Bank, 2011) <https://documents1.worldbank.org/curated/en/633671468194645126/pdf/646640PUB0fina00Box361543B00PUBLIC0.pdf> accessed 30 April 2022.

7 See, for example, See Joint Stock Companies Act 1856, s 2; Companies Act 1862, ss 3–4.

8 By separate legal personality, we mean that the legislature of a country recognises a company validly incorporated according to the laws of its land as a separate legal (juristic) person, different to its officers, shareholders and other stakeholders. By limited liability, we generally mean that, in a company whose share capital is limited by shares, the liability of shareholders to contribute to the repayment of the company's debt is according to the law of the land limited to the amount, if any, unpaid on the shares held by the shareholder ('limited by shares' in contradistinction to 'limited by guarantee').

9 For a judicial discussion of this point in *Salomon v Salomon* in relation to the Companies Act 1862, see [1897] AC 22, at 23–27.

10 See J Armour and others, 'What Is Corporate Law?' in R Kraakman and others (eds), *The Anatomy of Corporate Law: A Comparative and Functional Approach* (3rd edn, OUP, 2017) ch 1.

11 These rules implement the Basel III agreement on bank capital adequacy standards and include: (a) Capital Requirements Regulation – CRR I and II; and (b) Capital Requirements Directive – CRD IV and V. As a basic rule, the amount of capital required depends on the risk attached to the assets of a particular bank.

12 For a brief consideration of the policy and legal response to systemically important banks or the notion of 'too big to fail,' see the next section titled 'Bank Insolvency Law: Precis.'

13 See, for example, an unsuccessful suit for breach of fiduciary duty brought by the shareholders of Lloyds TSB Group Plc against directors of the bank in relation to the takeover of Halifax Bank of Scotland (HBOS) on the back of the 2008 financial crisis in *Sharp v Blank* [2019] EWHC 3096 (Ch).

14 See Directive (EU) 2017/1132, Art 45. In the UK, this minimum requirement was transposed as £50,000 – Companies Act 2006, s 763. By way of comparison with some developing economies: Nigeria – ₦2,000,000, Companies and Allied Matters Act 2020, s 27(2)(a); Ghana – abolished the minimum capital requirement and replaced it with the concept of 'stated capital' in Companies Act 2019 (Act 992), s 68. Foreign entities with a trading company, however, may have to invest a minimum capital of up to not less than $1,000,000 (USD) – Ghana Investment Promotion Centre Act 2013 (Act 865), s 28; Uganda – similar to the position of stated capital in Ghana, Companies Act 2012, ss 6–7.

15 Subject to rules on distribution and reduction of capital, a company's capital is, generally, to be applied in furtherance of its business.

16 See (n 11) above and accompanying text.

17 For an overview of bank insolvency law, see 'Bank Insolvency Law: Precis' later.

18 See, generally, K Akintola, *Creditor Treatment in Corporate Insolvency Law* (Edward Elgar, 2020).

19 This expression is, admittedly, nebulous. In common law jurisprudence for example, it has been taken as admitting the following contexts: 'doubtfully solvent' – *Brady v Brady* [1988] BCLC 20, p 40 (Nourse LJ); 'parlous financial state' – *Facia Footwear Ltd v Hinchliffe* [1998] 1 BCLC 218, p 228f–228g (Sir Richard Scott V-C); 'in financial difficulties' – *Re MDA Investment Management Ltd* [2004] 1 BCLC 217 [70] (Park J); 'near insolvency' – *Liquidator of Wendy Fair Ltd v Hobday* [2006] EWHC 5803 (Ch) [66] (Peter Smith J); and 'borderline solvency' – *Eastford Ltd v Gillespie* [2012] BCC 303 [15] (Lord Hardie). A review of the authorities will also be found in *BTI 2014 LLC v Sequana SA* [2019] EWCA Civ 112, [2019] 2 All ER 784.

20 See for example, *Liquidator of West Mercia Safetywear Ltd v Dodd* (1988) 4 BCC 30; *BTI 2014 LLC v Sequana SA* [2022] UKSC 25; Companies Act 2006, s 172(3).

21 In law, the balance sheet test (where liabilities exceed assets) and cash-flow insolvency test (where the entity is unable to pay its debts as they fall due) are 'deemed' indicators of insolvency. A commercial approach to the use of these tests will be found in the UK Supreme Court decision in *BNY Corporate Trustee Services v Eurosail-UK 2007–3BL Plc* [2013] UKSC 28.

22 See *Foley v Hill* (1848) 2 HLC 28 (HL); *Foskett v McKeown* [2001] 1 AC 102 (HL) at 127 (Lord Millett).

23 See also *Zumax v FCMB & Ors* [2019] EWCA Civ 294.

24 For an overview of unsecured creditor outcomes in insolvency proceedings, see R Mokal, *Corporate Insolvency Law: Theory and Application* (OUP, 2005) ch 5; K Akintola, 'The Prescribed Part for Unsecured Creditors: A Pithy Review' (2017) 30 Insol Intl 54; K Akintola, 'The Prescribed Part for Unsecured Creditors: A Further Review' (2019) 32 Insol Intl 67; Akintola (n 18) chs 3–4.

25 On the question of priority of creditors in bank insolvencies, see also the brief discussion of the Financial Stability Board's (FSB) international standards for resolution regimes for banks and other financial institutions (Key Attributes, particularly Key Attribute 5) in the next section.

26 See for example the Financial Services Compensation Scheme in the UK (www.fscs.org.uk/what-we-cover/) and other deposit insurance schemes presented in subsequent chapters of this book. It is also worth noting that customers in common law jurisdictions with a recognised system of equity and trusts may, pre-insolvency, seek to retain a proprietary interest in the deposit by giving the funds to the bank for a particular purpose (other than in the ordinary course of ordinary banking activities) on the

understanding that the bank is not free to apply the money for any other purpose. See *Barclays Bank Ltd v Quistclose Investments Ltd* [1970] AC 567; *Cf Zumax v FCMB & Ors* (*supra*). This, of course, would hardly be convenient for routine bank customers seeking to make regular deposits.
27 *Tayeb v HSBC* [2004] EWHC 1529 (Comm).
28 Such restoration may not be possible where the payer has provided wrong bank account details and the payment is made to a wrong person, who has now absconded with the funds – see *Tidal Energy Ltd v Bank of Scotland Plc* [2014] EWCA Civ 1107. In England, a 'Confirmation of Payee' scheme has been introduced which allows a payer to check whether the details provided by the payee matches the name associated with the account number and sort code they are paying, and decide not to make the payment if necessary. Thus, the onus is still on a payer to ensure they are satisfied to continue the payment transaction.
29 Information available on <www.bankofengland.co.uk/payment-and-settlement/chaps?msclkid=3c86986cd11d11ecad4c49ae1a7f19d0> accessed 30 April 2022.
30 See, for example, Bank of England, *CHAPS Reference Manual* (January 2022), 6.8(f). A list of insolvency events are specified in 8.6(a) to 8.6(e) inclusive and 8.6(g).
31 UK SI 1999/2979.
32 ibid, part III, Regs 13–19. Regulation 20 provides that the modifications to the law of insolvency cease to apply to a transfer order which is entered into a designated system after insolvency, unless the transfer order is carried out on the same day as the insolvency and the relevant persons do not have notice of the insolvency at the time of settlement.
33 Useful reflections on the notion of 'too big to fail' will be found in G Tett, *Fool's Gold: How the Bold Dream of a Small Tribe at J.P. Morgan Was Corrupted by Wall Street Greed and Unleashed a Catastrophe* (Free Press, 2009); AR Sorkin, *Too Big to Fail: Inside the Battle to Save Wall Street* (Penguin, 2010).
34 See G Farrell, *Crash of the Titans: Greed, Hubris, the Fall of Merrill Lynch, and the Near Collapse of Bank of America* (Crown Business, 2010) 267.
35 See again *Sharp v Blank* [2019] EWHC 3096 (Ch) at [128].
36 We have already made the point in the preceding section that the fundamentals of corporate law, which also applies to banks, is about allocation of loss.
37 FSB, 'Key Attributes of Effective Resolution Regimes for Financial Institutions' (15 October 2014). <www.fsb.org/wp-content/uploads/r_141015.pdf> accessed 30 April 2022.
38 ibid, preamble and Key Attribute 1.
39 More information <www.bankofengland.co.uk/financial-stability/resolution> accessed 30 April 2022.
40 FSB (n 37) Key Attributes 3 and 7.
41 For a discussion of cross-border bank insolvencies and the UNCITRAL Model Law, see ch 8.
42 An example is the UK Bank Administration, see Banking Act 2009, part 3.
43 FSB (n 37) Key Attribute 3.2.
44 For a discussion of a pragmatic approach to the question of balance sheet and cash-flow insolvency tests, see the UK Supreme Court decision in *BNY Corporate Trustee Services v Eurosail-UK 2007–3BL Plc* [2013] UKSC 28.
45 Otherwise the creditors would be entitled to compensation. See FSB (n 37) Key Attribute 5.
46 See Banks and Building Societies (Depositor Preference and Priorities) Order 2014 (SI 2014/4386).
47 BOFIA 2020, s 41.
48 ibid s 12 (1)–(9).
49 ibid s 34 (2).

50 ibid s 41.
51 ibid ss 74–94.
52 See, generally, CAMA 2020, ss 275, 278, 307.
53 ibid chs 17–18.
54 See again, Wessels and Haentjens, 'Three Paradigm Shifts in Recent Bank Insolvency Law' (n 2) above.

2 Distressed Banks and Asset Management Companies

Evaluating AMCON as a Bank Resolution Tool for Managing Non-Performing Loans in Nigeria

Anthony Idigbe

Evaluating AMCON as Bank Resolution Tool for Managing Non-Performing Loans in Nigeria

According to a 2021 World Bank study, non-performing loans (NPLs) erode profitability, threaten banks' solvency and potentially financial sector stability.[1] The study found that effective insolvency and creditor/debtor rights (ICR) regimes facilitate debt recovery, reduce credit costs, increase access to finance, and improve NPL levels.[2] The International Monetary Fund (IMF) estimates that Africa's non-performing loans (NPL) total $35 billion as of 2017, and more than 30 African states have an NPL portfolio that is greater than 10% of their GDP.[3] Moreover, the World Bank estimates that the stock of NPLs in Africa is expected to rise because of the COVID-19 pandemic.[4]

The statistics on financial distress and liquidation in Nigeria are unreliable.[5] However, the International Monetary Fund (IMF) estimates that NPLs across Nigerian banks have doubled since 2015.[6] The Economic Confidential Annual States Viability Index (ASVI) reported that 17 (seventeen) out of the 36 (thirty-six) states of the federation were insolvent, with internally generated revenue (IGR) for 2017 far below 10% of their receipts from the Federation Account Allocation (FAA).[7] The sub-sovereign insolvency resulted in federal government bailout measures for the sub-sovereigns.[8] NPLs in Nigeria are complicated by the sub-sovereign states' insolvency, many of whom are highly indebted to the banks through loans and bonds. There is no procedure for managing sub-sovereign insolvency. The Nigerian Deposit Insurance Corporation (NDIC) and Central Bank of Nigeria (CBN) Annual Reports, over the period 2007 to 2019, indicate that the NPL portfolio of banks reduced from a high of 37.3% in December 2009 to 6% in December 2019.[9] Because NPLs can undermine the financial stability of the banking sector, several tools exist for managing NPLs, such as direct invention through asset management companies, an improved environment for ICR-based workout of NPLs and an active distressed asset market.[10] The paper seeks to understand the relationship between the noted drop in NPL in Nigeria between 2007 and 2019 and the application of the tools for managing bank financial distress, primarily the asset management tool.

DOI: 10.4324/9781003173984-3

The establishment of Asset Management Company of Nigeria (AMCON) in 2010, just after the peak of the effects in Nigeria of the 2007 to 2009 global financial crisis, was "for the purpose of efficiently resolving the non-performing loan assets of banks in Nigeria." The objective of AMCON is to assist eligible financial institutions (EFI) in disposing of their eligible bank assets (EBA). It achieves this by acquiring them efficiently, managing, disposing of, and obtaining the best possible return on such acquired assets.[11] On the other hand, ICR-based regimes seek to address financial distress between the debtor and creditors using the court system and without any third party or public fund involvement.

The Act empowers the Central Bank of Nigeria (CBN) to issue guidelines designating any class of bank assets as EBA.[12] AMCON may purchase such assets within three (3) months or other extended periods up to three (3) years, as the CBN may approve.[13] The consideration to be furnished by AMCON for the eligible assets is a 7 (seven) year bond or other security instrument issued by it and approved by the CBN.[14] The CBN can also specify the maximum percentage of the eligible class of bank assets that an eligible financial institution may retain in its books.[15] It is required to offer any EBA above the specified percentage to AMCON for purchase. The NDIC may also recommend EBAs for purchase.

The law's objective is that AMCON would fully recover the value of the NPLs it has purchased through NPL consolidation and extensive recovery powers vested in AMCON.[16] Also, the law upsets and reverses contractual rights and securities law priorities and giving precedence to AMCON in disputes with bank debtors over collaterals and contracts.[17] These powers raise potential issues of breach of guaranteed constitutional property rights. However, under the regular ICR regime, it is not unusual for the procedure to adjust creditors' and debtors' rights, and settled contractual and security principles become unsettled with the required level of consent. For instance, under the United States Bankruptcy Code, filing a Chapter 11 bankruptcy results in an automatic stay, meaning that secured creditors could no longer exercise their security rights.[18] Similarly, the Companies and Allied Matters Act 2020 (CAMA 2020) now provides that on the appointment of an administrator, no step shall be taken to enforce security over the company's assets, repossess goods in the company's possession, enforce landlord forfeiture, commence or sustain legal proceeding, without the administrator's consent or court's permission.[19] The AMCON Act introduces many general insolvency restructuring concepts.[20] However, AMCON's use of these tools is not in the context of a collective proceeding of all creditors, as AMCON is the only creditor. Under the regular corporate insolvency regime, the proceedings are usually joint.

In meeting its objective, AMCON, from inception till 2020, acquired the EBAs or NPLs of various EFIs in three tranches.[21] The top 5 EFIs represent 58.18% of the 12,743 purchased EBAs. AMCON "bought 12,743 Eligible Bank Assets (EBAs) but has so far resolved about 4,000 EBAs while more than 8,000 EBAs are still outstanding."[22] The data confirms that the AMCON resolution success rate is about 30%. The justification for bank resolution regimes such as the AMCON intervention in Nigeria is that the regular corporate insolvency system is inadequate for managing bank financial distress.[23] The distress of banks can have a significant impact on the economy and lead to systemic collapse.[24] Apart from providing credit and liquidity, banks' other functions, such as payment processing and 'transmission belt for monetary policy to the economy,' render them too valuable to liquidate because of distress alone.[25] Bank resolution allows for applying unique restructuring and insolvency options for banks not necessarily available under ICR systems.

In many ways, Nigeria's regular corporate insolvency regime has lagged behind the bank resolution regime. The World Bank asserts that effective insolvency and creditor rights systems are essential for financial system stability and improve NPL levels.[26] However, between 1990 and 2016, government policy reform and the law on general creditor rights and insolvency in Nigeria were slow. In particular, before the global financial crisis of 2008 to 2009, there was no special insolvency regime for managing bank insolvency, and banks either failed or got bailed out with no middle way of restructuring their assets, which AMCON intervention now offers. While bank resolution provided resolution tools to resolution authorities such as the CBN and the NDIC through laws like the NDIC Act and the AMCON Act, the reform of creditor rights and the insolvency regime only picked up pace between 2017 and 2020. The enactment of the Credit Reporting Act, 2017, Secured Transaction in Movable Assets 2017 and the Companies and Allied Matters Act 2020 improved creditor rights by auditing the persons available for good credit, expanding access to credit by enabling the creation of security interest in movable assets and for creating new restructuring procedures such as administration and company voluntary arrangement.

The chapter is in four sections with Section: "Design of Effective Creditor Rights and Insolvency System to Manage Financial Distress" considering the design of effective ICR and bank resolution regimes to manage financial distress. Section: "Bank Regulation and the NPL Problem in Nigeria" discusses bank regulation and resolution and the NPL problem in Nigeria. Section: "Non-Performing Loans and Implementation of AMCON Intervention Tool" evaluates the performance of the AMCOM resolution tool in managing NPLs. Section: "Dealing With the Limitations of the AMCON Resolution Tool" evaluates the policy responses to the AMCON intervention's limitations regarding enhancements to the device and improvement in the ICR regime. The paper does not consider the impact of the COVID-19 pandemic on NPLs.

The paper concludes that the ICR and AMCON resolution regimes' misalignment explains the low exit percentage of 30% from EBAs acquired by AMCON. A financial distress management system must provide for financial emergencies, epidemics, or panic to be managed through bank resolution when they occur before returning to a regular ICR regime when the distress abates. An effective ICR regime reduces the build-up of NPLs and eases exit from bank resolution to a distressed asset market. There is a dependency between the corporate insolvency framework and the bank resolution regime. The cycle is complete when corporate insolvency effectively supports the bank resolution regime.

Design of Effective Creditor Rights and Insolvency System to Manage Financial Distress

According to Stijn Claessens et al., if the government takes no action to manage financial distress, significant sections of the economy may remain distressed for an extended period, resulting in large, socially unacceptable losses in output and employment.[27] Consequently, in a systemic crisis, the government's first role is to define rules that lead to practical private restructuring efforts.[28] Following a review of the East Asian financial crisis of 1997–98, they found that the absence of adequate insolvency regimes considerably complicated and slowed down the process of corporate restructuring and institutional reform, an issue not given much priority despite the rapid economic growth before the economic downturn of that time.[29] Stijn Claessens et al. contend that a vicious cycle of self-reinforcing financial distress requires government intervention in the form of an efficient insolvency and restructuring framework for the private restructuring of debts and liquidations as appropriate without the need for public intervention.[30] Finally, they argue that the injection of new government funds is the most challenging aspect of restructuring. The government should not, in principle, be in the business of paying for private companies and financial institutions' mistakes except for the limited purpose of reflating the economy.[31]

Therefore, the government's utilisation of intervention tools should be short-term, while long-term intervention would involve rules that encourage a private restructuring regime.[32] Since the AFC, there have been two other financial crises.[33] The Financial Stability Board (FSB) is the multilateral body established following these financial crises to promote global financial stability by coordinating national financial institutions and international standard-setting bodies.[34] It reviewed the 2008 Global Financial Crisis (GFC) and developed the Key Attributes for an Effective Financial Resolution Regime to avoid a similar global crisis.[35] FSB Key Attributes recommends that the regulator in a global financial institution's home state has a clear mandate and power to intervene, independence to act, adequate resources, corrective and remedial powers, and improved techniques that focus on the outcome.[36] Lehmann argues that bank resolution is key to avoiding a repetition of a global financial crisis requiring a bailout of failing financial institutions with taxpayers' money.[37] It permits the recapitalisation of banks or winding them down in an orderly fashion without creating systemic risk.[38] Ari et al. of the International Monetary Fund (IMF) found that reducing pre-crisis vulnerabilities and promptly addressing NPL problems during a crisis is essential for post-crisis output recovery.[39]

The use of AMCs to manage the toxic assets in banks' books was one of the tools available under the post-financial crisis bank resolution regime. NPLs are loans and mortgages on which the debtors cannot make the scheduled payments to cover interest or capital reimbursement for over 90 days from the due date or loans assessed as unlikely to be repaid by the debtor.[40] The European Central Bank (ECB) issued its Guidance on Non-Performing Loans for the prudential regulation of NPLs.[41] The Guidance adopted the strategy of mass standardisation and application of short and long-term forbearance measures to enable the conversion of NPLs to tradable instruments. NPLs, once standardised and tradable, can be easily disposed of to third parties through sale to AMCs on securities exchanges. Besides, it can be the basis for settlement, restructuring or liquidation.[42] Mansilla-Fernandez, Arner et al. argue that balance sheet restructuring and AMCs to deal with NPLs are often the best choices in a systemic financial crisis.[43] They also argue that the bail-in procedure is the best approach for non-systemically important financial institution failures occurring outside of the systemic crisis.[44]

However, dealing with NPLs involves more than bank resolution using balance sheet restructuring and AMCs because it requires reducing pre-crisis vulnerabilities and effective ICR that improve NPLs.[45] Aiyar et al. early study of the problem found that dealing with NPLs would typically involve four components: tightening supervisory policies (prudential regulation), insolvency reforms, skills and capacity building, and development of the distressed debt market.[46] Baudino and Yun argue that key country characteristics can constrain NPL resolution.[47] They identified vital country characteristics as the size of the NPL problem and NPL resolution, the macroeconomic context and structural banking sector issues, the type of underlying assets, fiscal space and legal and judicial constraints.[48] They then suggest an approach that recognises the limitation imposed by country-specific characteristics on expanding the proposed NPL resolution toolkit. They conclude that ensuring adequate interaction between the resolution policy and other macroeconomic and macroprudential policies mitigates the NPL problem.[49] Such an approach would reveal the policy space for NPL resolution, which can accommodate country-specific characteristics.[50]

Using limited public funds to resolve bank financial crises has not substantially changed from what Claessens et al. proposed.[51] The current approach is towards eliminating any short-term public funding of bank resolution schemes through additional measures such as recovery and resolution plans targeted at using creditors' funds before resorting to public funds.[52]

The other aspect of designing a framework for managing financial distress is the corporate restructuring framework consisting of a business rescue or reorganisation scheme and formal liquidation.[53] However, as Westbrook pointed out, an insolvency system's design involves more than liquidation and restructuring. It must include effective creditor rights and other support systems such as tax and court administration.[54] Using the health industry as the comparator, he argues that systemic corporate distress is like an epidemic.[55] It requires special rules to deal with it based on a robust structure of an effective insolvency regime of regulations and experienced administrators.[56] He suggests that the system returns to normal after overcoming the financial epidemic. The regular ICR should deal with reorganisation or business rescue, liquidation, priorities, secured creditors' rights and limitations, and transnational cooperation. It should also involve institutional reform and reform of related areas of law and administration.[57] Explaining these relationships, Westbrook argues that an efficient and effective individual collection system ensures that debts and collaterals are fully collected and forces insolvent persons into bankruptcy proceedings to avoid collection.

On the other hand, an inefficient system creates NPLs as insolvent companies continue incurring more irrecoverable debts.[58] A recent World Bank study confirms that the more efficient the ICR system, the greater its ability to deal with insolvent companies without the stockpiling of NPLs in banks' books, leading to bank financial distress and risk contagion or systemic collapse.[59] The regular insolvency system could deal with normal corporate insolvency. Still, Westbrook recognises that there may be a need for additional measures that must be preplanned and ready to be activated in a financial pandemic, just like public health epidemic measures. Bank resolution offers this assurance for managing banks' financial distress because banks play a crucial role in the financial system.[60]

In the context of corporate insolvency, the orthodox focus of bankruptcy, from liquidation to restructuring, is to maximise returns to the creditor and provide honest and viable debtors with a second chance.[61] However, maximising returns to creditors is no longer the only focus of insolvency regimes. Insolvency now recognises dealing with financial distress and seeking the "next best alternative" as a significant area of focus. The COVID-19 pandemic has further drawn attention to the need to preserve businesses and employment rather than creditors' interest in a pandemic. Various measures by many states restrict creditors' right to commence winding up or bankruptcy proceedings and offer generous workout terms to debtors.[62] The US Chapter 11 Bankruptcy Code has never been based on proof of insolvency but on good faith that the petitioner is in financial difficulty requiring intervention. The EU and the UK have adopted a similar approach to the US. There is a movement towards convergence on bankruptcy intervention occurring at first sight of financial distress to save the business and employment other than creditors. New procedures such as preventive orders, cross-class cram-down and other concepts based on relieving financial difficulties before insolvency now blur differences between the US and Eurocentric bankruptcy traditions.[63]

Bank Regulation and the NPL Problem in Nigeria

Nigeria is the biggest economy in Africa and has the largest population of 200.9 million as of 2019.[64] It is one of the few countries where the indigenous people had early access to the banking business.[65] Indigenous banks mushroomed even though the colonial government doubted the indigenous people's ability to do business or provide banking services.[66] The colonial government also had a strategy of encouraging only British and European banks and companies.[67] Before 1952, banking was unregulated in Nigeria, and there was an absence of a concise definition of banks and banking business.[68] Macro and micro factors contributed to the failure of banks both before and after independence, including the rapid increase of indigenous commercial banks with weak management.[69] Since colonial interest did not favour the existence of indigenous businesses' the usual remedy for insolvency of firms, inclusive of banks, was liquidation and, at times, prosecution of their promoters and managers.[70]

However, bank financial distress has a broader implication than ordinary firms' collapse because of its contagion effect and the government's need to encourage credit expansion, maintain the payment processing system and execute monetary policy through banks.[71] Eva Hupkes argues that special entry regimes for banking business and prudential regulation became well established by the 1930s.[72] International Monetary Fund (IMF) studies of the Asia banking crisis of the late 1990s showed an additional need for a special insolvency regime for bank restructuring.[73]

The history of banking in Nigeria follows the same pattern. The system started as unregulated, and then, following the Paton Report, the Bank Ordinance was enacted in 1952. Subsequently, the government introduced prudential regulation and a special insolvency regime for bank resolution. Establishing entry requirements and prudential regulation in Nigeria intends to improve banks' management and reduce financial distress risk.[74] The entry and prudential requirements included licensing, capital adequacy ratios, reserve and inspection.[75] According to the Paton Report, these entry and prudential regimes aimed to safeguard bank depositors by improving management.[76] Based on the Paton Report, the Central Bank of Nigeria (CBN) was set up in 1958 to regulate the banking industry.[77] From 1958 to 2008, the CBN applied entry requirements and prudential regulation as the primary way of regulating banks. When a bank was in financial distress, and prudential and internal restructuring efforts had failed, the preferred means by which the CBN resolved bank insolvency was liquidation in line with the regular corporate insolvency regime.[78]

The government established the Nigeria Deposit Insurance Corporation (NDIC) in 1988 to secure bank depositors' priority within the regular insolvency regime.[79] The NDIC operates as an insurance scheme with special priority ranking rules favouring bank account holders.[80] It also acts as the liquidator for insolvent banks that have lost their banking licence.[81] The loss of banking licences and liquidation of banks had reduced banks from about 90 to 25 following the December 2005 recapitalisation requirement of CBN.[82] Ogowewo and Uche argue that the bank recapitalisation exercise of 2005 was a misguided approach to the industry's consolidation.[83] Depositors were shut out of their deposits until NDIC could pay a dividend. The system could not take another lockout for depositors so soon when the Nigerian capital market and banking system experienced financial distress between 2008 and 2009 following the GFC or Global Meltdown.[84] Unfortunately, existing measures, such as banks' liquidation and recapitalisation exercises, were insufficient to respond to Nigeria's bank failures following the GFC.[85] The government, therefore, adopted other measures, such as bridge banks and the establishment of AMCON, among other bank resolution measures, to deal with the crisis.[86] Adeyemo provides a comprehensive account of regulatory responses to bank financial distress in Nigeria, including an analysis of the recently enacted Banks and Other Financial Institutions Act 2020 (BOFIA 2020), which has limited the use of the NDIC-style liquidation approach to managing bank insolvency.[87] Adeyemo argues that despite these measures, banking regulation in Nigeria is reactive and not proactive and has not achieved the regulatory objective.[88]

Hupkes argues that banks require a special insolvency regime to prevent contagion, maintain access to credit, continue payment processing and ensure monetary policy implementation.[89] She further contends that although other companies could render some of those services, only banks could perform all of them.[90] Buckley et al. discussed the ever-recurring regulatory systems' financial crisis despite sophisticated risk management and regulatory tools from the international perspective.[91] They sought to determine their causes and proffer solutions to them.[92] Following their discussion of the Asian Financial Crisis (AFC) of 1997–98, the GFC of 2007–2009 and the European Financial Crisis (EFC) of 2010, Buckley et al. concluded that the differences between the three crises may be more significant than their similarities, and suggested that the next crisis may be different in causes and consequences.[93] They argue that states' ability to overcome financial crises depends on their appetite for centralised regulation and robust crisis management, early intervention and resolution framework.[94] They assert that a purely country-based solution was no longer feasible because of increased interconnectedness, which can quickly spread contagion across borders.[95]

The GFC of 2008 affected Nigeria's capital and money markets, and the government responded to the crisis by intervening in both markets.[96] The crisis's immediate macro cause was the global meltdown resulting from the United States' housing crisis.[97] However, there were also other endemic micro causes of financial distress in Nigeria.[98] Alawiye-Adams argues that micro causes of non-performing loans arose from financial and operational mismanagement of financial institutions.[99] Poor credit processing and outright credit fraud caused loan failures and losses, resulting in banks' capital erosion until their shareholders' funds and reserves' exhaustion.[100] Kuye et al., quoting Sanusi L. Sanusi, the CBN Governor, attributed the bank financial crisis to the economy's absorptive capacity. The economy lagged behind the excess liquidity generated from bank consolidation, oil revenues and foreign investment inflows. In turn, the excess liquidity gives rise to significant flows to non-priority sectors and the capital markets, mainly in the form of margin loans and proprietary trading camouflaged as loans.[101] These risky investments built up NPLs to 37.3% in December 2009, diminishing the banks' capital base.[102] With reduced capital, the banks became technically insolvent, ultimately requiring capital injection by the existing or new investors. If those options fail, the liquidation or government's direct intervention through the resolution intervention vehicle, AMCON, becomes inevitable. Nonetheless, other scholars argue that supervisory failure was primarily responsible for the 2008 financial crisis in Nigeria.[103]

Bank resolution measures are special insolvency regimes to address the macro and micro causes of bank financial distress with the objective of an outcome better than liquidation for bank creditors, particularly bank depositors who enjoy statutory priority. However, a result better than in liquidation for bank depositors is not the primary focus of AMCON resolution measures. Instead, it offers relief for banks by removing toxic assets from their books and only indirectly benefiting bank depositors. It follows that an outcome better than liquidation is a desirable consequence for bank depositors and not the objective of the AMCON resolution tool. Therefore, the broader insolvency framework must work effectively to support bank resolution measures so banks can continue to maintain access to credit, preserve the centralised payment system, and ensure the implementation of monetary policy during bank restructuring.

Non-Performing Loans and Implementation of AMCON Intervention Tool

AMCON expects to recover the purchased assets' value fully, and extensive powers are vested in it.[104] AMCON Act upsets and reverses contractual rights and securities law priorities and gives precedence to AMCON in disputes with bank debtors over collaterals and contracts.[105] It provides the resolution authority legal basis for the management of NPLs.[106] AMCON restructures the banks by removing toxic assets from their books and injecting fresh funds, aligning with corporate insolvency restructuring principles. By so doing, bank account holders retain their deposits because they have confidence in the financial system, assuring banks' ability to honour their obligation. AMCON then manages the acquired EBA preparatory to their disposal. In so doing, AMCON can grant relief to eligible bank debtors seeking and obtaining forbearance or compromise; in other words, a sort of reorganisation or business rescue for the debtors and managing the banks' financial distress by taking out the toxic asset from banks' books.[107] By acquiring many EBAs, AMCON can consolidate them and structure them into marketable securities, creating a secondary market for NPLs. If AMCON is a unique restructuring tool designed to deal with an epidemic and the system is supposed to return to regular corporate insolvency after the epidemic, why has AMCON remained in existence since 2010, a period of over ten years.

The sunset clause of ten years in the AMCON Bill did not make it into the law during the legislative process.[108] The special regime created for AMCON is now a permanent feature of Nigeria's insolvency framework. The battle to stipulate a sunset for AMCON is ongoing, but the organisation seeks more powers outside of and parallel to the general insolvency laws to realise its assets.[109] There is a lack of understanding among government policymakers of the limited role of AMCs in the broader scope of financial distress management. Instead of improving the general insolvency law, which supports the special bank insolvency regime, Nigeria's approach infused AMCON with more powers for a long time. It also means that the special resolution regime became a substitute for regular corporate insolvency, which it was not suited to handle. Best practice in designing a bank financial distress management framework, which justifies a special insolvency regime for bank financial distress, expects exit from its deployment by selling the acquired asset or the intervention scheme's closure when financial panic abates.[110] The challenge with the absence of a sunset date under the AMCON Acts is that it deviates from the best practice by perpetuating government intervention. As Claessens et al. contend, a vicious cycle of self-reinforcing financial distress requires government intervention only in an efficient ICR framework for the private restructuring of debt without public intervention. Apart from the controversy over a sunset for

AMCON, there are other criticisms of bank resolution through AMCON, which border on allegations of political interference.[111] Westbrook suggests that a way to manage the risk of political interference with the special insolvency regime for managing financial panics is for the framework to provide "limited discretion" to the resolution authority.[112]

Nigeria's critical country-specific characteristics constrain the policy space for the resolution of NPLs through AMCON. Supervisory failure, weaknesses in prudential regulation and creditor rights, absence of restructuring options and distressed asset market and lack of skills and capacity among professionals reduced the effectiveness of AMCON as a resolution tool. These factors could explain the low percentage of 30% achieved by AMCON on acquired EBAs sales after ten years of existence. However, policymakers have made efforts to expand the policy space and reduce the constraints. For instance, the BOFIA 2020 enables the CBN to sell or transfer EBAs to private asset management companies.[113] The next section overviews the limitations in the policy environment and the various attempts to tackle them.

Dealing With the Limitations of the AMCON Resolution Tool

Pre CAMA 2020 Position

Aiyar et al. proposed that the success of a special insolvency regime for the resolution of bank NPLs depends on four supporting components outside of the bank resolution tools.[114] Based on Aiyar et al. proposition, the problem with NPL resolution through AMCON is not with the device itself but the soundness of the corporate insolvency system that supports it. Before the enactment of CAMA 2020, the Nigerian insolvency system was liquidation focused.[115] The World Bank ROSC report found three primary deficiencies and weaknesses in the Nigerian insolvency framework. They are the absence of a rescue framework, unregulated insolvency profession and lack of public administration.[116] Also, the Nigerian public administrative structure for insolvency is weak and underfunded. The unregulated insolvency profession left inexperienced and inadequately qualified professionals to dominate the practice and administration of bankruptcy.[117] The related laws on debt collection and collateral creation and realisation are weak or not properly implemented.

Although the scheme of arrangement provisions under CAMA 1990 could encourage business recovery, the jurisprudence did not take the opportunity.[118] The conflict between the CAMA 1990 provision of 75% majority[119] and the Investment and Securities Act 2007 (ISA) provision of 90% majority for the approval of a buyout of dissenting minority[120] and the approach of the Securities and Exchange Commission (SEC) to the interpretation of those provisions practically took the sail off schemes of arrangement as a business rescue tool. Further, the requirement to appoint a provisional liquidator only after the advertisement of the winding-up petition hampers suspension of the exercise of security rights (moratorium) and achievement of restructuring.[121]

The Supreme Court effectively frustrated the availability of a moratorium on the commencement of winding up proceedings by its judgment in *FMBN V NDIC*.[122] The decision limited the s.417 CAMA 1990 stay provisions to actions or proceedings pending or instituted in the Federal High Court except with the leave of court where a provisional liquidator was appointed for a company. By this decision, s.412 of CAMA 1990, which empowers the grant of stay, is only applicable to proceedings before the Federal High Court, the court with jurisdiction in bankruptcy cases.[123] The consequence of the decision is that filing a winding-up proceeding does not operate as an automatic stay of all legal proceedings, as the state courts exercise jurisdiction on many civil and commercial matters.[124] Moreover, the decision circumscribes the bankruptcy court's (Federal High Court) inherent power to bind everyone by a stay order on the threat of contempt. As a result, creditors and debtors resorted to various antics to gain "priority" or obtain a "moratorium."[125] No doubt, a moratorium is crucial to any rescue regime.[126]

The Bankruptcy Act of 1979 has not been effective regarding personal insolvency because it requires obtaining and executing a judgment as a condition for compulsory bankruptcy.[127] Also, the ineffective discharge provisions render voluntary bankruptcy an unattractive option for individual debtors.[128] Furthermore, the absence of a regulated insolvency profession before the Companies and Allied Matters Act (CAMA 2020) also meant no basis exists for developing a pool of skilled, experienced and knowledgeable practitioners to drive and operate the insolvency framework administrative and judicial structure. Furthermore, Nigeria has no specific legislation to recognise foreign insolvency proceedings, orders, or judgments, establish cooperation between domestic and foreign courts, coordinate proceedings, or communicate information. Indeed, CAMA 2020 did not remedy the situation because it did not adopt the UNCITRAL Model Law on Cross-Border insolvency and BOFIA 2020 deals with bank resolution and not general ICR legislation.[129]

AMCON Effort at Coping Without ICR Support

The weaknesses in the four ICR support components for the AMCON resolution tool increased NPLs between 2010 and 2015. AMCON and the policymakers responded to the external deficiencies affecting AMCON's performance in several manners.

Apart from enabling banks to resolve their EBAs, AMCON also provides a channel for eligible bank debtors to seek and obtain forbearance or compromise on their debts acquired by AMCON; in other words, reorganisation or business rescue for AMCON debtors.[130] The restructuring procedure under the AMCON Acts is non-collective because it does not involve all the debtors' creditors, unlike in regular corporate insolvency.[131] At AMCON's intervention, the bank debtors whose EBAs with EBIs it acquired were already insolvent. Moreover, AMCON only accepts EBA in default for a minimum of 90 days. Consequently, the window for resolution by restructuring is narrow, pushing AMCON to liquidate through sales or enforcement of rights against third parties such as guarantees.

Further, the efficiency of resolution through court action against third parties or authorisation of asset liquidation was retarded by the slow court process. The Federal High Court adopted AMCON Practice Directions intended to speed up recovery cases to alleviate the situation.[132] We argue that the general creditor rights regime's improvement is not determined by AMCON Practice Direction but by improving the regular court dispute mechanism to improve debt collection.

AMC and bridge bank resolution tools exempting banks from the regular insolvency regime and subjecting them to a special resolution regime are justified because they tend to take a large chunk of the economy when banks fail.[133] However, as Smith and Hall pointed out, bridge banks, as a resolution tool, are intended to warehouse the banks temporarily before being sold to new investors.[134] The same principle applies to NPLs. Indeed, in the US, where resolution trust companies managed NPLs during the savings and loans crisis in the 1980s, the tool is no longer used, and the resolution trust companies have wound up.[135] In Korea and Japan, the resolution authority used asset management tools on a short-term basis.[136] In Europe, AMCs were proposed only as a short-term intervention measure with a three-year exit limit.[137] China maintains 4 (four) asset management corporations, but they have been practically investment banks.[138] The Chinese policy on using asset management companies to manage NPLs is gradualism and legislative forbearance in its transition from a centrally controlled economy to a socialist market economy.[139] Hsu et al. have argued that the policy, though a pragmatic approach to a problematic issue, exposes China's continued development to the risk of weakening the rule of law's progression.[140]

In analysing the development of the asset-based securities (ABS) market in China, Schena argued that from the experience of the Asian financial crisis, restructuring through the use of ABS markets is one component of the broader approach to ABS market development.[141] Others include strengthening the financial soundness and reputational integrity of China's banks, the liberalisation of alternative asset markets to promote, in parallel with securitising NPL portfolios, and the broad-based securitisation of other assets.[142] The experience in Thailand is like that of Nigeria, where the public does not perceive the resolution authority as the panacea for resolving NPLs.[143]

The exit strategy could be selling the NPLs to new investors due to the inability to restructure with the existing debtors. In that case, NPL resolution requires an efficient insolvency framework for recovery by the new investors. According to the World Bank Doing Business 2019 Report on Nigeria, 2 (two) years would be a reasonable estimate of the time to resolve insolvency.[144] Still, if the debtor resists (including the delays and appeals) during the process, it could go up to five years for a receiver to realise an asset.[145] The resolution rate of just 30% of EBAs achieved by AMCON suggests limited exit options. The performance of AMCON leads to the conclusion that once a bank's NPL is sold to AMCON or any of the private AMCs or shadow banks to clean the books of the bank, the debtor aggressively resists collection by the purchaser, leading to a liability discount, which discourages activity on the secondary NPL market.[146] The weak ICR framework without a restructuring option menu meant a weak secondary market for distressed assets and enforcement and realisation of creditors' rights. Therefore, the need for policy action by the government to fill the regulatory gap remained imperative. Meanwhile, the government bore the carrying cost of the 70% unresolved NPLs cost, which AMCON saddles.

The government is now tired of being the sole permanent funder of AMCON.[147] In addition to the 2015 AMCON Act requiring banks to contribute, the CBN has authorised private asset management companies to diversify the asset management and debt resolution business.[148] However, private debt factoring is not fully developed, and licenced banks control them indirectly.[149] AMCON has focused on debt restructuring and liquidation and has not pursued the securitisation option to manage NPLs.[150] The change in policy direction toward diversification of funding sources for bank resolution reflects in BOFIA 2020, which authorises the transfer of EBAs to private AMCs. Also, BOFIA 2020 established a Resolution Fund domiciled with CBN for use exclusively as part of bank resolution measures in defraying the operating costs of bridge banks and transferring a bank or financial institution's business.[151] The CBN and NDIC contribute N10 billion and N4 billion or such amount as CBN may decide at commencement and first business day subsequent years to the Fund. All banks and financial institutions also pay an annual levy into the Fund on or before 30 April. The law prohibits a bank or financial institution that fails to pay its levy from paying dividends and bonuses to shareholders. Adeyemo describes the Bank Sector Resolution Fund as one of the core regulatory innovations of BOFIA 2020.[152]

AMCON is concerned about the resurgence of huge toxic loans in the banking sector. Ahmed Lawan Kuru, AMCON Managing Director/Chief Executive Officer, called on the financial regulators to revisit the Failed Bank Act to make bankers accountable for their actions and banks to strengthen their risk management framework to stem the negative growth.[153] By this call, AMCON admits that CBN improving the prudential regulation of banks will reduce the build-up of NPLs requiring AMCON intervention. AMCON also pursued a strategy of strengthening its resolution toolkit by adding more powers to its already vast arsenal. It followed a legislative agenda for more capabilities. By the 29th day of July 2019, President Mohammed Buhari signed the Asset Management Corporation of Nigeria (Amendment No. 2) Act 2019, which bolstered the powers and defences available to AMCON to realise its NPLs.[154]

Prudential Regulation, CAMA 2020, and Enhancement of Creditor Rights

The explanation for the fall of NPLs from 37% in 2009 to a low of 9.6% in 2019 is improving policy and legal framework, prudential regulation and ICR supporting components for effective bank resolution. Recent reports suggest a drop in bank NPLs to a single-digit figure as a percentage of bank loans.[155] The upside growth in credit can reduce the ratio of NPLs that form loan stock, resulting in banks' reluctance to deal with the NPL problem.[156] However, the reduction in NPLs is a misnomer because the collection rate remains low.[157] The misnomer has led to the outcry of AMCON on the need for better risk management by the banks.[158] Also, the secondary market for NPLs is practically non-existent.[159] The debt market for securitisation is growing.[160] However, it focuses on primary debt issuance, and the conditions for listing in the market are unattractive for NPL securitisation because of requirements for dividend payment history, among others.[161] As part of prudential regulations, the CBN now requires banks to achieve a loan-to-deposit ratio (LDR) of 60%,[162] a drop-down from the previous level of 80%. However, the banks still are struggling to comply, meaning that they have been investing in perceived more secure treasury bills rather than creating more credits. NPL's prudential regulation is getting more desperate, with new rules seeking to access debtors' funds in other banks to settle the debt in another bank, signalling that the problem is not decreasing.[163] In terms of lessons, the European Financial Crisis of 2010 was traced partly to banks' preference to invest in safe Treasury bills.[164] Hence the banking crisis eventually morphed into a sovereign debt crisis as the markets declined to roll over Greek treasury debt, necessitating placing the country under an IMF and EU rescue programme.[165] An underlying NPL problem still exists in Nigeria with increasing provisioning under IFRS 9 and low loans to deposit ratio (LDR), meaning that banks are investing in safe treasury bills, which can suddenly erupt if other safety valves are weak.[166]

Despite the tightening of AMCON laws and the noted weaknesses of prudential regulation, the government policy action achieved significant law reform results for the general ICR regime between 2017 and 2020, and, arguably, those improvements contributed to the drop in NPL levels. For example, the Credit Reporting Act of 2017 provides credit information sharing among credit bureaus, deposit lenders, and other credit service institutions. As a result, financial institutions can determine customers' creditworthiness before making a credit decision. Section 1(e) of the Act sets its objectives as "to promote responsibility in the credit market by encouraging responsible borrowing, avoidance of over-indebtedness and fulfilment of financial obligations by consumers and discouraging reckless credit granting by credit providers and contractual default by consumers." Babatunde Popoola argues that credit infrastructure such as credit bureaus, collateral registries, and sound bankruptcy laws and practices enhance access to consumer credit.[167] It achieves this by reducing bad loans, a significant bane of Nigeria's banking industry.

The Secured Transactions in Movable Assets Act (STMAA) came into force in 2017.[168] However, the jurisprudence on this law has not developed in the courts.[169] The law was introduced by CBN, with PEBEC actively involved.[170] It created the National Collateral Registry (NCR) to register security interests in movable assets by filing a financial statement. The order of registration at the NCR determines security priority in movable assets under the STMAA.[171] Section 34 provides circumstances where registered security could gain priority over the execution of judgment, raising questions about whether registration of an unexecuted judgment would give the judgment creditor priority. In an unconcluded execution process, the jurisprudence on cross-border insolvency suggests that a judgment execution creditor is not a secured creditor, even over the judgment debtor's attached asset.

Until completion of execution, the judgment execution creditor is an unsecured creditor.[172]

The STMAA is a substantial improvement in Nigeria's general ICR regime. In addition, overcoming the challenges of creating security over movable assets expands access to credit as most Nigerians only have movable assets as available collateral.[173]

The BOFIA 2020 repealed the BOFIA Cap B3 LFN, 2004 as the significant legislation for regulating and supervising the operations and activities of Banks and other financial institutions in Nigeria.[174] In addition, the Act introduced provisions pertinent to the rescue of failing banks and other financial institutions.[175]

The CBN is the apex regulatory agency authorised to issue and revoke banking, including offshore banking licences.[176] Specifically, no bank shall enter into an agreement or arrangement for restructuring, reorganisation, merger, and disposal of banks without the prior written consent of the Governor of CBN.[177]

On the prudential side, BOFIA 2020 explicitly provides for banks' duty to maintain a statutory reserve fund, restrictions on paying dividends, disclosure of interest by directors, managers and officers in advance, loan or credit facility, prohibition of inter-locking directorship, etc.[178] These provisions appear to ensure the security of depositors' funds with the bank. Furthermore, the Act restricts a bank or other financial institutions from granting any advance, loan or credit facility against the security of its shares, any unsecured advance, loan or credit facility except in line with the bank's regulation on collateralisation without the prior written approval of CBN.[179] In addition, banks are to keep proper books of account for all transactions and make relevant monthly returns to CBN showing their assets and liabilities, an analysis of advances and other assets at their head office and branches, and subsidiaries within and outside Nigeria.[180]

On the bank resolution side, BOFIA 2020 provides for the CBN to intervene in a failing Bank to acquire its shares and control the bank, amongst other measures, if the bank will not meet its obligations under the law or is about to suspend payment to any extent or is insolvent.[181] In addition, the CBN can order the transfer of the bank, the whole or part of the banking business, to third-party private purchasers as may be necessary to ensure the survival and revival of the bank.[182] Where all intervention measures by CBN to rescue the failing bank fails, CBN may revoke the banking licence.[183] After that, the NDIC shall apply to the Federal High Court for a winding-up order[184]. However, to ensure the survival of systemically important financial institutions (SIFIs) described as banks that control 12.5% or more of the total assets in the industry or 12.5% or more of the total industry deposits, the Act mandates cooperation, assistance, waivers, or forbearances to resolve the crisis occasioned by SIFI distress.[185]

The CBN may bail in a failing bank or other financial institution by cancellation, modification or conversion of any eligible instrument issued by the bank or other financial institution or to which it is a party or subject. These measures are used if the CBN believes that it would facilitate the rescue of the bank or if the available assets of the bank are unlikely to support the payment of due bank liabilities.[186] The Act provides a moratorium on all claims and judgment debt enforcement regarding an eligible instrument existing or being pursued as of the date of the bail-in certificate. They are automatically suspended and unenforceable against the bank or other financial institution during the period covered by the bail-in certificate or any period as may be determined by the Governor of CBN by written notice.[187]

Moreover, the CBN may, without the consent of the shareholders of the bank, transfer the assets of a bank or other financial institution to one or more private asset management vehicles to maximise their value for an eventual sale or organised and measured winding up.[188] The private asset management vehicle owes no duty to the shareholders or creditors of the bank or other financial institution. Also, it has no liability to them for acts and omissions in the discharge of its duties unless in the event of fraud or gross misconduct, which directly affects the rights of such shareholders or creditors. The CBN can also utilise the sale of business tools to sell on commercial terms shares or other instruments of ownership issued by the bank and all or any asset, right or liability of the bank.

Other reforms introduced by BOFIA 2020 include establishing the Banking Resolution Fund, Special Tribunal for Enforcement of Eligible Loans, recognition of Fintechs as financial institutions, reduction of the role of NDIC as resolution authority and enhancement of CBN's role as resolution authority.[189] Furthermore, despite reservations about the policy objectives of some of the reforms, in line with Aiyar et al. support proposition, BOFIA 2020 substantially improves the environment for bank prudential supervision and provision to the CBN of additional resolution tools to support AMCON intervention in the NPL management.[190]

Another policy reform that has impacted the ICR framework in Nigeria is CAMA 2020, which repealed and replaced CAMA 1999. It introduced two new insolvency and restructuring procedures: Company Voluntary Arrangement (CVA) and Administration.[191] Under these new procedures, debtors can now propose a business rescue plan to creditors through a CVA without displacing the management, unlike the previous receiver-manager procedure.[192] The board of a debtor company or qualified creditors can also appoint an administrator (management displacing procedure) who can make a similar business rescue proposal to the creditors on a statutory moratorium against creditors enforcing their securities.[193] CAMA 2020 retains the old techniques of receivership and managership, winding-up and arrangements, and compromise in varying degrees.[194] However, given the new law's provisions, the receiver-manager will likely fade over time, favouring administration.[195] Nevertheless, the scheme of arrangement will continue to be helpful as a way of achieving business rescue.[196]

CAMA 2020 rearranged the priorities of creditors in involuntary liquidation or winding up. In descending order, the new priority ranking places secured creditors at the top, followed by administration and liquidation costs, preferential payments, floating charge holders, unsecured creditors, and contributories claims.[197] Other creditors like critical suppliers and post-commencement of insolvency finance providers now have recognition under the law and can even improve their priority ranking.[198] CAMA 2020 offers clear protection and the highest priority ranking to secured creditors in liquidation, reorganisation or rescue of a company's business.

Another innovation introduced by CAMA 2020 is the regulation of the insolvency profession. The law vested in the CAC regulation of the insolvency profession by recognising professional bodies that appear to meet the law's requirements.[199] The law recognises the Business Recovery and Insolvency Practitioner Association of Nigeria (BRIPAN) as a professional body.[200] The CAC's responsibility is to ensure that insolvency professional bodies "meet acceptable requirements as to education and practical training and experience" and are "fit and proper" to practise as insolvency practitioners.[201]

To the extent that mergers and acquisitions are ways of managing insolvency, the enactment of the Federal Competition and Consumer Protection Act 2018 (FCCPA) and the creation of the Federal Competition and Consumer Protection Commission (FCCPC) add to the improvement of the regime for managing insolvency.[202] Before enacting FCCPA, mergers and acquisitions were regulated by the Securities and Exchange Commission (SEC) as established by the Investment and Securities Act 2007 (ISA 2007). SEC's regulatory role in mergers and acquisitions is now limited to public companies and determining whether shareholders are treated fairly and are well informed about the impending merger. At the same time, the FCCPC addresses merger control to eliminate anti-competitive practices.[203]

It is noteworthy that the FCCPA has slightly redefined mergers compared with the repealed portion of ISA 2007. Some of the notable distinctions include recognising a joint venture as a merger.[204] It also reclassifies the types of mergers to small and large, allowing the public's invitation to provide written submissions on the proposed threshold for mergers calculation method, amongst others.[205] The FCCPC, under Sections 17, 18 and 163 of the FCCPA, issued the Merger Review Regulations 2020 with ancillary instruments to govern the notification and review of mergers under Part XII, FCCPA.[206] Sections 92(2) and 92(3) of the FCCPA define control. Section 92(2) states that an undertaking has control over the business or undertaking of another if it: beneficially owns more than one half of the issued share capital, is entitled to cast majority votes, and can appoint or veto the appointment of the majority of the directors of the undertaking. Assessment of mergers is against the test of "substantial lessening or prevention of competition" and "on substantial public interest grounds."[207] In the case of an undertaking that is a trust, control means the ability to influence the majority of trustees' votes, appoint a majority of the trustees, or appoint or change the majority of the trust beneficiaries. The implication is that merger control issues may arise where an NPL's resolution involves combining the undertaking of two or more companies. A predictable framework for merger control improves the chance for the resolution of NPLs through mergers and acquisitions, and the FCCPA has, subject to its effective implementation, the potential to positively impact NPL resolution.

The law reforms discussed earlier strengthened the AMCON NPL resolution and ICR regimes. In addition, credit reporting, secured transactions in movable assets, insolvency and business rescue provisions of CAMA 2020, and merger control have impacted the reduction of NPLs even though the CAMA reforms are still in implementation infancy. The improvements in bank resolution measures for CBN under BOFIA 2020 also enhance the support for AMCOM. Popoola argues that credit reporting relying on data, technology, and a legal framework ensures an effective credit system that encourages responsible borrowing and lending, improving consumer credit access.[208]

The data from the NCR indicate improvement in the creation of secured debt using movable assets. As of 1 March 2020, the total number of filings was 87,674, and the value of the registered Financing Statement with the NCR was = N=1,604 Billion, $ 1.2 Billion and €6.3 Million.[209] Only 31,707 filings were by women for the total value of =N=110 Billion and USD 444,000.[210] NCR has registered about 23 collateral classes totalling 157,752 collaterals against 237153 debtors as of 1 March 2020.[211] Out of the 157752 collaterals, motor vehicles remain the most popular, with 28,303, followed by consumer/household goods with 19920 and inventory with 19823. The data is consistent with those from other countries, which indicates that motor vehicles are the most popular or available collateral for secure transactions in movable assets.[212]

Government policy and law reform achieved between 2016 and 2020 address the gaps in the insolvency framework identified by the 2007 World Bank ROSC report on Nigeria.[213] The ICR regime has improved its efficiency in that payday loans are now processed virtually using Bank Verification Number (BVN) or National Identity Number (NIN), credit report and a mobile telephone.[214] Recent reports suggest a drop in bank NPLs to a single-digit figure as a percentage of bank loans.[215] With an improved legal and technological framework that ensures responsible borrowing and lending, the likelihood of accumulating NPLs that would require an AMCON resolution tool is limited to when there is panic in the system. The current COVID-19 pandemic is one such situation that justifies a separate bank resolution regime, no matter how efficient the general ICR regime may be.[216] This paper argues that after discounting the impact of the increase in credit expansion, the explanation for reducing NPLs in Nigeria between 2009 and 2019 is the improvement of the ICR system.

All may not yet be Uhuru if there is another explanation for the reduction of NPLs. Arguably, upside credit growth can reduce the percentage of NPLs that form loan stock, resulting in banks' reluctance to deal with the NPL problem.[217] The reduction in NPLs is a misnomer where the collection rate remains low.[218] Even AMCON has cried out on the banks' need for better risk management.[219] Also, the secondary market for NPLs is practically non-existent.[220] An underlying NPL problem still exists in Nigeria with increasing provisioning under IFRS 9 and a low LDR ratio, which could suddenly erupt if other safety valves are weak.[221] While critical blocks of the credit and insolvency framework that support a bank resolution system for NPLs are now in place, a lot still has to be done. In many ways, it is still a work-in-process. There are lessons to be learnt from global norms and the experiences of other countries.

Lessons From Abroad

As stated initially, the World Bank study found a relationship between the ICR regime and the level of NPLs.[222] The EU recognised the relationship between an inefficient restructuring and insolvency framework and the rise in NPLs in banks' books when it observed that preventive insolvency "could contribute to reducing the risk that loans become non-performing loans in cyclical downturns, thus reducing the related negative impact on the financial sector."[223] The EU has since adopted the EU Directive on Preventive Restructuring Framework introducing new insolvency procedures to rescue businesses before their financial distress and allowing cross-class cram-down.[224] The UK also enacted the Corporate Insolvency and Governance Act 2020 (CIGA) to relieve debtors even before financial distress.[225] The EU and UK have shifted the goal post by recognising that early intervention in businesses' distress reduces the chance of their loans becoming non-performing loans in a cyclical downturn. The Indian experience confirms the relationship between NPLs and efficient general insolvency law. India enacted a new Insolvency and Bankruptcy Code in 2016.[226] The Code was amended in 2018.[227] The Modi government made the reform of India's business environment its top priority, and the new law's implementation was pursued aggressively as a signature achievement.[228] It introduced fast-track procedures for small and unlisted companies through regulations.[229] About 17% of all loans in India in the sum of between 150–200 Billion US Dollars are NPLs.[230] Before the Code, recovery of NPLs was at 25% over 4 (four) years.[231] Now, recovery is at 45% over 1 (one) year.[232] Also, the Code induced a substantial change in the behaviour of debtors and creditors.[233] Creditors and borrowers act more quickly once they see a sign of distress by selling, attacking the cash-flow problem and other measures.[234] The improved collection experience in India spurned the active NPL secondary market enabling realisation of the bank resolution regime objective of NPL securitisation.

This paper argues that critical structural weaknesses in the Nigerian ICR framework pressure the need for bank resolution measures as companies pile up debts as NPLs in banks' books. These structural weaknesses include the lack of reorganisation provisions, excessive priority for secured creditors, non-inclusion of secured creditors in the insolvency process, and a weak judicial process, leading to a lengthy collection period. Another weakness of the Nigerian ICR regime is the non-adoption of the UNCITRAL Model Law on Cross-Border Insolvency (the Model Law). Although the UNCITRAL Model Law does not apply to banks, it helps resolve corporate insolvency by ensuring the cooperative management of their financial distress in such a way as to reduce pressure on the NPLs of banks, obviating the need for intervention through bank resolution measures.[235] Buckley et al. noted that because of the increasing globalisation of companies, a purely country-based solution to NPLs resolution was no longer feasible because of the increased interconnectedness of businesses.[236] Again, the EU remarked in its proposal for the preventative insolvency measures directive that insolvency has a broader cross-border dimension as companies have an international supply chain.[237]

Before the recent reforms discussed earlier, the public administrative structure for insolvency was weak and underfunded in Nigeria. Insolvency practice was unregulated. Inexperienced and unqualified professionals dominated the practice and administration of insolvency.[238] The related laws on debt collection, secured credit in movables, credit reporting, business rescue, collateral creation, and realisation were weak or not properly implemented. In addition to the weaknesses in the ICR regime, the bank resolution tools for managing bank financial distress were also weak.[239] It may be overkill to expect AMCON, a limited resolution tool for NPLs, to address all prudential or policy challenges of the banking system rightly vested in the CBN and government. Indeed, it is the responsibility of CBN and not AMCON to address prudential issues, while AMCON focuses on the special resolution regime for managing banks' financial distress. Nevertheless, weaknesses in the ICR framework and CBN bank resolution tools affect AMCON's effectiveness.

However, as has occurred in India, the regulatory framework that will improve collection experience is a modern, efficient and effective general creditor rights and insolvency regime. So, there is a link between the ICR framework and the special bank resolution regime, and both must work in harmony for the most effective outcome from the bank resolution regime.

In this regard, a small but dedicated mass of insolvency practitioners under the aegis of the BRIPAN, with the support of INSOL International, engaged in reform agenda setting, lobbying, and collaboration with receptive public and private sector entities like the Nigerian Bar Association (NBA) Section on Business Law, the Presidential Enabling Business Environment Council (PEBEC), which implements the government's plan for ease of doing business in Nigeria under the office of the Vice President, Corporate Affairs Commission (CAC), the CBN and the National Assembly.[240] The abundance of local expertise partly defines policy success.[241] With increased interconnectedness, no country, sector or arm of government can work in isolation.[242] Therefore, achieving law reform in Nigeria resulted from the public and private sector and domestic and international cooperation.[243] The Nigerian reforms have had long to come but bear the inklings of impending NPL resolution transformation through enhanced bank resolution tools and improved ICR regimes.

A solid ICR framework is the foundation for rehabilitating businesses that can be resuscitated and allowing only the severe cases to be the subject of liquidation or government intervention through a resolution trust company like AMCON. The Etisalat 9Mobile case supports the need for a formal framework for the resuscitation of failing but viable companies.[244] Before 2020, a formal framework for business rescue was non-existent in Nigeria. CAMA 2020 is, therefore, a game-changer with its CVA and administration procedures. Another significant law reform is BOFIA 2020, which has provided the CBN with improved bank resolution tools to support AMCON's focus on NPLs. However, there are still policy spaces to be filled. For instance, the personal bankruptcy law requires urgent reform and the need for an insolvency regime for small and medium scale enterprises (SMEs). There is also a need to align the new reforms, such as creating special tribunals with AMCON practice direction courts and regular bankruptcy and credit courts. The practical support of the ICR and BOFIA rescue regimes implies that the AMCON resolution tools, as envisaged by the best practice design of the financial distress management framework, handles extreme cases with systemic or cyclical impact. Like in the public health pandemic, the unique AMCON resolution tool is expected to be recalled to standby mode upon overcoming the emergency.

Conclusion

Public policy must recognise NPL resolution policy interacts with the broader key country characteristics. The efficiency and effectiveness of prudential, creditor rights, insolvency, and restructuring framework affect resolution tools for NPLs. The AMCON experience indicates that special resolution powers for an AMC alone without supporting components from the regular insolvency and bank resolution infrastructure may result in underperformance by the resolution authority and elongated government support and intervention in the financial epidemic. On the other hand, the collective pursuit of government reform initiatives with private-sector norm entrepreneurs yields the fruit of a robust insolvency law framework to resolve ordinary corporate organisations' financial distress.[245] The outcome of an efficient ICR regime, in turn, would improve the effectiveness of the bank resolution regime for dealing with NPLs, including the resolution of those assets into a viable secondary market for NPLs.[246]

The drop in NPLs in Nigeria by 2019 is attributable to the improvements in the AMCON resolution toolbox and the ICR regime through law reform on credit reporting, secured transactions in movable assets and merger control. In addition, the additional business rescue tools introduced by CAMA 2020 in the form of CVA and Administration have widened the support base for the management of NPLs before they become toxic to be referred to AMCON for resolution and to ensure the existence of a secondary market for NPLs. Furthermore, BOFIA 2020 has provided CBN with additional tools for prudential regulation and resolution measures for banks in financial distress. While these reforms do not meet current best practices toward preventive restructuring frameworks, they amount to substantial progress, given the previous divide between bank resolution tools and the ICR regime.

Notes

1 World Bank Group, *How Insolvency and Creditor-Debtor Regimes Can Help Address Nonperforming Loans* (World Bank Group, 2021) 5.
2 ibid.
3 IMF Data 2017 quoted in presentation slides of Antonia Menezes, *Bank Resolution and Recovery in Africa: Features, Challenges and Opportunities* (Virtual Colloquium on Resolution of Financially Distressed Financial Institutions, 14 September 2020).
4 ibid.
5 Anthony Idigbe, *Ranking of Claims in Post-Commencement Finance in Business Rescue in Nigeria* (Lagos Nigeria Four Points by Sheraton Oniru VI, 2018).
6 'IMF: Nigeria's Non-Performing Loans Have Doubled Since 2015 | TheCable' <https://perma.cc/2WWL-QCTR> captured 18 September 2018 at 10.30 am.
7 'Half of Nigeria's 36 States Insolvent – Report – Premium Times Nigeria' <https://perma.cc/VQ7A-PEED> captured 8 September 2018 at 10:31:04; Punch Newspaper, 'Debts Exceed Statutory Revenues in 32 States, Says FRC' (*Punch Newspaper*)

<https://punchng.com/debts-exceed-statutory-revenues-in-32-states-says-frc/> accessed 18 September 2018 at 10:31:04.

8 'Perma | FEC Approves N2.7 Trillion to Settle Nigerian Govt Debts to Contractors, Pensioners, Others – Premium Times Nigeria' <https://perma.cc/99M5-M3GE> captured 8 September 2018 at 10.53 am.

9 CBN, 'Central Bank of Nigeria | CBN Annual Report and Statement of Accounts' <https://perma.cc/8QL4-JC6W> captured 7 April 2021 at 9.37 am; For NDIC 2019 Annual Report see <https://perma.cc/NDS3-Z54R> captured 7 April 2021 at 9.49 am.

10 S Aiyar and others, *A Strategy for Resolving Europe's Problem Loans* (IMF Staff Discussion Note No 15/19, International Monetary Fund, 2015); Patrizia Baudino and Hyuncheol Yun, *Resolution of Non-Performing Loans – Policy Options* (Bank for International Settlements, 2017); Anil Ari, Sophia Chen and Lev Ratnovski, *The Dynamics of Non-Performing Loans During Banking Crises: A New Database* (International Monetary Fund, 2019); Menezes (n 3).

11 Section 4 of the AMCON Act 2010.

12 S.24 AMCON Act 2010.

13 ibid s.25(1).

14 The corporation raised its N5.6 trillion take-off capital from bonds it issued at 6% for a discounted value of N4.042 trillion (face value of N5.6 trillion) for the acquisition of Non-Performing Loans (NPLs) and the recapitalization of Eligible Financial Institutions (EFIs). Communication Week, 'CBN, Others Push for Winding Up of AMCON' (*Nigeria Communication*, 16 November 2019) <https://nigeriacommunicationsweek.com.ng/cbn-others-push-for-winding-up-of-amcon/> accessed 14 May 2022 at 7.12 pm.

15 S.25(2) AMCON Act 2010.

16 Concentrating NPLs in a single AMC can create economies of scale because it could realise profits, while freeing the bank's balance sheet at the same time avoiding fire sales in illiquid markets thus limiting the need and cost of restructuring banks: José Manuel Mansilla-Fernández, 'Institutions – European Economy' <https://perma.cc/NVX8-47NF> captured 14 May 2022 at 7:16:15 pm.

17 For detailed discussions on the powers of AMCON under the statute, see Anthony Idigbe and Okorie Kalu, 'Dealing with Bank Insolvency: Asset Management Company of Nigeria Act (2010)' <https://perma.cc/T62X-RQMD> Under the 2019 Amendment Act, additional information, surveillance and tracing powers are added to AMCON whilst the Corporation is at the same time pretty much insulated from any enforcement proceedings, suits for breach of rights or monetary claims or any injunctive orders. accessed 14 May 2022 at 9:40:33 PM.

18 See s.365 US Bankruptcy Code 'U.S. Code: Title 11 | U.S. Code | US Law | LII / Legal Information Institute' <https://perma.cc/78CD-HVVG> captured 15 May 2022 at 2.05 AM but see recent SCOTUS case of City of Chicago v. Fulton, 592 U.S. _ (2021), delivered 14 January 2021 holding that a secured creditor retention of collateral may not amount to breach of automatic stay as s.362 only applies to affirmative acts of breach.

19 CAMA-NOTE-BOOK-FULL-VERSION.pdf s.480.

20 For instance, the AMCON Act 2019 (amended s.48(7) (a) and (b)) provides for automatic one-year extendable stay period for a statutory receivership appointed by AMCON and cram down on other creditors but the appointment is not in the context of any collective proceeding and it is not clear whether AMCON as a creditor is bound by the automatic stay. It seems like a defensive mechanism to stay all other creditors apart from AMCON.

21 <https://amcon.com.ng/achievements.php> accessed 3 March 2021 at 7.30 pm US ET.

22 Week (n 14) See also <https://amcon.com.ng/achievements.php>.

23 Eva Hupkes, 'Insolvency – Why a Special Regime for Banks?' in *Curriculam Development Monetary Finance Law* (International Monetary Fund, 2003) 459.

24 ibid.
25 ibid.
26 World Bank Group (n 1) 5.
27 ibid.
28 ibid.
29 ibid.
30 ibid.
31 ibid.
32 Aiyar and others (n 10); J Garrido, E Kopp and A Weber, *Cleaning Up Bank Balance Sheets: Economic, Legal, and Supervisory Measures for Italy* (IMF Working Paper No. 16/135, International Monetary Fund, 2016); RD Haas, Bojan Markovic and Alexander Plekhanov, 'Reducing Non-Performing Loans in Europe' (*European Economy*, 5 July 2017) <https://european-economy.eu/2017-1/reducing-non-performing-loans-in-europe/>, post-GFC resolution strategists all agree that strategy for dealing with NPLs must include insolvency reform.
33 Ross P Buckley, Emilios Avgouleas and Douglas W Arner, 'Three Major Financial Crises: What Have We Learned' (2018) <https://papers.ssrn.com/abstract=3247455> Also https://perma.cc/T5KM-AYVF accessed 14 May 2022 at 22:25:54.
34 'About the FSB – Financial Stability Board' <https://perma.cc/ZV5V-B26C> accessed 14 May 2022 at 22:43:11.
35 Financial Stability Board, 'FSB Key Attributes of Effective Resolution Regimes' (October 2011) <https://perma.cc/MRR7-S3B3> accessed 14 May 2022 at 10.52 PM.
36 ibid.
37 Matthias Lehmann, 'Bail-In and Private International Law: How to Make Bank Resolution Measures Effective Across Borders' (2017) 66(1) Int Comp Law Q 107.
38 ibid; See also Recitals (45) and (46) of the EU BRRD which provides the justification for bank resolution regime in spite of existence of normal insolvency regime being to avoid systemic collapse, ensure financial stability by continuity of critical infrastructure and protection of covered depositors: European Union, *EU Directive on Recovery and Resolution of Credit Institutions and Investment Firms Directive 2014/59/EU of the European Parliament and of the Council of 15 May 2014* (Official Journal of the European Union, 2014).
39 Ari, Chen and Ratnovski (n 10).
40 Padraic Kenna, 'Mortgage Law Developments in the European Union' (2018) 4 J Prop Soc 45 at 64; Central Bank of Nigeria, *Central Bank of Nigeria Prudential Guidelines for Deposit Money Banks in Nigeria* (Central Bank of Nigeria, 2010) Clause 12.1 (b) 2 provides that: a credit facility should be deemed as non-performing when any of the following conditions exists: (i) interest or principal is due and unpaid for 90 days or more; (ii) interest payments equal to 90 days interest or more have been capitalised rescheduled or rolled over into a new loan (except where facilities have been reclassified as specified in 12.1[d] later).
41 European Central Bank, *Guidance to Banks on Non-Performing Loans* (ECB, 2017) <www.bankingsupervision.europa.eu/ecb/pub/pdf/guidance_on_npl.en.pdf>, also captured <https://perma.cc/9AXY-5CUK> accessed 15 May 2022 at 1.06 PM.
42 See also Haas, Markovic and Plekhanov (n 32) who argue that though resolution schemes involve three option of use of specialised AMCs, specialised servicers and or securitization, success still depends on seven important policy choices such as existence of secondary market, standardization, incentives, growth, access to capital, access to public funding and availability of expertise.
43 José Manuel Mansilla-Fernández, 'A Bird Eye (Re)view of Key Readings' (*European Economy*, 5 July 2017) <https://european-economy.eu/2017-1/a-bird-eye-review-of-key-readings-2017-1/> accessed 15 May 2022 at 1.12 pm; Douglas W Arner and others, 'Overstating Moral Hazard: Lessons from Two Decades of Banking Crises' (2017) <https://papers.ssrn.com/abstract=2929574> accessed 15 May 2022 at 1:30:31 pm.

44 Arner and others (n 43).
45 Ari, Chen and Ratnovski (n 10); World Bank Group (n 1).
46 Aiyar and others (n 10); Garrido, Kopp and Weber (n 32); Haas, Markovic and Plekhanov (n 32).
47 Baudino and Yun (n 10).
48 ibid.
49 ibid.
50 ibid; See also the seven policy choices for success of Haas, Markovic and Plekhanov (n 32).
51 European Union (n 38). Recital (16) recognises that effective intervention may require the use of public funds, but Recital (31) indicates that resolution plan should not assume access to extraordinary public financial support or exposure of tax payers to the risk of loss.
52 ibid.
53 World Bank, *The World Bank Principles and Guidelines for Effective Insolvency and Creditors Rights Systems* (The World Bank, 2001); World Bank Group (n 1).
54 Jay Lawrence Westbrook, 'Systemic Corporate Distress: A Legal Perspective' in Stijn Claessens, Simeon Djankov and Ashoka Mody (eds), *Resolution of Financial Distress: An International Perspective on the Design of Bankruptcy Laws* (The World Bank, 2001).
55 ibid.
56 ibid.
57 ibid 50.
58 European Commission, *Proposal for a Directive of the European Parliament and of the Council on Preventive Restructuring Frameworks, Second Chance and Measures to Increase the Efficiency of Restructuring, Insolvency and Discharge Procedures and Amending Directive 2012/30/EU* (European Commission, 2016).
59 World Bank Group (n 1).
60 Hupkes (n 23).
61 Charles Jordan Tabb, 'The History of the Bankruptcy Laws in the United States' (1995) 3(1) Am Bankr Inst Rev 5 at 32; Vern Countryman, 'A History of American Bankruptcy Law' (1976) 81(6) Com LJ 226 (1976) 81(6) Com LJ 226; Louis Edward Levinthal, 'Early History of Bankruptcy Law' (1917) 66(3) U Pa Rev 223; David A Skeel Jr, 'The Genius of the 1898 Bankruptcy Act' (1999) 15(2) Emory Bankr Dev J 321.
62 For an overview of emergency insolvency measures and preventive insolvency measures taken by various states in response to COVID-19 pandemic, see Antonia Menezes and Akvile Gropper, *Overview of Insolvency and Debt Restructuring Reforms in Response to the COVID-19 Pandemic and Past Financial Crises: Lessons for Emerging Markets* (Virtual Colloquium on Resolution of Financially Distressed Financial Institutions, 8 March 2021); See also, World Bank Group and INSOL, *Global Guide: Measures Adopted to Support Distressed Businesses Through the COVID-19 Crisis* (INSOL International and World Bank Group, 2020).
63 Corporate Insolvency and Governance Act 2020 c.12 (CIGA) 'www.legislation.gov.uk' <https://perma.cc/W897-2EEV> accessed 15 February 2021 at 9.25 AM and also, Re DeepOcean 1 UK Ltd [2020] EWHC 3549 (Ch) sanctioning creditors meetings and Re DeepOcean I UK Ltd & Ors [2021] EWHC 138 (Ch) approving the restructuring plan where one or more classes did not vote in favour, if the plan is sanctioned, none of the members of the dissenting class would be worse off than in the event of the 'relevant alternative' (if the plan were not confirmed); and the plan has been approved by at least one class who has a genuine economic interest in the 'relevant alternative.'; See also, Directive (EU) 2019/1023 of European Parliament and Council of 20 June 2019 on Preventive Restructuring Frameworks and others 'EUR-Lex – 32019L1023 – EN – EUR-Lex' <https://perma.cc/N2DD-42VN> accessed 15 February 2021 at 9.42 am.

64 'These Are the Biggest Economies in Africa – IMF | IOL Business Report' <www.iol.co.za/business-report/economy/these-are-the-biggest-economies-in-africa-imf-15929339> <https://perma.cc/E88R-BTAU> accessed 15 May 2022, 12.25 am; 'Population, Total – Nigeria | Data' <https://perma.cc/R6X9-N6Q9> accessed 4 March 2021 at 12.07 am.

65 Chibuike Ugochukwu Uche, *Banking Developments in Pre-Independence Nigeria: A Study in Regulation, Control and Politics* (A thesis submitted for the degree of Doctor of Philosophy to Department of Accounting and Finance, The London School of Economics and Political Science, University of London, 1997).

66 ibid.

67 ibid.

68 GD Paton, Nigeria and Legislative Council, *Report on Banks and Banking in Nigeria* (Government Printer, 1948) 9; Folashade A Adeyemo, *Banking Regulation in Africa: The Case of Nigeria and Other Emerging Economies* (1st edn, Routledge, 2021) 7, 12.

69 Uche (n 65); Adeyemo (n 68) 6.

70 Uche (n 65).

71 Hupkes (n 23) 460–61.

72 ibid 459–61.

73 ibid.

74 Uche (n 65) see also, Banking Ordinance 1952.

75 ibid.

76 Paton, Nigeria and Legislative Council (n 68) 9; Tunde I Ogowewo and Chibuike Ugochukwu Uche, '(Mis)Using Bank Share Capital as a Regulatory Tool to Force Bank Consolidations in Nigeria' (2006) 50(2) J Afr L 161 at 167; see also OSFI Canada, *Osfi Supervisory Framework* (Office of the Superintendent of Financial Institutions Canada, 1999) for explanation of such intervention in Canada.

77 Central Bank of Nigeria Ordinance 1958.

78 Adeyemo (n 68) 105.

79 'NDIC | NDIC History' <https://ndic.gov.ng/about-ndic-3/ndic-history/> stating that: Government established the Corporation to administer the deposit protection scheme on its behalf and to serve as a vehicle for implementing failure resolution options for badly managed insolvent banks. accessed 1 March 2019, 9:19:30 pm and 15 May 2022 at 5.56 pm WAT.

80 ibid.

81 ibid.

82 Charles C Soludo, 'Consolidating the Nigerian Banking Industry to Meet the Development Challenges of the 21st Century' (2004) 43 Bank Int Settl Rev <www.bis.org/review/r040727g.pdf> presenting and arguing CBN rationale for its Nigerian banks consolidation and global competitiveness agenda. accessed 8 March 2022, 7:34:05 PM EST.

83 Ogowewo and Uche (n 76).

84 OL Kuye, OJK Ogundele and Andrew Otike-Obaro, 'Nigeria's Bank Failures from 2008 to 2009' (2013) 4(8) Int J Bus Soc Sci <https://scholar.google.com/scholar?hl=en&as_sdt=0%2C5&q=Nigeria%E2%80%99s+bank+failures+from+2008+to+2009+&btnG=#aHR0cDovL3d3dy5pamJzc25ldC5jb20vam91cm5hbHMvVm9sXzRfTm9fOF9TcGVjaWFsX0lzc3VlX0p1bHlfMjAxMy8xNi5wZGZAQEAy> at 176 arguing that the home grown governance and prudential breaches were responsible for the 2008 to 2009 bank failures and not the Global Meltdown and intervention was only justified because of the systemic risk banks posed to depositors. accessed 10 April 2021 at 11:36:57 pm; Edwin M Egboro, 'The 2008/2009 Banking Crisis in Nigeria: The Hidden Trigger of the Financial Crisis' (2016) 12(2) Br J Econ Manag Trade 1–16 on the other hand showing by empirical study that the exit of foreign investment from the Nigerian capital market following the responses

abroad to the Global Meltdown was directly responsible for the bank financial crisis of the period.

85 Kuye, Ogundele and Otike-Obaro (n 84) 178.

86 Sanusi L Sanusi, 'Global Financial Meltdown and the Reforms in the Nigerian Banking Sector' (2011) 2(1) CBN J Appl Stat 93–108 for comprehensive narration of government and CBN response to the impact of the Global Meltdown on the Nigerian banking system.

87 Adeyemo (n 68) Chapter 4.

88 ibid 2, 23.

89 Hupkes (n 23) 460–61.

90 ibid 461.

91 Buckley, Avgouleas and Arner (n 33).

92 ibid.

93 ibid 30.

94 ibid 31.

95 Buckley, Avgouleas and Arner (n 33).

96 Adeyemo (n 68) 109–12.

97 'The 2008 global financial crisis led to an increased risk of insolvency among firms worldwide due to declining demand for goods and services, decreasing availability of external finance, declining investments, and reductions in remittances' – Elena Cirmizi, Leora Klapper and Mahesh Uttamchandani, 'The Challenges of Bankruptcy Reform' (2011) World Bank Res Obs Adv Access; Buckley, Avgouleas and Arner (n 33) For detailed discussion of the causes of the three primary financial crisis.

98 Adewale Adegoke Alawiye-Adams, 'AMCON: Professional Abuse of the Lending Function by Banks in Nigeria and the Invocation of the Assets Management Corporation to the Rescue by the Central Bank of Nigeria – A Treatise' <https://papers.ssrn.com/sol3/papers.cfm?abstract_id=1936153>; Kuye, Ogundele and Otike-Obaro (n 84).

99 Alawiye-Adams (n 98).

100 ibid.

101 Kuye, Ogundele and Otike-Obaro (n 84) 176.

102 CBN (n 9).

103 Olumide Famuyiwa, 'The Nigerian Financial Crisis' (2013) 2(1) J Sustain Dev Law Policy 36–64; Adeyemo (n 68) 109–12.

104 Concentrating NPLs in a single AMC can create economies of scale because it could realise profits, while freeing a bank's balance sheet at the same time avoiding fire sales in illiquid markets thus limiting the need and cost of restructuring banks: José Manuel Mansilla-Fernández, 'Institutions' (*European Economy*, 5 July 2017) <https://european-economy.eu/2017-1/institutions-2017-1/> accessed 17 August 2019, 11:24:24 pm.

105 For detailed discussions on the powers of AMCON under the statute, see Anthony Idigbe and Okorie Kalu, 'Dealing with Bank Insolvency: Asset Management Corporation of Nigeria Act' (2010) <www.internationallawoffice.com/newsletters/detail.aspx?r=21338> Under the 2019 Amendment Act, additional information, surveillance and tracing powers are added to AMCON whilst the Corporation is at the same time pretty much insulated from any enforcement proceedings, suits for breach of rights or monetary claims or any injunctive orders.

106 ibid.

107 S.6(7) AMCON Act 2010 gives AMCON power to compromise and debt and grant forbearance and waiver.

108 Mansilla-Fernández (n 16) argues in his proposal for a European wide AMC that there should be a 3-year limit for exit by selling with provision for compensation for shortfall recourse mechanism and clawback mechanism for losses. Most scholars

agree that there should be an exit limit for a specific asset and a sunset date for particularly public-funded AMC.

109 Week (n 14).

110 Westbrook (n 54) 47 and 59 arguing that special insolvency regime like special medical rules and practices during a public health epidemic is based on sound existing insolvency or health regime to which the system reverts when emergency rules are lifted.

111 There are other criticisms of the implementation of the AMCON Act. For instance, Adewale contends that it has been used as an instrument to achieve a political agenda to dispose some persons of ownership of banks or reduce their significance in the economy through arbitrary and selective enforcement of realization and grant of forbearance on eligible bank assets Alawiye-Adams (n 98); See also for argument of expropriation through AMCON: Chinenyeze Amechi and Folashade A Adeyemo, 'A Comparative Analysis of the Asset Management Corporation of Nigeria and the US Troubled Asset Relief Programme' <www.academia.edu/36490815/A_Comparative_Analysis_of_the_Asset_Management_Corporation_of_Nigeria_and_the_US_Troubled_Asset_Relief_Programme> accessed 22 August 2019, 4:49:31 am; Tobechukwu Chikwendu, 'Amcon and Toxic Assets: Optimizing the Securitization Option | LinkedIn' <www.linkedin.com/pulse/amcon-toxic-assets-optimizing-securitization-option-chikwendu/> referred to IMF advise to Nigeria to terminate AMCON. accessed 22 August 2021, 4:09:45 am; 'IMF and the AMCON Sunset Debate – Businessday NG' <https://businessday.ng/opinion/article/imf-and-the-amcon-sunset-debate/> accessed 6 September 2019, 6:08:58 pm.

112 Westbrook (n 54) 59.

113 s.41 BOFIA 2020.

114 Aiyar and others (n 10). These are 1. tightening supervisory policies (prudential regulation), 2. insolvency reforms, 3. skills and capacity building, and 4. development of the distressed debt market.

115 For more details on the Nigerian jurisprudence showing conflict between forces of liquidation and those of business rescue and how practitioners manoeuvre the terrain, see Ikemefuna Idigbe (n 5).

116 World Bank, *Report on Observance of Standards & Codes Nigeria Insolvency and Creditor Rights Systems* (The World Bank, 2007).

117 Haas, Markovic and Plekhanov (n 32) presence of expertise is one of the key elements for resolution policy success.

118 Anthony Idigbe, *Transforming the Nigerian Economy: Aligning the Nigerian Business Rescue Practice with Global Trends* (Metropolitan Club Victoria Island Lagos, 2013).

119 See, generally, Companies and Allied Matters Act 1990, Part XVI.

120 See, generally, Investment and Securities Act 2007, Part XII, ss 129–130, 146–147.

121 See *Savannah Bank of Nigeria Plc v Nigeria Deposit Insurance Corporation* [2006] 9 N.W.L.R (pt 986) 424 at 441, paras E – H holding that until a winding up petition is filed a provisional liquidator could not be appointed by the court; See also Rule 21(1) CWR and *General and Aviation Services Ltd v Thahal* (2004) 4 SC (pt 1) 109 at 127.

122 (1999) 2 NWLR 591, p. 333.

123 See s.251 of the 1999 Constitution as amended.

124 Nigeria is a federation of 36 states and one federal capital territory (FCT), Each state and the FCT has its own court, and there is a Federal High Court which deals with bankruptcy and insolvency exclusively.

125 Idigbe (n 5).

126 The Companies and Allied Matters Act 2020 has made significant provisions for a moratorium as the further discussion later will disclose.

127 Chapter B2 Laws of the Federation (LFN) 2004, see sections 2, 3, 4 and 8.
128 ibid and sections 28–31 on discharge including automatic discharge after 5 years.
129 The Bill adopted the UNCITRAL Model Law on Cross Border Insolvency but the provision did not survive the legislative process and so was not adopted in CAMA 2020. Further article 3 of the UNCITRAL Model Law allows treaty obligations to prevail over the Model Law in which case bank resolution measures under the Basel framework implemented by BOFIA 2020 are exceptions to the Model Law.
130 Section 9(l) AMCON Act 2010 empowers AMCON to compromise any claim or forgive or forebear any debt or other obligation owed to the Corporation in respect of a specified class of eligible bank assets.
131 For instance, the AMCON Act 2019 (amended s.48(7) (a) and (b)) provides for automatic one-year extendable stay period for a statutory receivership appointed by AMCON and cram down on other creditors but the appointment is not in the context of any collective proceeding and it is not clear whether AMCON as a creditor is bound by the automatic stay. It seems like a defensive mechanism to stay all other creditors apart from AMCON.
132 AMCON Practice Directions (APD) 2013 as amended in 2018, and made pursuant to the powers conferred on the Chief Judge of the Federal High Court by s.254 of the Constitution of the Federal Republic of Nigeria 1999, s.44 of the Federal High Court Act, ss.53 and 61 of the AMCON Act, 2010 and Order 57 Rule 3 of the Federal High Court (Civil Procedure) Rules, 2009. The fundamental objective of the APD as set out in Part 1.2 is enabling proper case management and assisting the Court to deal with AMCON claims quickly and efficiently. The AMCON Track Judge with the assistance of the parties and counsel is required to give effect to the fundamental objective of the APD at every stage of an AMCON claim. Also, note that AMCON Act 2015 included a requirement for a receiver appointed by AMCON to submit to AMCOM a Rehabilitation Plan within 30 days of his appointment.
133 Stephen J Lubben, 'A Functional Analysis of SIFI Insolvency' (2018) 96 Tex Rev 1377.
134 Brian W Smith and Melissa R H Hall, 'Troubled Banks and Failed Banks: Opportunities for Investment' (2008) 4 Pratts J Bankruptcy Law 483; There are others issues of concern with use of bridge banks such as valuation of shares of previous owners Thomas C Baxter, *Resolving the Unresolvable: The Pathway to Ending, Too Big to Fail* (Columbia University, 2013). See also Adewale's contention of political interference and use of AMCON to dispossess or favour people (n 3) supra. Alawiye-Adams (n 98).
135 Gary Shorter, *The Resolution Trust Corporation: Historical Analysis* (CRS, 2008) Shorter argues that between 1989 and 1995, when the RTC was terminated, it was alternately criticised for dumping thrift assets and for taking too much time to dispose of them.
136 Charles D Booth and William S Richardson, *Japan & China (including Hong Kong): Introduction to the Tools Available for Corporate Rescue & Cross-Border Insolvency, American College of Bankruptcy Course on International Bankruptcy* (American College of Bankruptcy, 2018).
137 Mansilla-Fernández (n 104).
138 Booth and Richardson (n 136).
139 Berry Fong-Chung Hsu, Douglas Arner and Qun Wan, 'Policy Functions as Law: Legislative Forbearance in China's Asset Management Companies' (2006) 23 UCLA Pac Basin Law J 129.
140 ibid; for additional discussion on the legal framework for AMC and trust companies in China see Xusheng Yang, 'Asset Management's Big Bang' (2013) 32 Intl Fin Rev 20.

141 Patrick J Schena, 'Banks, Distressed Loans, and the Development of Chinese Markets for Asset-Backed Securities' (2005) 29 Fletcher F World Aff 35.
142 ibid.
143 Cynthia M Pornavalai, 'Thai Asset Management Corporation – Objectives and Powers' (2002) 30 Intl Bus Law 174 Pornavalai observed that 'bankers do not think of TAMC as a panacea to the problem of NPLs [non-performing loans].'
144 World Bank Group, *Doing Business Report 2020 Nigeria* (World Bank, 2020) 99 <www.doingbusiness.org/content/dam/doingBusiness/country/n/nigeria/NGA.pdf> accessed 16 May 2022, 12.29 am wat.
145 ibid 107.
146 Geoff Simms, AJCapital Advisory speaking on similar challenges in Southeast Asia at INSOL Fellows Forum at INSOL Conference, 2 April 2019, Singapore.
147 The AMCON Act 2015 introduced cost-sharing with the banks through the set-up of a Resolution Trust Account to which both the government and the banks are required to contribute annually.
148 The CBN Exposure Draft of the Framework for Licensing, Regulation and Supervision of Private Asset Management Companies in Nigeria, specifies that the provision for the establishment of Private Asset Management Companies (PAMC) was premised on the evolving nature of the financial industry and the need to proactively widen the space for the management of non-performing loans; licenced as a privately owned Other Financial Institution (OFI) to acquire, manage, restructure and dispose of eligible assets of banks, OFIs and Banks in Liquidation Central Bank of Nigeria, *Draft Framework for the Licensing, Regulation and Supervision of Private Asset Management Companies in Nigeria* (2017) accessed 16 May 2022 at 1.40 am.
149 The active local AMCs are subsidiaries of bank holding companies even though CBN regulation require separation from the banks.
150 Chikwendu (n 111).
151 The annual levy paid by the banks and other financial institutions remains tax deductible for the purpose of companies' income tax. See Chapter D- Part IX of the BOFIA 2020.
152 Adeyemo (n 68) 95.
153 'AMCON Seeks Reintroduction of Failed Bank Act' (*Guard Niger News – Niger World News*, 21 March 2019) <https://guardian.ng/business-services/amcon-seeks-reintroduction-of-failed-bank-act/> accessed 14 April 2019, 6:22:27 pm.
154 See notes 40, 86, 104 and 105 above.
155 'CBN: NPLs Rate Drops to 9.6% in 40 Months' (*Nation Newspaper*, 19 August 2019) <https://thenationonlineng.net/cbn-npls-rate-drops-to-9-6-in-40-months/> accessed 20 August 2019, 2:49:49 pm.
156 Haas, Markovic and Plekhanov (n 32).
157 World Bank Group (n 144) at 99 Collection rate in Nigeria is 27.5 cents on the US Dollar compared to 85.3 cents in the UK. AMCON collection rate at 30% of EBAs is only marginally better than the general ICR rate.
158 'AMCON Seeks' (n 153).
159 Chikwendu (n 111).
160 'About' (*FMDQ Security Exchange*) <www.fmdqgroup.com/about/> accessed 26 August 2019 at 2:48:15 am. A market now exists for the execution, clearing and settlement of financial market transactions across the debt capital, foreign exchange and derivatives markets, through the FMDQ Entities – FMDQ Securities Exchange PLC, FMDQ Clear Limited and FMDQ Depository Limited.
161 FMDQ, *FMDQ Bond Listing and Quotation Rules* (FMDQ OTC Securities Exchange, 2014) www.fmdqgroup.com//wp-content/uploads/2017/07/FMDQ-Bond-Listing-and-Quotation-Rules-Dec.-2014.pdf.
162 note 155.

163 'CBN Adopts New Measure to Tackle Loan Default, Rising NPLs' (*Guard Niger News – Niger World News*, 27 August 2019) <https://guardian.ng/business-services/cbn-adopts-new-measure-to-tackle-loan-default-rising-npls/> See ss. 49, 50 and 50A of recently enacted AMCON (Amendment No. 2) Act 2019 and notes 84 and 85 above.
164 Elizabeth Buckel, 'Curbing Comity: The Increasingly Expansive Public Policy Exception of Chapter 15 (Washington, DC)' 2013 44(3) Georget J Int Law 1281–311 at 24.
165 ibid.
166 Communication Week, 'Banks Lose N1.1trn to IFRS 9 Rule on Bad Loans' (*Nigeria Communications*, 20 August 2019) <https://nigeriacommunicationsweek.com.ng/banks-lose-n1-1trn-to-ifrs-9-rule-on-bad-loans/>.
167 Babatunde Popoola, *Improving Consumer Credit Through Credit Reporting* (CRC, 2021).
168 Published in Official Gazette No 58 Volume 104-page A37–60 Lagos 31 May 2017. PEBEC data indicate 1.7 trillion Naira value in 39000 registered financial statements and only 58,843 collaterals registered with the registry so far.
169 For more detailed discussion of the STMAA 2017 see George Etomi, 'Analysis of the Secured Transactions in Movable Assets Act 2017 | Lexology' <www.lexology.com/library/detail.aspx?g=c2d10dcd-dfa8-42ef-845f-bb18b5440fae> accessed 3 March 2019 at 7:28:15 pm.
170 The Presidential Enabling Business Environment Council (PEBEC) was set up in July 2016 by His Excellency, President Muhammadu Buhari, to remove impediments to doing business in Nigeria.
171 Sections 23–26 STMAA.
172 Anthony Idigbe, 'Overview of the Regulatory Framework for Secured Transactions in Movable Assets' (2022) 1 Bripan Law Rev 79–110 at 93–94 for details of the impact of the STMAA on collateral realisation.
173 ibid for a more detailed discussion and overview of the STMAA.
174 s.130 BOFIA 2020.
175 ss. 34–42 (Part IV) BOFIA 2020 Adeyemo (n 68) 87–98 for detailed discussion on the prudential and bank resolution measures introduced by BOFIA 2020.
176 s.5, 8 and 12 BOFIA.
177 s. 7 BOFIA. This is without prejudice to the provisions of the Federal Competition and Consumer Protection Act. See subsection 6 and section 53 BOFIA.
178 Part II, s.15–18 BOFIA.
179 s.19 BOFIA.
180 s. 23 BOFIA.
181 s.34 (3) BOFIA.
182 s.34 (2h) BOFIA.
183 s.34(4) BOFIA.
184 s.35 BOFIA.
185 See s.36 BOFIA. Agencies include Corporate Affairs Commission, Federal Inland Revenue Service, Nigeria Deposit Insurance Corporation, Federal Ministry of Finance, Budget and National Planning and any ministry, department or agency as may be determined by the CBN Governor.
186 ss.37 and 38 BOFIA 2020 Adeyemo (n 68) 91–92 arguing that by these provisions the bail-in measures could be at the coat of other stakeholders such as creditors and depositors.
187 s. 39 BOFIA.
188 s. 41 BOFIA Interestingly, the shareholders or creditors of the bank or other financial institutions and other third parties shall not enforce any right, judgment or claim howsoever described against the assets transferred to the private asset management vehicle.

189 Adeyemo (n 68) 87–98 while Adeyemo commends BOFIA as a welcome development, it is worrisome that some of its provision introduce duplications that can hamper the policy environment. For instance, multiplicity of courts by creation of a tribunal could result in jurisdiction disputes instead of substantive decisions. Reform of personal bankruptcy law and creation of credit court under the Federal High Court may have been more effective.
190 Aiyar and others (n 10).
191 See Chapters 17 and 18 CAMA 2020 respectively.
192 See Chapter 17 CAMA 2020.
193 See sections 484–513 CAMA 2020.
194 See Chapter 19 on receivership and management, Chapter 20, on winding-up and Chapter 27 on arrangements and compromise.
195 Section 452(4) CAMA 2020 provides that appointment of a receiver under a floating charge amounts to administration. An administration is only invalid against a receiver appointed pre-CAMA 2020 by section 454. However, fixed charge holder can appoint a receiver and appointment of administrator required consent of fixed charge holder – see sections 476 and 450 of CAMA 2020.
196 See section 710 of CAMA 2020.
197 See sections 204, 207, 647, 657, 665 and 675 of CAMA 2020.
198 See sections 503, 537(2), 537(3) and 655 of CAMA 2020.
199 See sections 705–7 CAMA 2020.
200 See section 705(1) c.
201 See sections 705 (1) c and 705 (1) b CAMA 2020.
202 For history of the FCCPA see, Anthony Idigbe, 'Overview of Development of Competition Law in Nigeria | Afronomicslaw' <https://perma.cc/4Q2R-T62C> Section 3 of FCCPA established the FCCPC.
203 https://thenationonlineng.net/mergers-acquisitions-sec-to-realign-rules-as-new-commission-takes-off/.
204 S. 92(1) (iii) of the Federal Competition and Consumer Protection Act 2018.
205 S. 93 (3) of the Federal Competition and Consumer Protection Act 2018.
206 'Mergers – Federal Competition and Consumer Protection Commission Mergers | Federal Competition and Consumer Protection Commission' <https://perma.cc/46WB-WBA3> It also issued the FCCPC Administrative Penalties Regulations, 2020.
207 Section 94 FCCPA.
208 Popoola (n 167) at slide 26 Popoola is the CEO of one of Nigeria's credit reporting agencies.
209 National Collateral Registry, *National Collateral Registry (Ncr) Statistics as at 1st March, 2020* (National Collateral Registry, 2020); See also Idigbe (n 172) at 106–9 arguing that the STMAA has provided an opportunity for data integration among various registries such as the CAC, NCR, Land and Court registry.
210 National Collateral Registry (n 209).
211 ibid.
212 The most common PMSI (Purchase Money Security Interest) transaction in the United States is automobile financing: John Ukegbu, *Uniform Commercial Code: The Anatomy of an Automobile Financing Transaction* (La Cours Hotel Lagos, 2019) 10.
213 World Bank (n 116).
214 Ratna Sahay and others, *The Promise of Fintech: Financial Inclusion in the Post COVID-19 Era* (International Monetary Fund) at 2, 13, 20–22.
215 note 155.
216 For discussion on measures taken to deal with the pandemic, see note 62.
217 Haas, Markovic and Plekhanov (n 32).

218 World Bank Group (n 144) at 90 Collection rate in Nigeria is 27.5 cents on the US Dollar compared to 85.3 cents in the UK.
219 'AMCON Seeks' (n 153).
220 Chikwendu (n 111).
221 Week (n 166).
222 World Bank Group (n 1).
223 European Commission (n 58) at 3.
224 Corporate Insolvency and Governance Act (n 63).
225 ibid C.12.
226 For preview of the law see H Jayesh, Aditi Bagri and Aaheree Mukherjee, 'A New Look to the Indian Corporate Insolvency Regime' (2016) 10(1) Insolv Restruct Int 34; Abhishek Saxena and Akshay Sachthey, 'The Insolvency and Bankruptcy Code, 2016 a Fresh Start for India's Insolvency Regime' (2016) 10(2) Insolv Restruct Int 22. The 2016 Code came into force on the 1st of December 2016.
227 The Insolvency and Bankruptcy Code (Amendment) Ordinance 2018 effective 6 June 2018. For key highlights of the amendment, see Khushnuma Khan, 'Insolvency and Restructuring in India' (2019) 13(1) Insolv Restruct Int 23–26.
228 Nikhil Shah, The MD of Alvarez & Marsal, India Speaking on a Panel on Dealing with Non-Performing Loans at INSOL Conference, 3 April 2019, Singapore.
229 Insolvency and Bankruptcy Board of India (Fast Track Insolvency Resolution Process for Corporate Persons) Regulations, 2017, see Khan (n 227).
230 See Shah (n 94).
231 ibid.
232 ibid.
233 ibid.
234 ibid.
235 Although UNCITRAL Model Law on Cross-Border Insolvency is not applicable to banks because the Model Law uses the courts as the site for cooperation and coordination while the banks use the supervisor or regulator as the site for cooperation, the norm of cooperation and coordination underlay both regimes under the Model Law as well as the FSB Key Attributes for Effective Financial Resolution Regime particularly for G-SIFIs.
236 Buckley, Avgouleas and Arner (n 33).
237 note 58 at 3.
238 Haas, Markovic and Plekhanov (n 32) presence of expertise is one of the key elements for resolution policy success.
239 Adeyemo (n 68) arguing that bank resolutions measures are reactive not proactive; Alawiye-Adams (n 98) arguing that AMCON intervention has not resulted in improved prudential discipline.
240 Anthony Idigbe, 'Progress of Insolvency Law Reform' Int Law Off <https://perma.cc/X9CG-R8UE> accessed 11 October 2021 at 6:09:19 pm.
241 Haas, Markovic and Plekhanov (n 32).
242 Buckley, Avgouleas and Arner (n 33).
243 Idigbe (n 240).
244 The collapse of Etisalat, the fourth largest telecommunication company in Nigeria, now 9mobile, further betrays the need for a general business recovery law 'Perma | 17 Important Things to Know About Etisalat Nigeria Debt Crisis – Premium Times Nigeria' <https://perma.cc/HE6F-FAT7> accessed 11 October 2018, 1:17:46 PM; The judicial orders obtained to support the restructuring process leading to the sale of the company to new investors is currently under legal challenge 'Court Declares Sale of Etisalat Illegal | The Guardian Nigeria News – Nigeria and World NewsBusiness – The Guardian Nigeria News – Nigeria and World News' <https://guardian.ng/business-services/court-declares-sale-of-etisalat-illegal/> accessed 6 April 2019, 8:43:13 am;

'Court Warns CBN, NCC, Others Against Concluding Etisalat's Sale' (*Guard Niger Newsp – Niger World News*, 11 February 2019) <https://guardian.ng/news/court-warns-cbn-ncc-others-against-concluding-etisalats-sale/> The Etisalat insolvency could have been easily resolved under CAMA 2020 with a CVA, Administration or Scheme of Arrangement. accessed 11 February 2022, 5:11:00 pm.

245 Martha Finnemore and Kathryn Sikkink, 'International Norm Dynamics and Political Change' (1998) 52(4) Int Organ 887–917.

246 Leora Klapper, 'Saving Viable Businesses Viewpoint Public Policy for the Private Sector' (2011) Note Number 328 World Bank Group Financ Priv Sect Dev Vice Pres.

3 Unravelling the Mystery Behind Bank Insolvencies in the East African Community (EAC) – The Case for Uganda, Kenya and Tanzania

Hamiisi Junior Nsubuga

Introduction

Bank insolvency in the East African Community (EAC) is no longer breaking news on media platforms and outlets as it is a common occurrence in the region. Since the last global financial crisis of 2007–2009, over 25 banks have been liquidated by Central Banks in Uganda, Kenya and Tanzania.[1] In the last five years, over 15 banks have been liquidated, including the recent high profile liquidations of Dubai Bank, Imperial Bank and Chase Bank in Kenya, Crane Bank, National Bank of Commerce and Global trust Bank Ltd in Uganda and a total of seven banks liquidated by the Central Bank in Tanzania in 2018 alone. These included the high-profile liquidations of Bank M, coupled with Covenant Bank, Kagera Farmers' Co-operative Bank, Njombe Community Bank Ltd, Efatha Bank Ltd and Meru Community Bank Ltd.[2]

Regulation and supervision of commercial banks in these Member States is mandated to the Central Banks. Corrective measures prescribed by banking laws and regulations in these Member States encompass optional and flexible remedial measures to be taken by Central Banks while dealing with financially struggling banks. However, these remedial measures are discretionary which risks permissiveness and laxity in supervisory and regulatory proficiency by the Central Banks.[3] Very often, the preferred remedial measures taken by Central Banks do not consider rescue of financially distressed-but-viable banks and financial institutions as the main priority, preferring receivership and liquidation measures, due to lending structures and security arrangements.[4]

This chapter analyses the collapse of banks and financial institutions in Uganda, Kenya and Tanzania, three of the key Member States of the EAC. The causes and impact of bank insolvencies in these Member States' banking sectors are examined. The chapter begins with a historical overview of banking and its evolution in these Member States prior to the 2007–2009 global financial crisis, and the response to this crisis, examining the safeguards that were implemented by these Member States to combat subsequent financial crises. This is followed by analysis of factors that have inhibited the functionality of these safeguards, leading to a high number of bank insolvencies in these Member States. The

DOI: 10.4324/9781003173984-4

chapter concludes by calling for a regional cross-border banking and resolution framework across the EAC as a measure that would combat bank insolvencies in the region.

Historical Overview of Banking in the EAC

Uganda

Uganda's banking sector is tiered into commercial banks, credit institutions and microfinance deposit-taking institutions under the regulation and supervision of the Central Bank of Uganda (CBU). However, the scope of this chapter focuses only on clearing/commercial banks. The CBU has the mandate to supervise and regulate all operations of commercial banks and financial institutions in the country.[5] This mandate is enshrined in legislations such as the Bank of Uganda Act 1969, Bank of Uganda Act 2000, Financial Institutions Act 2004, Financial Institutions Amendment Act 2016, Micro Deposit Taking Institutions Act 2003 and Tier 4 Microfinance Institutions Money Lenders Act 2016.[6] As at 30 June 2019, commercial banks accounted for 95.2 percent of the banking sector total assets of USh.31.8 trillion.[7]

Almost 80 percent of banks and financial institutions in Uganda are foreign owned, with bigger financially stable banks from South Africa, Kenya, India etc., acquiring/opening subsidiaries as part of their wider banking groups. These include for example, Standard Chartered Bank, Stanbic Bank, Development Finance Company of Uganda Bank Ltd (DFCU), Equity Bank, Bank of Africa among other banks. This played out to the detriment of Uganda when the global financial crisis hit its banking sector in 2007–2009. The concern was that because of the foreign ownership parent banks would make huge withdrawals from subsidiaries in Uganda to offset other liquidity deficits in parent banks or other subsidiaries within the EAC region.[8]

At the turn of the millennium in 2000, Uganda's banking sector witnessed a significant evolution where a majority of indigenous commercial banks and financial institutions experienced financial difficulties and were either declared insolvent and taken over by the Central Bank, or sold to other stronger banks.[9] For example, International Credit Bank (ICB), Greenland Bank, Cooperative Bank, Global Trust Bank and National Bank of Commerce, with assets worth Ush164 billion ($42.8 million) were sold and liquidated by the CBU.[10] Other banks were ultimately sold to foreign-owned banking conglomerates. These included, for example, Nile Bank Uganda Limited – sold to British-owned Barclays Plc. in 2007, which merged with the already existing subsidiaries of Barclays Bank (Uganda) and Uganda Commercial Bank (UCB) – the then stronghold of Uganda's banking sector, sold to Standard Bank of South Africa, giving birth to the present Stanbic Bank Uganda Ltd.[11]

Following the 2007–2009 global financial crisis, like any other sectors of the economy, Uganda's banking sector was also gravely impacted as a majority of banks went through a readjustment period.[12] A majority of commercial banks declared financial difficulties and while corrective measures were taken by the CBU to address these difficulties, not many of the banks could be supported/rescued by the CBU and were liquidated. In 2012, the CBU liquidated and closed down National Bank of Commerce (Uganda), selling some of its assets to Crane Bank (U) Ltd, the then fastest growing commercial bank in the country. However, Crane Bank did not also survive for long, as in 2016, it was also taken over by the CBU, placed under receivership and formally liquidated in 2018.[13]

Kenya

Kenya's banking crisis dates back to circa five decades ago, but the crises of 1986 to 1989, and 1993/1994 to 1998 were heralded as one of the worst in Kenya's banking history in recent years. Thirteen banks collapsed in 1993 alone and 5 banks collapsed between 1996 and 1999 and the main causes for such failures were premised on under-regulated insider lending and corporate governance failings.[14] The most recent banking crisis took place between October 2015 and early 2018 but the most critical period was between August 2015 – April 2016 when major commercial banks such as Dubai bank were put under receivership, followed by Imperial Bank and Chase bank in April 2016.[15]

The banking sector in Kenya is governed and regulated by the Central Bank of Kenya (CBK).[16] According to the CBK's directory of licenced commercial banks and financial institutions, the number of commercial banks and financial institutions as of 30 March 2021 stood at 42, with 28 classified as domestic and 14 as foreign owned.[17] These banks and financial institutions are further classified into tiers: Tier 1 – consisting of large banks with a huge financial and asset base, and therefore at low risk of financial instability, Tier 2 – consisting of medium-sized banks and Tier 3 – consisting of smaller banks with low capital and asset bases.

Prior to the 2007/2008 global economic recession, about 11 multinational and Kenyan owned banks were using Kenya as their regional hub/headquarters to expand their operations into the EAC region by opening up subsidiaries. These banks included, for example, KCB Bank (with branches in Rwanda, Tanzania and Uganda), Equity Bank (with branches in Tanzania, Uganda, Rwanda and South Sudan), Fina Bank (with branches in Rwanda and Uganda), and the Commercial Bank of Africa (with branches in Tanzania, Rwanda and Uganda). These banks had, in total, 63 branches/subsidiaries outside Kenya (16 in Tanzania, 31 in Uganda and 16 in Rwanda).

However, this rapid growth has continually been set aback by banking and financial institutions instabilities as recently witnessed by the collapse of Chase Bank, Dubai Bank and Imperial Bank between 2015 and 2018 thereby affecting customer confidence in the banking sector.[18] Established in 1982, Dubai bank was one of the fastest growing but small high street banks in Kenya, headquartered in Nairobi, with other branches in Nairobi, Nakuru and Mombasa. However, on 14 August 2015, management of the bank was taken over by the CBK and placed under receivership for one year.[19]

The CBK appointed the Kenya Deposit Insurance Corporation (KDIC) as the main receiver to oversee the receivership process courtesy of sections 53(2) and 54(1) (a) of the Kenya Deposit Insurance Act, 2012.[20] In its report on the financial condition of the bank to the CBK on 24 August 2015, the KDIC as the main receiver, concluded that the bank was beyond rescue and recommended that liquidation of the bank was the most feasible option.[21] According to the CBK, the bank was suffering from capital and liquidity deficiencies as it had failed to fulfil its financial commitments and obligations, including *inter alia*, inability to meet daily cash reserve ratio (CRR), honouring loan commitments, such as that with Bank of Africa Kenya and other regulatory non-compliance and managerial failings.[22]

Another bank, Chase Bank Ltd, was placed into receivership by the CBK on 7 April 2016, citing among other reasons, failure to meet the statutory banking ratios and administrative under-reporting of vital information, particularly, of insider loans and other financial products.[23] It was reported that the bank had made huge amounts of insider loans to directors totalling to Kshs. 13.62 billion without due-diligence and compliance with corporate governance requirements. Chase Bank was itself a product of the failed United Bank (Kenya) which had been put in receivership and was under statutory management by the CBK in 1995. However, in 1996, United Bank rebranded to Chase Bank Ltd following several stakeholders acquiring over 60 percent shareholding in the failed United Bank Kenya. However, within a decade in operation, Chase Bank found itself subject to financial difficulties, struggling to maintain its place within Kenya's banking sector. Like was the case with Dubai Bank, the CBK later appointed the KDIC as the statutory receiver to take over the management of Chase Bank.

Following two years in receivership, Chase Bank was taken over by a Mauritius based SMB Bank in 2018 while other parts of the loans/assets were still under management of the KDIC.[24] On 7 April 2021, KDIC submitted the receiver's report to CBK in which it recommended that Chase Bank in receivership be liquidated. The decision was premised on the bank's weak and susceptible financial position to sustain its presence in the banking/financial market and therefore, liquidation was the only feasible option. The CBK later confirmed that it had assessed the KDIC recommendation and concluded that liquidation was the only option to facilitate the orderly resolution of residual assets and liabilities of the collapsed bank as rescue of the bank was no longer possible.[25]

Imperial Bank also collapsed in 2015. Established in 1992 as a finance and securities company, it transformed into a commercial bank in 1996 and licenced by the CBK to operate financial and banking services in Kenya. Prior to its demise in 2015, the bank's total asset base was recorded at US$498 million (equivalent to Kshs. 43 billion), with shareholders' equity of approximately US$66.2 million (equivalent to Kshs. 5.719 billion) in December 2013, making it one of the financially stable medium sized banks in Kenya.[26]

However, in October 2015 the bank was put under statutory receivership by the CBK and on 21 June 2016, NIC Bank was appointed as its asset and liabilities consultant, to work alongside the CBK.[27] Consequently, NIC Bank was allowed *inter alia*, to acquire some of Imperial Bank's assets and assumption of some liabilities including satisfaction of customer deposits.[28] NIC Bank became responsible for returning funds to the failed bank's deposit customers, while other assets were sold to KCB Bank. Amidst all of this, the CBK appointed the KDIC as the official receiver of Imperial Bank and liquidation proceedings were initiated.[29]

Tanzania

Like Kenya and Uganda, Tanzania's banking sector comprises a mix of commercial banks, community banks, micro-finance institutions and Savings and Credit Co-Operative Societies (SACCOs). These banks are both domestic and foreign owned. Until 1991, Tanzania's banking sector was mainly state controlled with two of the leading state-owned banks; the Cooperative Rural Development Bank (CRDB) and the National Micro-Finance Bank (NMB) accounting for over 40 percent of deposits and 35 percent of total assets.[30]

However, the banking sector underwent a privatisation drive in mid-1990s that witnessed a host of foreign banking groups, such as the South African banking group, Absa Group Limited, acquiring a majority stake in the National Bank of Commerce (NBC) in 1997 and Rabobank of the Netherlands acquiring 49 percent in NMB Bank. In late 2000s, that is, prior to the global financial crisis in 2007/2008, a host of several new banks such as Exim Bank, Access Bank, Azania Bank, and other regional banks from the EAC Member States, such as Equity Bank, Ecobank, Citi Bank etc. joined Tanzania's formal banking sector. As of 31 March 2021, there are 36 commercial banks, five community banks, two development banks and four micro-finance institutions in Tanzania.[31]

Between 2015 and 2019, Tanzania's banking sector experienced an economic slump that did not only affect the economy at large, but the banking sector in particular, experiencing a systemic shock. This shock was precipitated by *inter alia*, risky and aggressive lending without adequate Know Your Client (KYC) checks, uncontrolled insider lending and other corporate governance non-compliance that further amplified the reporting of non-performing loans across the banking sector.[32] For instance, in 2017 alone, the NPL ratio in Tanzania's banking sector was peaking at 11.5 percent, the highest to be recorded in over a decade, with the worst affected banks reporting an NPL ratio of over 55 percent.[33]

In an IMF Report released on 4 December 2018 on Tanzania's financial systems stability assessment, it was reported that more than half of commercial banks in Tanzania's banking sector were highly susceptible to financial shocks and harboured a high risk of future insolvency.[34] The susceptibility to market/financial shocks was mainly caused by high rise in NPL ratios, risky lending/loans, high dollarisation amplifying vulnerabilities to liquidity shocks, among other factors.[35] This Report was released at a time when Tanzania's banking sector was going through a banking crisis and when a total of 8 banks were experiencing financial difficulties in a single year.

In January 2018, the Central Bank of Tanzania (CBT) placed five banks under compulsory liquidation by appointing the Deposit Insurance Board of Tanzania as official receiver to oversee the liquidation processes. These banks included Covenant Bank For Women Ltd, Efatha Bank Ltd, Njombe Community Bank Ltd, Kagera Farmers' Co-operative Bank Ltd and Meru Community Bank Ltd.[36] According to the then governor of the CBT, Professor Benno Ndulu, the closures were mainly precipitated by persistent undercapitalisation – inability to maintain Tanzanian Shillings – (Tshs. 2 billion (equivalent to $891,180), non-compliance with other liquidity requirements and the high rates of non-performing loans.[37]

On 2 August 2018, Bank M, which had been incorporated and licenced by the CBT in 2007 to operate as a commercial bank was also placed under liquidation by the CBT due to failure to meet capital liquidity requirements.[38] In January 2019, Bank M's assets and liabilities, then estimated at about US$500 million, were transferred to Azania Bank by the CBT, officially, liquidating Bank M.

On 19 November 2020, the CBT, once again, took over temporary control over China Commercial Bank for 90 days as a resolution mechanism was being sought.[39] Incorporated in 2013, the bank had only been in operation for just over six years. However, it had failed to fulfil minimal capital requirements in addition to other managerial con-compliance. In March 2021, the CBT decided to transfer all assets and liabilities of China Commercial Bank to NMB Bank Plc, one of the largest banks in the country, as liquidation proceedings ensued.[40]

However, a vital point to note in relation to bank insolvencies within the EAC region is that the key causes are all interlinked. These are, in particular, high levels of non-performing loans, corporate governance systemic failings and the absence of efficient banking resolution framework. These are the same key causes reported in Tanzania, Kenya and Uganda at large. These factors are analysed later, followed by suggested recommendations on how these causes may be countered/remedied to devise an efficient banking resolution framework that can be adopted across the EAC region.

Banks and Financial Institutions Insolvency – The Causes Analysed

Non-Performing Loans

Non-performing loans (NPL) are globally linked to bank failure as well as financial crises but the term has no globally adopted definition as country definitions differ. This is because, it has been accepted that what is appropriately accepted/categorised as an NPL in one country may not be so in another.[41] However, a key feature of an NPL is that a loan is non-performing where payments of interest and/or principal are past due by 90 days or more, or interest payments equal to 90 days or more have been capitalised, refinanced, or delayed by agreement, or payments are less than 90 days overdue, but there are other good reasons – such as a debtor filing for bankruptcy – to doubt that payments will be made in full.[42]

Within the EAC, NPLs have been identified as one of the prime causes of bank failures, mainly precipitated by factors, such as imprudent lending policies and strategies, insider lending as almost half of the failed banks' losses were attributed to bad loans and high interest rate loans.[43] In Kenya, it had been highlighted that most of the so-called big local banks' financial difficulties and failures such as those of Continental Bank and Pan African Bank, were exacerbated by excessive insider lending, often to politicians.[44] The collapse/liquidations of other banks, such as Dubai Bank, Imperial Bank and Chase Bank were also blamed to a larger extent, on NPLs. For example, the report published following the collapse of Chase Bank indicated that NPLs within the bank had risen from Kshs. 3 billion in 2014 to Kshs. 11 billion in 2015, but mainly attributed to insider loans.[45]

In Uganda, the main reason given by the CBU for the liquidations of the National Bank of Commerce in 2012, Global Trust Bank in 2014 and Crane Bank Uganda Ltd in 2016 was the high rate of NPL that affected the financial stability of these banks in addition to other corporate governance failings.[46] In its 2019 Annual Financial Stability Report, the CBU indicated that gross loans and advances within the commercial banking sector had increased by 11.2 percent, compared to the 11.0 percent in the year ending June 2018.[47] The report also highlighted that asset quality, as measured by the ratio of non-performing loans to total loans (NPL ratio), had worsened across the banking sector over the year ended September 2020. The commercial banks' aggregate NPL ratio rose from 4.4 percent in September 2019 to 5.1 percent in September 2020.[48]

In Tanzania, the 2020/2021 Monetary Policy Statement published by the CBT in June 2020, indicated that Tanzania's banking sector was stable as banks had enough capital reserves to sustain the impact COVID19 had caused to the financial sector in general.[49] The Statement also indicated that banks and financial institutions maintained appropriate liquidity levels as per minimum requirement of 20 percent. However, the Report highlighted that banks had reported a higher increase in NPLs as the ratio of the NPLs to gross loans was recorded at 11 percent as of April 2020 compared to 10.7 percent reported previously, in June 2019. This slight increase was largely attributed to the impact of COVID19 that slowed-down business transactions in the country and regional and international lockdowns.

Following the CBT's policy measures to tackle the effects of COVID-19, banks have restructured loans to their customers by reducing interest rates, extension of repayment periods, and moratoria relief (payment holidays of between 3–6 months) to customers.[50] However, despite these strategies, customers were still struggling to service their loans due to economic slow-down and business closures. As a result, NPLs were still recorded by banks and financial institutes at a level higher than the 5 percent targeted by the CBT by December 2020.[51]

Therefore, with NPLs being one of the major factors inhibiting banking and financial stability and efficiency across the EAC region, a coherent regulatory framework on bank governance, loan and credit supervision and prudential data/information sharing through a regional cross-border banking resolution framework ought to be adopted. This aspect is broadly analysed later at 4.0–4.2.4.

Corporate Governance Concerns

In the banking sector a key aspect of corporate governance is fiduciary duty and accountability by the board of directors and top management.[52] This is the need for directors and top management officers to ensure that good governance across all levels is maintained. This includes ensuring that stronger governance policies on financial reporting, capital and liquidity adequacy management and compliance, financial risk assessment and management and clear flow of information with insider and outsider constituents, such as the Central Bank is maintained.[53] This is to enable openness and transparency, within the bank/financial institution and the sector at large.

In the case of Chase Bank's collapse in Kenya, following an extended audit, it was reported that although the bank had attributed the biggest cause of its financial difficulties to poor accounting and management of its Islamic banking assets, there were more serious implications pointing towards governance failings. It was reported that the bank had made large amounts of loans to its directors, in excess of Kshs.1.35 billion per director (equivalent USD 13.5 million) without adequate financial affordability assessments among other know your client (KYC) validation checks.[54] This activity further raised questions of bank directors' fiduciary duties and obligations towards the bank itself and shareholders, especially, on how such huge loan amounts could be approved without due diligence.[55]

In Uganda, the recent collapse of Crane Bank Ltd exposed extensive corporate governance failings, especially in relation to the bank's mismanagement. A report compiled by accounting firm Price Waterhouse Coopers (PwC), in December 2016 on request by the CBU concluded that the board of directors of the bank, chaired by Mr Sam Muwanguzi, and Mr Ruparelia (the majority shareholder) failed in their primary responsibility and fiduciary duty to ensure that the bank was run efficiently.[56] The board was found to be complicit in the irregular shareholding of Mr Ruparelia who concealed his true shareholding in the bank and sanctioned irregular transfer of the bank's properties to other associated companies.[57]

Another corporate governance concern highlighted by the failed banks was in relation to structure and ownership settings. In Uganda, Kenya and Tanzania, and much like in developing economies, there are mainly two ownership structure types: concentrated ownership and dispersed ownership.[58] The major issue was that where ownership was concentrated either in a family controlled or business/banking group setting, the majority shareholders exercised more control with less scope for accountability from minority shareholders. This had the impact that governance failings such as unassessed insider loans or lending to connected parties, and noncompliance with lending regulations were side-stepped.[59] This was the case in Crane Bank's failings in Uganda, Dubai and Chase Banks in Kenya as discussed earlier.

In its Financial Systems Stability Assessment Report of 4 December 2018 on the state of Tanzania's financial systems, the IMF recommended that CBT should replace the Guidelines for Boards of Directors with a new Corporate Governance Regulation with a specific requirement for a Code of Conduct and Conflicts of

Interest Policy.[60] The Report also recommended a requirement for bank, or group-wide compensation policies that incorporate current Basel I guidance on ensuring alignment of incentives with the long term best interests of the banks.[61]

Ineffective Banking Insolvency Resolution Framework

One of the key factors that impact the effectiveness of a banking resolution framework, especially in developing economies is the absence of, or/poor enforcement of contract and insolvency laws that establish contractual commitments on the one hand, and the enforcement of such contractual commitments on the other hand.[62] An efficient resolution framework, especially, in a cross-border setting can help incentivise amongst other things, the development of local and regional financial markets through effective policies that can hedge risk exposures, such as interest rate risks, or credit risks that may lead to defaults within the banking/financial sector. This can have the advantages of enhancing the flow and allocation of capital and opportunities for diversification of banking/financial portfolios across borders.[63]

However, despite the significance of an efficient banking resolution framework as revealed in the recent global financial crisis as being one of the key factors that exacerbated the global financial recession, most African countries, let alone regions/communities such as the EAC have not acted swiftly to either establish such resolution frameworks or improve the ones in place.[64] Yet, an efficient banking resolution framework can inhibit excessive risk-taking during the good financial health of banks/financial institutions and also, triggers cause for concerns upon signs of imminent financial difficulties. Where this is the case, banks/financial institutions become more risk-averse[65] to such issues and prompt corrective actions either by the banks themselves, or the central banks as the main supervisors/regulators may be taken.

An efficient banking resolution framework can also strengthen the role of Central Banks as regulators of banking/financial sectors by sanctioning these institutions upon failure to adhere to the laws and regulations set by the resolution framework, which in turn reduces the necessity for bailouts.[66] Prior to the global financial crisis of 2007/2008, crisis management in the banking sector was differently and minimally regulated globally, premised on extant national laws and policies, with less emphasis on the global or regional aspects of this area of law.[67]

This was because the traditional view on bank insolvency and crisis management was mainly aimed at satisfying creditor interests and courts were looked at as the supervisors and arbiters of the process. However, post-global financial crisis, bank insolvency, crisis management and resolution has witnessed a paradigm shift towards a more inclusive approach. This approach considers not only creditor interests, but also, those of other interest holders, such as the bank itself, and the society at large.[68] This paradigm shift has impacted the evolution of bank insolvency and restructuring law as an area of interest, not only at a global, but also, at regional and national levels.[69]

As a result, many countries and regions across the world have either made amendments to existing laws or introduced new banking insolvency laws on key aspects, such as capital requirements, supervisory and resolution regimes, regional cooperation and compliance. However, most African States and regions/communities have witnessed a slow approach to this aspect, yet these amendments or new laws would take as a priority, coherent crisis management and preventive regimes as the main drivers that would shift the focus from the traditional creditor protection on insolvency, to a more inclusive model, taking into account, extant interest holders, including the economy and financial system.[70]

For instance, the European Union (EU) instigated a regional integration post-crisis through the introduction of the Banking Union to ensure that EU banks were stronger and better supervised with harmonised banking rules and regulations across Europe/Euro Zone.[71] This has to a certain extent, accelerated a European integration in the area of banking insolvency and restructuring law.[72] Although this would be a bit of a big ask for African nations/regional communities, such as the EAC to adopt, it must be submitted, the African response to bank insolvencies has been relatively slow and this has led to the recent surge in bank insolvencies in EAC as discussed earlier.

Recommendation for a Regional Cross-Border Banking and Resolution Framework

Cross-border banking in the EAC has seen a significant increase across Member States since the 2007/2008 global economic crisis with many banks across the region opening up branches. This increase has led to significant improvement in financial infrastructure needed to support financial services and financial markets, enhancing the development of cross-border payment systems, such as Mobile Money Services/M-PESA, clearing and settlement and credit registry systems.[73] Therefore, having a cross-border banking framework within the EAC would impact regional development and coordination to ensure banking and financial services provisions across the region are governed and regulated prudently.

The argument is that within the EAC, Kenya is heralded as one of the top countries with a modern banking and financial system in Sub-Saharan Africa, and the best in the EAC.[74] Therefore, Kenya's membership to the EAC may help impact and develop EAC's cross-border banking and resolution framework that can operate a more advanced cross-border model and can provide a platform upon which differences in legal and procedural frameworks could be reconciled/balanced to tailor a uniform regional banking resolution framework.[75]

For instance, if the CBU's policy approach to enforcement of mobile money tariffs for cross-border services transactions is significantly different to that of the KCB's, and therefore, impacting the regulation and supervision of such financial products/services in Kenya, it might be challenging to provide such a service across the region. This might not only impact customer services but also, efficient financial coordination and stability in the region which in turn, impacts the banking and financial sectors at large. There would therefore be a need to devise a balanced cross-border banking resolution framework that would remedy these divergences.

In a 2005 IMF policy report on bank behaviour in developing countries, evidence from the EAC countries (Uganda, Kenya and Tanzania) premised on structure, performance, and role of banking systems, showed that large foreign international banks were more efficient and active in lending than domestic banks due to weaker institutional policies that did not impact competitiveness and improved banking services provision.[76] Another study conducted by the IMF in 2013 highlighted that banks head-quartered in Uganda, Kenya and Tanzania but with subsidiaries in other EAC Member States had lower spreads and were more efficient than other private domestic banks with no subsidiaries in the region.[77] These banks (with regional branches/subsidiaries) were also recorded as being highly profitable in their domestic markets than other private banks due to liquidity support as part of a group that provided a sort of safety buffer from losses and financial shocks.[78]

Why a Regional Banking and Resolution Framework?

Some of the major impediments to attaining full regional banking and financial integration within the EAC have been cited as being: (i) the lack of a common tax regime; (ii) diverse national regulatory and supervisory frameworks prescribed by central banks; (iii) poor regional infrastructure, such as IT connectivity within the banking and financial sectors; (iv) the lack of a centralised data sharing network; and (v) the existence of diverse capital movement polices among other factors.[79] However, these impediments or/constrictions may be overcome by making good use of the EAC institutional framework to tailor a regional-integrated framework, especially within the banking and financial services sector.

Within the EAC, banks and financial institutions have historically been ahead of the curve in assessing the potential of the EAC regional market. This is because several banks have to a certain degree adopted a regional business model incentivised by a range of factors including but not limited to; diverse client base, corporate structures, common currency model – (the Shilling) being the main regional currency in Uganda, Kenya and Tanzania.[80] This is in addition to close-linked infrastructure along the regional trade corridors, such as the Mombasa Port that serves the main region. In addition, Uganda, Kenya and Tanzania as the three founding members of the EAC share a somewhat long history of trade and administrative cooperation, traceable to over a century, knitted by a shared colonial history by the British, leading to a shared legal system based on English common law which is an added advantage.

The EAC has a regional customs union adopted in 2005, and a Common Market Protocol adopted in November 2009 which have both strengthened regional trade cooperation.[81] These agreements map-out the agenda on liberalisation of trade in financial services (including banking) within the region which led to elimination of barriers to the free movement of capital in 2015. In essence, EAC Member States have progressively, in accordance with the Schedule on the Removal of Restriction on the Free Movement of Capital: (i) removed restrictions on the movement of capital belonging to the persons resident in the EAC; (ii) removed discrimination based on the nationality or on the place of residence of the persons or on the place where the capital is invested; (iii) removed any existing restrictions on the movement of capital and on the current payments and transfers; (iv) removed restrictions relating to current payments connected with the movement of goods, persons, services or capital.[82]

Another important factor that would support the argument for the introduction of a cross-border banking resolution framework across the EAC region is the regional legislative assembly, the East African Legislative Assembly – (EALA).[83] The EALA is the legislative organ of the EAC that has the mandate to legislate on all aspects of the law relating to the region, with power to pass laws overriding national laws. The EALA is supplemented by the Judiciary and the Secretariat – with three top-level committees; the Monetary Affairs Committee (MAC) comprised of the central bank governors, with subcommittees covering banking and insurance issues, the Fiscal Affairs Committee, comprised of the Ministers of Finance, dealing with harmonisation of taxes and duties; and the Capital Markets Development Committee, dealing with securities regulatory affairs.[84]

Therefore, this would support the establishment of a regional (single) licensing regime/framework to govern/regulate banking and financial services across the region. This in turn, would remedy inherent barriers to regional inter-connectedness mainly caused by separate domestic laws and regulatory restrictions, such as capitalisation requirements for banks and their regional subsidiaries. This would further, enable cross-border branching/subsidiaries, especially by powerful and stable banks across the region which is key to regional banking and financial integration.[85]

Benefits of an EAC Regional Banking and Resolution Framework

Cross-Border Harmonised Legal and Regulatory Framework

One of the key challenges in regulating cross-border banking services is that these services are governed/guided by various national or/domestic banking systems, built on different legal and regulatory structures. Therefore, the coordination of these diverse banking regulations becomes particularly onerous as different regulatory frameworks in different jurisdictions require different compliance frameworks.[86] Financial reporting is one such requirement. In the EAC for example, banks have to comply with banking and financial reporting requirements for the different jurisdictions they operate in due to absence of a regional coordinated regulatory framework.[87]

For example, Ecobank operates in several of EAC Member States, with five branches in Tanzania, eighteen branches in Kenya, and fourteen branches in Uganda (plus its presence in other EAC Member States, Rwanda, Burundi and South Sudan). However, each of these Member States have their own set of banking and financial rules and regulations on financial reporting. Where certain regulatory changes, such as capital adequacy requirements are introduced by one Member State, other branches or subsidiaries in other Member States may need to either recapitalise or decapitalise to comply with new regulations. This has the impact of creating capital imbalances across the region that affects the economies of scale in maximising capital movement/profits to both the consumer and the Member States within the region. This can however, be remedied by adopting a harmonised cross-border regulatory framework that can be adopted by EAC Member States and used as a regional regulatory framework.

Progress has been made between Uganda, Kenya and Tanzania to harmonise their bank payments transfer system by integrating their real time gross settlement systems (RTGS)[88] across borders. This harmonisation, if fully operative, could lead to the adoption of a single-regional licensing framework across the EAC region that would significantly enhance regional coordination in cross-border banking services provision aided by a regional banking and resolution framework.

Mutual Recognition of a Single Licensing Regime

Adopting a single licensing regime would be an important aid to further regional banking integration within the EAC region. If introduced for banks and financial institutions, it would significantly and procedurally reduce cross-border transaction times and costs. A single-licensing regime would also lead to or improve regional mutual recognition of broadly defined regional policies and principles among domestic regulators, such as the Basel core principles for bank supervision,[89] that can be regionally adopted by the EAC Member States among other principles.

Strengthening Cross-Border Supervision and Coordination

Establishing strong regional links between banks and financial institutions between EAC Member States would strengthen regional regulatory and supervisory cooperation especially from Member States' central banks. In the banking and financial sectors, prudential domestic regulation and supervision is very important to ensure compliance. However, for regional integration and coordination, both domestic and regional consolidated financial supervision are important in ensuring enforcement of financial compliance and risk management.[90] This would ensure, for example, that weaknesses in one Member State's bank/financial institution with subsidiaries in other Member States do not put the regional financial system at risk. To this effect, data sharing on regional cross-border banking or trading in financial products/services would be enhanced to remedy the data-gap caused by Member States' procedural and regulatory restrictions that may obscure cross-border linkages that mask the benefits of regional integration.[91]

Establishment of a Regional EAC College of Supervisors (CoS)

According to the Basel Committee on Banking Supervision,[92] College of Supervisors are multilateral working groups of relevant supervisors that are formed for the collective purpose of enhancing effective and consolidated supervision of international banking groups. This is to ensure that both home and host supervisors work as effectively as possible by clearly outlining expectations in relation to college objectives, governance, communication and information, as well as potential areas for collaborative work.[93]

Where established, supervisory colleges would enable the home State supervisors to exercise effective supervision of groups and their subsidiaries on a consolidated basis, but also, affording host State authorities a chance to be adequately represented in the regulatory and supervisory cross-banking affairs across the region. However, despite the presence of large supervisory colleges in developed jurisdictions, particularly, in the Western European banking groups, supervisory colleges are somewhat a new phenomenon within the African banking groups.[94] Nevertheless, in the EAC region, Kenya has pioneered on this front by setting up a supervisory college for its largest cross-border banks – the Kenya Commercial Bank Supervisory College, launched in Nairobi in October 2012 assisted by the IMF East AFRITAC.[95] Arrangements were also made in 2014 by the KCB for the opening of three more supervisory colleges.[96]

It is also envisaged that once created, the structures of the supervisory colleges will not only provide for supervisors/personnel providing expertise during the good financial health of banks/financial institutions within the region, but will also, provide for supervisors/experts that would provide resolution and fiscal expertise in relation to financial crisis management, be it to individual banking groups within a Member State, or to a regional systemic banking/financial set-up. This would help to foster key information sharing, regional coordination and consolidated enforcement of banking/financial activities to combat imminent financial crises/bank insolvencies in the region.

The only concern perceived in respect to supervisory colleges lies in the fact that supervisory colleges are not statutory bodies with law making powers. This would raise the question as to whether such colleges would be in a position to pass binding decisions/resolutions to bind other banking supervisors in other Member States. For instance, would a supervisory college in Kenya pass a decision/resolution, such as making changes to recapitalisation requirements impacting a subsidiary in Uganda that would be binding on the parent bank's supervisors in Uganda? Yet such a decision lies with Uganda – the home State to the parent bank?

The answer to this question lies in the effectiveness of regional integration and coordination within the EAC. The presence of provisions like the Common Markets Protocol and Customs Union and organs such as the regional legislative assembly (EALA) may support binding resolutions, such as a directives and regulations at a regional level, with a binding effect to be adopted. Where this is the case, regional directives/regulations would guarantee a binding effect of the decisions of supervisory colleges across Member States, like is the case with the supervisory colleges set-up under the framework for micro prudential supervision in the European Union through the work of the European Banking Authority (EBA).[97]

Conclusion

Banking insolvency within the EAC has been a key topic of discourse amongst extant stakeholders for decades but such discourses have gained pace in the last decade as several high-profile commercial banks and financial institutions across the region have been liquidated by respective Central Banks after suffering from irredeemable financial difficulties. The high-profile liquidations of National Bank of Commerce in 2012, Global Trust Bank in 2014 and Crane Bank Uganda Ltd in 2016 in Uganda, coupled with the liquidation of Chase Bank, Dubai Bank and Imperial Bank between 2015–2018 in Kenya and the liquidation of Covenant Bank for Women Ltd, Efatha Bank Ltd, Njombe Community Bank Ltd, Kagera Farmers' Co-operative Bank Ltd and Meru Community Bank Ltd in 2018 alone further highlight the plight of banking insolvencies in the region.

The outbreak of the global COVID19 pandemic at the beginning of the year 2020 that prompted not only national, but regional and international lockdowns further exacerbated a fragile state of banking and financial services provisions within the EAC as the timing of the outbreak coincided with already existing banking crisis in the EAC region. As a result, COVID19 induced lockdowns measures have greatly impacted the flow of capital and movement across borders which have further impacted the financial performance of bank and consumers' abilities to service their loans with banks which has further contributed to high NPLs reporting across EAC banking sectors, pausing a major threat to banking insolvency in the region.

As discussed in this chapter, the key causes of these banking insolvencies have been identified as high levels of NPLs, corporate governance failings and lack of or/poor banking resolution frameworks within EAC Member States. After close analysis of these factors and efforts taken by these Member States to address these concerns, the chapter recommends adoption of a regional cross-border banking resolution framework across the EAC as measure that can tailor regional coordination in the banking and financial services sectors as way of attaining efficient supervision and regulation of banking and financial services provision in the region. The chapter has argued that as these Member States share somewhat similar/common problems in relation to banking insolvencies, they should adopt a concerted approach to remedy these concerns, which is through adoption of a regional banking resolution framework.

Notes

1 Beatrice Materu, 'Panic as Tanzania Closes Five Banks' *The East African* (Nairobi, 6 January 2018) <www.theeastafrican.co.ke/business/Panic-as-Tanzania-closes-five-banks/2560-4253830-yd7mr9z/index.html> accessed 12 April 2022; B. Busulwa, 'Uganda's Central Bank Takes Control over Crane Bank' *The East African*, (Kampala, 20 October 2016), <www.theeastafrican.co.ke/business/Uganda-central-bank-takes-control-of-Crane-Bank/2560-3423876-108c3v0z/index.html> (accessed April 2022); Dicta Asiimwe, 'Report Indicts BOU for Illegal Closure of Banks' *The East African*, (Kampala, 22 September 2018) <www.theeastafrican.co.ke/

business/Report-indicts-BoU-for-illegal-closure-of-banks/2560-4772380-c1y0t7z/index.html> (accessed May 2022).

2 Busulwa (n 1); Hamiisi Junior Nsubuga, 'The Role of the Central Bank in Financial Distress Management and Resolution in Developing Economies' (2020) 35(5) J Int Bus Law Rev 208, 214.

3 ibid Nsubuga (n 2) 11.

4 M Brownbridge, 'Resolving Bank Failures in Uganda: Policy Lessons from Recent Failures' (2002) 20(3) Dev Pol Rev 279, 291.

5 These institutions include but are not limited to commercial banks, credit institutions, microfinance deposit taking institutions (MDIs) and forex bureaus.

6 These Acts of Parliament and other operational regulations are listed on the Bank of Uganda website at <www.bou.or.ug/bou/supervision/supervision_acts_regulations.html> accessed 11 May 2022.

7 Bank of Uganda, 'Financial Stability Report' (30 June 2019) <www.centralbanking.com/central-banking/official-record/1592844/bank-uganda-financial-stability-report> accessed 2 April 2022.

8 World Bank, 'Financial System Stability Assessment (FSSA): East African Community' (2013).

9 Brownbridge (n 4) 279, 291.

10 Asiimwe (n 2) accessed April 2022.

11 Honest P. Ngowi, 'The 2008 Economic Crisis: Implications and Responses in the Banking Sector' (2015) 3(1) Afr J Econ Rev 100–15.

12 World Bank, 'Uganda's Economic Update: Step by Step – Lets Solve the Finance Puzzle to Accelerate Growth and Shared Prosperity' (7 February 2017) <https://openknowledge.worldbank.org/handle/10986/26038?locale-attribute=en> accessed 10 March 2022.

13 Busulwa (n 1).

14 A Kithinji and NM Waweru, 'Merger Restructuring and Financial Performance of Commercial Banks in Kenya' (2007) 2(4) Econ Manag Financ Mark J 9–39.

15 Robert M Gathaiya, 'Analysis of Issues Affecting Collapsed Banks in Kenya from Year 2015–2016' (2017) 7(3) Int J Bus Manag Stud 9–15.

16 This power is mandated to the Central Bank of Kenya courtesy of the Central Bank of Kenya Act Chapter 491, Laws of Kenya, and as provided for its establishment under the Constitution of Kenya 2010, Art.231.

17 Central Bank of Kenya, 'Directory of Licenced Commercial Banks, Mortgage Finance Institutions and NOHCs' <www.centralbank.go.ke/wp-content/uploads/2020/01/Directory-of-Licensed-Commercial-Banks-Mortgage-Finance-Institutions-Bank-NOHCs.pdf> accessed 10 March 2022.

18 Nanjala Nyabola, 'What the Collapse of a Major Bank Says About the Rise of Kenya's Powerful Social Media Spaces' *Yahoo Finance* (Nairobi, 13 March 2019) <https://finance.yahoo.com/news/collapse-major-bank-says-rise-170115778.html> accessed 10 March 2022.

19 Allan Olinga, 'Central Bank of Kenya Names Liquidator for Dubai Bank' *The EastAfrican* (Nairobi, 24 August 2015) <www.theeastafrican.co.ke/tea/news/east-africa/central-bank-of-kenya-names-liquidator-for-dubai-bank–1339704> accessed 18 March 2022.

20 Kenya Deposit Insurance Act, 2012, ss.53(2) and 54(1) (a).

21 Anon Reporter, 'Receiver KDIC Says Dubai Bank Kenya Should Be Wound Up' *Business Daily Africa* (Nairobi, 24 August 2015) <www.businessdailyafrica.com/bd/economy/receiver-kdic-says-dubai-bank-kenya-should-be-wound-up-2094720> accessed 10 March 2022.

22 See, Central Bank of Kenya Press Release on 14 August 2015 'Dubai Bank Kenya Ltd Under Receivership' www.centralbank.go.ke/images/docs/media/2015/Dubai Bankpressrelease.pdf> accessed 14 March 2022.

23 See, 'Agony of Depositors as CBK Closes Chase Bank Over Sh16 Billion Loans' *The Standard* (Nairobi, 8 April 2016) <www.standardmedia.co.ke/business/article/2000197518/pain-and-agony-as-chase-bank-depositors-fail-to-access-their-money> (accessed 17 April 2022).

24 Otiato Guguyu, 'Chase Bank Officially Transforms to SBM Kenya' *The Standard* (Nairobi, 20 August 2018) <www.standardmedia.co.ke/business-news/article/2001292696/chase-bank-is-now-officially-sbm-kenya> accessed 18 March 2022.

25 Patrick Alushula, 'CBK Okays Liquidation of Chase Bank' *Business Daily Africa* (Nairobi, 16 April 2021) <www.businessdailyafrica.com/bd/markets/capital-markets/cbk-okays-liquidation-of-chase-bank-3364896> accessed 18 April 2022.

26 Gathaiya (n 15) 9–15.

27 Standard Reporter, 'NIC Appointed Asset and Liability Consultant for Closed Imperial Bank' *The Standard* (Nairobi, 21 June 2016) <www.standardmedia.co.ke/business-news/article/2000206031/nic-appointed-asset-and-liability-consultant-for-closed-imperial-bank> accessed 21 March 2022.

28 Gathaiya (n 15) at 11.

29 Macharia Kamau, 'KDIC Opens Door for Other Lenders to Buy Imperial Bank' *The Standard* (Nairobi, 16 November 2019) <www.standardmedia.co.ke/business-news/article/2001349613/kdic-opens-door-for-other-lenders-to-buy-imperial-bank> accessed 19 March 2022.

30 S Wagh and others, 'Scaling-Up Regional Financial Integration in the East African Community' (2012) World Bank Working Paper No. 69337 <http://hdl.handle.net/10986/13031> accessed 30 March 2022.

31 The list of banks and financial institutions in Tanzania is maintained and updated by the Central Bank of Tanzania. See: <www.bot.go.tz/Publications/Filter/1> accessed 14 April 2022.

32 Preetam Kaushik, 'A Cautionary Tale of Banking in Tanzania and the Dangers of Inadequate KYC' (*Arachnys*, 16 October 2019) <www.arachnys.com/a-cautionary-tale-of-banking-in-tanzania-and-the-dangers-of-inadequate-kyc/> accessed 21 April 2022.

33 John Mitchell, 'Tanzania's Banking Sector Returns to Stability' *The Banker* (Online, 1 May 2019) <www.thebanker.com/World/Africa/Tanzania/Tanzania-s-banking-sector-returns-to-stability?ct=true> accessed 20 April 2022.

34 International Monetary Fund, 'United Republic of Tanzania: Financial Sector Assessment Programme' (2018) IMF Country Report No. 18/346 at 11.

35 ibid 12–13.

36 Materu (n 1).

37 See, 'Real Reasons Behind Closure of Five Banks' *The Citizen* (Dar es Salaam, 6 January 2018) <www.thecitizen.co.tz/news/Real-reasons-behind-closure-of-five-banks/1840340-4252932-152kt97/index.html> (accessed 12 March 2022).

38 C Kidanka, 'Tanzania's Bank M Placed Under Receivership' *The East African* (Nairobi, 2 August 2018) <www.theeastafrican.co.ke/tea/business/tanzania-s-bank-m-placed-under-receivership-1399560> accessed 20 April 2022.

39 Pursuant to the Banking and Financial Institutions Act 2006, s.56.

40 Nuzulack Dausen, 'Tanzania's Central Bank Transfers Assets of Local Lender China Commercial Bank' *Reuters* (Online, 4 March 2021) <www.reuters.com/article/uk-tanzania-banking-idUSKCN2AW1PB> accessed 20 April 2022.

41 H Fafack, 'Non-Performing Loans in Sub-Saharan Africa: Causal Analysis and Macroeconomic Implications' (2005) World Bank Policy Research Working Paper No. 3769.

42 International Monetary Fund, 'Compilation Guide on Financial Soundness Indicators' (30 July 2004) <www.imf.org/external/np/sta/fsi/eng/2003/051403.htm> accessed 12 May 2022.
43 M Brownbridge, 'The Causes of Financial Distress in Local Banks in Africa and Implications for Prudential Policy' (1998), UNCTAD OSG/ DP/ 132.
44 N Waweru and VM Kalani, 'Commercial Banking Crisis in Kenya – Causes and Remedies' (2009) 4(4) Afr J Acc Econ Fin Bank Res 12.
45 Gathaiya (n 15) 9–15.
46 See, further, Nsubuga (n 2) 208, 214 where I discuss the collapse of Crane Bank Uganda.
47 Bank of Uganda (n 7) accessed May 2022.
48 ibid.
49 A Ayub and T Msinjilli, 'Bank of Tanzania's Monetary Policy and Non-Performing Loans in Light of COVID-19' *Mondaq* (Online, 18 August 2020) <www.mondaq.com/fiscal-monetary-policy/976966/bank-of-tanzania39s-monetary-policy-and-non-performing-loans-in-light-of-covid-19> accessed April 2022.
50 Bank of Tanzani, 'Measures to Increase Credit to Private Sector and Containing Non-Performing Loans' Circular No. FA.178/461/01/02 <www.clydeco.com/Clyde/media/Awards/BOT-Circular-IRO-Measures-to-Increase-Credit-to-Private-Sector-Contain.pdf> accessed 12 April 2022.
51 Tenda Msinjili and Amreen Ayub, 'Tanzania: COVID-19 Update on the Policy Measures Introduced by the Bank of Tanzania' *Mondaq* (Dar es salaam, 21 May 2020) <www.mondaq.com/fiscal-monetary-policy/976966/bank-of-tanzania39s-monetary-policy-and-non-performing-loans-in-light-of-covid-19> accessed 21 April 2022.
52 S Claessens and N Horen, 'Foreign Banks: Trends and Impact' (2014) 46(1) J Money Credit Bank 295–326.
53 A Koch and H McDonald, 'Post-Crisis Bank Liquidity Risk Management Disclosure' (2013) 5(1) Qual Res Financ Mark 65–84.
54 Danielle Piskadlo, 'Is Weak Governance to Blame for Bank Collapses in Kenya?' *Centre for Financial Inclusion* (Nairobi, 25 April 2016) <www.centerforfinancialinclusion.org/is-weak-governance-to-blame-for-bank-collapses-in-kenya> accessed 29 March 2022.
55 ibid.
56 Price Waterhouse Coopers, 'Project Nyonyi Report on the Preliminary Forensic Review at Crane Bank' (16 December 2016) <www.coursehero.com/file/75698835/Project-Nyonyi-Forensic-audit-report-21-December-2016-1pdf/> accessed 21 April 2022.
57 E Mukiibi, '12 More Face Charges Over Crane Bank Mess' *Daily Monitor* (Kampala, 31 July 2017) <www.monitor.co.ug/News/National/12-more-face-charges-Crane-Bank-mess/688334-4039854-8srh1uz/index.html> accessed April 2022.
58 E Mang'unyi, 'Ownership Structure and Corporate Governance and Its Effects on Performance: A Case of Selected Banks in Kenya' (2011) 2(3) Int J Bus Adm 1–18.
59 ibid 8.
60 International Monetary Fund (n 34) Principle 14 at 57.
61 ibid.
62 Koch and McDonald (n 53) 65–84.
63 I Salami, 'Derivatives Markets in Africa – Legal and Regulatory Issues' (2012) 27(10) J Int Bank Law Reg 416–28.
64 T Beck and others, *Financing Africa: Through the Crisis and Beyond* (The World Bank, 2011).
65 A 'risk-averse' company or institution is one which chooses to invest in business transactions with known risks that may provide low returns than unknown risks with higher predictable returns.

66 See for example; 'Tanzanian Central Bank Fines Lender for Breaching Rules' *Reuters* (Dar es salaam, 13 July 2019) <www.reuters.com/article/us-tanzania-banking/tanzanian-central-bank-fines-lender-for-breaching-rules-idUSKCN1U80DC> accessed 21 April 2022.
67 Alexandria Carr, 'Bank Structural Reform: Too Big to Fail, Too Big to Save and Too Complex to Manage, Supervise and Resolve?' in M Haentjens and B Wessels (eds), *Research Handbook on Crisis Management in the Banking Sector* (Edward Elgar, 2015) 283–307, ch 12.
68 Matthias Haentjens and B Wessels, 'Three Paradigm Shifts in Recent Bank Insolvency Law' (2016) 31(7) J Int Bus Law Rev 396–400.
69 ibid.
70 Federico Lupo-Pasini and Ross P Buckly, 'International Coordination in Cross-Border Bank Bail-ins: Problems and Prospects' (2015) 16(2) Eur Bus Organ Law Rev 203.
71 D Busch and G Ferrarini, *European Banking Union* (OUP, 2015).
72 Matthias Haentjens and Pierre de Gioia-Carabellese, *European Banking and Financial Law* (Routledge, 2015).
73 Wagh and others (n 30).
74 Brownbridge (n 43) 13.
75 I Salami, 'Cross-Border Banking in Africa: Legal and Regulatory Challenges' (2014) 29(12) J Int Bus Law Rev 728–42.
76 M Cihak and R Podpiera, 'Bank Behaviour in Developing Countries: Evidence from East Africa' (2005) IMF Working Papers 05/129.
77 World Bank (n 8).
78 ibid.
79 Salami (n 75).
80 Cihak and Podpiera (n 76).
81 Hamiisi Junior Nsubuga, 'The Call for Harmonisation of Cross-Border Insolvency Laws to Enable Cross-Border Filing and Litigation in the East African Community' (2019) 30 (12) Int Com Comm Law Rev 659–68.
82 E Binda, 'Free Movement of Capital and East African Monetary Union' in E Ugirashebuja and others (eds), *East African Community Law: Institutional, Substantive and Comparative EU Aspects* (Brill, 2017) ch 13.
83 Established under the Treaty for the Establishment of the East African Community, Art. 9(f).
84 See further, W Kaahwa, 'The Institutional Framework of the EAC' in E Ugirashebuja and others (eds), *East African Community Law: Institutional, Substantive and Comparative EU Aspects* (Brill, 2017) ch 2.
85 Wagh and others (n 30).
86 Salami (n 75) 728–42.
87 See, World Bank (n 8).
88 This is the payments/funds transfer system where the transfer of money or securities takes place from one bank to any other bank on a 'real-time' and on a 'gross' basis as soon as the payment is made without subjecting such transaction to any waiting period.
89 Basel Committee on Banking Supervision, 'Good Practice Principles on Supervisory Colleges' <www.bis.org/publ/bcbs177.pdf> accessed 10 March 2022.
90 B Wessels, 'Giving Legal Effect to Foreign Resolution Measures in the Financial Sector' (2015) 28(3) Intl Insolv Rev 44–45.
91 Koch and McDonald (n 53) 65–84.
92 Basel Committee on Banking Supervision (n 89).
93 ibid, principles 2–4.
94 I Salami, *Financial Regulation in Africa: An Assessment of Financial Integration Arrangements in Emerging and Frontier Market* (Routledge, 2016) Chs 2–3.

95 East AFRITAC is a collaborative venture between the International Monetary Fund (IMF), the recipient countries (Eritrea, Ethiopia, Kenya, Malawi, Rwanda, Tanzania (including Zanzibar), and Uganda), and bilateral and multilateral development partners to increase technical assistance and capacity building. See, <www.eastafritac.org/aboutus?title=About%20us> accessed 21 March 2022.

96 See, 'Making Finance for Africa – Kenya: CBK Lines Up Three More Supervisory Colleges' <www.mfw4a.org/news/kenya-cbk-lines-three-more-supervisory-colleges> accessed 5 March 2022.

97 The EBA set up guidelines that provide *inter alia*: i) guidance on the operational functioning of colleges and (ii) guidance on the joint assessment of banks' risks, and joint decisions on the adequacy of cross border banks' capital for supervisory colleges. See, <www.eba.europa.eu/regulation-and-policy/colleges-of-supervisors> accessed 1 April 2022.

4 Towards Early Intervention in the Resolution of Banks' Financial Distress in Ghana

Kenneth N.O. Ghartey

Introduction

The Ghanaian economy, in 2022, is still recovering from the effects of severe turmoil in its banking and finance industry. This crisis eventually led to the revocation of the licences of over 400 "weak, dormant and insolvent" regulated financial institutions between 2017 and 2019 by the Bank of Ghana (BoG), the country's Central Bank and primary banking business regulator.[1] In 2019 alone, the BoG revoked the licences of 347 microfinance institutions, 39 microcredit companies, 16 savings and loans companies, 7 finance houses, a leasing company and a money remittance company.[2] Among these regulated financial institutions whose licences were revoked were both established and relatively new banks, namely UT Bank, Capital Bank, Unibank Ghana Ltd, Construction Bank, GN Bank[3], Sovereign Bank, Royal Bank, The Beige Bank, Premium Bank and Heritage Bank.

In the decade after the global financial crisis of 2008–2009, Ghana's finance industry grew steadily with acquisitions of new licences to operate financial institutions ranging from universal banks, specialised deposit-taking institutions (SDIs) such as savings and loans companies, microfinance institutions, microcredit companies and non-bank financial institutions (NBFIs) such as finance houses, leasing companies and money remittance companies.[4] While these other regulated financial institutions far outnumber universal banks in count, universal banks represent the main contributors to the size of Ghana's banking sector total assets. The banks held 91.12% of total combined assets in the banking sector[5] end-December 2020 and over 85% of the total assets of the financial system, end-December 2019.[6] The universal banks are therefore the greatest singular source of systemic risk in Ghana's financial system.

Before the drastic regulatory responses to the banking crisis, there were 34 universal banks and several hundred licensed financial institutions[7] in Ghana for an estimated population of 29.1 million[8], many of whom still remain outside of formal banking networks. This is compared to the 27 licensed banks[9] in Nigeria[10], Ghana's much larger West African neighbour with an estimated population of 190.9 million[11] in 2017. This reveals that Ghana had a comparatively high number of banks and other financial institutions, relative to its population. The reasons for this relatively large number of financial institutions to a small population can

DOI: 10.4324/9781003173984-5

be attributed to growing entrepreneurial venturing into small business finance and the use by unscrupulous businesspersons of regulated financial institutions to source public deposits to invest in their related business ventures.

In 2017, the new leadership of the Central Bank detected stress in the banking sector, with the recurring requests for liquidity support, increasing rates of impaired capital, and an increase in non-performing loans held by Ghanaian banks. In response, the BoG announced a new minimum paid-up capital of 400 million Ghana Cedis (GH¢) (about $100 million/GBP 70 million)[12] for universal banks in September 2017 to be fulfilled by December 2018.[13] This represented a 333.3% increase from the previous minimum capital requirement of GH¢ 120 million announced four years before in 2013.[14] The BoG recognised that high inflation and rapid currency depreciation in the intervening period had, in dollar terms, significantly depreciated banks' minimum capital in value. 'The new capital requirement was necessary to align banks' capital base more closely with macroeconomic realities.'[15]

Starting in August 2017, the BoG approved the takeover of some of the viable assets and liabilities of two distressed banks[16] by Ghana's largest indigenous bank[17] under a 'purchase and assumption'[18] order. In August 2018, the licences of five banks[19] were revoked on the same day and aspects of their businesses taken over by a new bank incorporated by the Government of Ghana as a bridge institution. By the end of 2018, the licences of a total of seven banks[20] had been revoked.[21] The banks which lost their licences in 2018 included Beige Bank and Construction Bank both of which had commenced business as universal banks only in the previous year.[22] The licences of two relatively new banks, Premium Bank and Heritage Bank, were also revoked in January 2019. The Central Bank conducted a sector-wide Asset Quality Review for the years 2016 to 2018. At the end of the process and the related revocation of licences, the total number of companies licensed to operate as universal banks in Ghana had gone from 34 at the end of 2017 to 23 in January 2019.[23] At the end of the first quarter of 2022, there are still 23 licensed universal banks.[24]

The failures of these banks undoubtedly placed depositors' funds and investments at risk of jeopardy and threatened the stability of the wider Ghanaian economy. The character of the government and BoG's overall resolution strategy was multi-headed. The first response in August 2017 was the approval of a 'purchase and assumption' order to GCB Bank to assume deposits and other assets of the failed Capital and UT Banks. Subsequently, the Ghanaian government aided by the Central Bank incorporated a bridge institution, Consolidated Bank Ghana Limited (CBG), to take over the remaining depositors' funds and other viable assets of seven of the eight other failed banks in August 2018.[25] BoG had approved an application to reclassify GN Bank as a Savings and Loans Company in 2018 before its license as a Savings and Loans company was revoked in August 2019. Customers and other creditors of GN Bank were not 'absorbed' into the new CBG as was done for the other banks. They were left to scramble under the mercy of the receivership process for GN's assets. Lastly, the government incorporated a special purpose vehicle, Ghana Amalgamated Trust Limited (GAT), to assist five other solvent indigenous banks to meet the new minimum capital requirements set by BoG, by direct capital injection.[26]

The cost of this so-called 'financial sector clean-up' by the Government of Ghana had, by early 2021, come at a cost of over GH¢21 billion (about 3.6 billion US Dollars at 2021 rates).[27] This is a large sum for a low middle-income developing economy. It represents roughly six percent (6%) of nominal GDP based on available 2019 estimates. It is, therefore, money that could have been used for critical public investments in education, transport, housing, utilities and healthcare. The government reports that the deposits of 4.6 million depositors were saved and that COVID-19 expenses, legacy energy sector contracts costs and the financial sector clean-up costs contributed to a budget deficit of 12.1% of GDP in 2021.[28] This pushed the national public debt stock as a percentage of GDP to 77.8% at the end of September 2021 from 76.1% in December 2020.[29]

This chapter therefore advocates for the swift use of early intervention procedures of remedial measures and prompt corrective actions for undercapitalised banks for distressed financial institutions. This would ensure the regulator avoids similar shocks to the economy in the future. The discussion in this chapter traces the circumstances which contributed to the financial services crisis. It considers the overhaul of the banking regulatory landscape with the passage of the Banks and Specialised Deposit-Taking Institutions Act 2016 (Act 930) (hereafter BSDIA 2016) which has significantly expanded the regulatory powers of the Central Bank as regulator of banking business. This chapter considers why despite the substantial regulatory powers before and after 2016, the BoG failed to intervene early towards resolving the factors which led to the eventual financial distress of the failed banks. We diagnose whether the crisis was an abdication of supervisory responsibilities of the Central Bank, risky practices by banks or difficult macroeconomic circumstances or a mix of all three factors.

Apart from this introduction, this chapter has four additional parts. The second section considers the causes of the financial sector turmoil in the recent past in Ghana. The third section provides an overview of the regulatory framework for banking business in Ghana, highlighting the regulatory players and the focus of the regulation of different types of licensed financial services providers in Ghana. The fourth section summarises the legal framework for the resolution of banks' financial distress highlighting the nature of the early intervention mechanisms for banks in financial distress and mandatory liquidation-related processes for irredeemably undercapitalised or insolvent banks. The fifth section makes a case for early intervention by discussing the Central Bank and Ghanaian government's responses to the crisis. The final section concludes the chapter. It offers recommendations aimed at avoiding the occurrence of another episode of mass insolvencies in Ghana's financial sector.

The Causes of the Financial Sector Turmoil in Ghana

The troubles in the financial sector between 2017 and 2019 were not primarily attributable to the wider macroeconomic troubles of 2013 to 2017. Between

2013 and 2016, Ghana was in the grip of significant electric power production shortfall which significantly affected industry productivity by driving up costs of production. Despite this energy crisis, Ghana's economy grew above the mean gross domestic product (GDP) for Sub-Saharan Africa between 2007 and 2017. Ghana's financial services sector started seeing increasing instability from 2013. This growing instability culminated in the mass revocation of operating licences of several types of financial institutions beginning in 2017. In a study investigating the insolvencies of microfinance institutions in the Ashanti Region of Ghana, Boateng and others[30] asserted that in spite of the macroeconomic instability in Ghana in 2013, the collapse of the large number of microfinance institutions was primarily due to "unduly risky, unethical and illegal practices. Mismanagement and disregard of due diligence" practices.[31] This also holds true for the major banks that went under in the period of the crisis.

The BoG has itself attributed the vulnerabilities in the collapsed institutions to poor corporate governance, poor risk management practices, weak credit administration, unsafe and unsound banking practices, diversion of customer deposits into unproductive ventures and general non-compliance with prudential norms.[32] These vulnerabilities identified by the regulators were generally traceable to unscrupulous related party activities between banks and their majority shareholders, key management personnel, directors, other employees, corporate affiliates, corporate associates, subsidiaries and their financial holding companies.[33] It created a fertile ground for the conflict-of-interest exploitations and other corporate governance risks that characterised the failure of the ten banks between 2017 and late 2019.

Overview of Banking Business Regulation in Ghana

Ghana's financial institutional regulatory landscape covers three types of entities: banks, specialised deposit-taking institutions and non-bank financial institutions. Banks and specialised deposit-taking institutions such as savings and loans companies, rural and community banks, microfinance companies and finance houses are regulated together under the Banks and Specialised Deposit-Taking Institutions Act 2016 (Act 930) (hereafter BSDIA 2016). Non-bank financial institutions are regulated under the Non-Bank Financial Institutions Act 2008 (Act 774). Non-bank financial institutions represent the second tier of the financial services industry in Ghana. Currently, the scope of Act 774 covers non-bank financial services such as leasing operations, relatively small-scale money lending operations, money transfer services, mortgage finance operations, non-deposit-taking microfinance and credit union operations.[34] Under Ghanaian law, the Bank of Ghana, is the regulator of all banking business[35] and has "overall supervisory and regulatory authority in all matters relating to deposit-taking business."[36] The regulatory framework for universal banks in Ghana is found within the BSDIA 2016.

Many of the entities which had been converted from lower tier financial institutions such as savings and loans companies into banks were often part of a wider corporate group and were therefore subject to potential shocks from dealings with corporate affiliates, corporate associates and their holding groups. The

BSDIA 2016 significantly enhanced the regulatory scrutiny of banks which were part of a financial holding group on a consolidated basis beyond what was available in the repealed Banking Act 2004 (Act 673). It is possible under the 2016 Act to decouple these banks from shareholders and corporate affiliates considered unfit to have controlling powers in the banking industry. This is to protect banks from undue risks arising from their relationships as members of a wider corporate group.[37]

Under the 2016 Act, the Central Bank's powers of supervision and control over banks operating in Ghana are exercised by way of directives, information and periodic returns, examinations, investigations, taking custody of records, verification of information, issuance of examination reports, follow-up actions on examination and other supervisory reports, the appointment of advisors and remedial measures, and other corrective actions against directors, key management personnel, significant shareholders and financial holding companies of banks.[38]

The BoG has power to issue directives to banks generally or a class of banks to secure the proper management of a bank and where 'it is necessary to prevent the affairs of banks from being conducted in a manner detrimental to the interest of depositors and other stakeholders or prejudicial to the interest'[39] of the bank. The law empowers the BoG to do so by specifying the minimum levels of capital for banks, prescribing prudential norms on asset quality, bad debt and write-offs, liquidity reserve requirements and net open position requirements, computation of on-going capital adequacy and lending limits on credits extended to insiders, limitations for advances or credit facilities to a single borrower among others.[40] These interventions are intended to promote the management of banks as viable businesses.

To this end, the BoG can require a bank to submit any information or data relating to its assets, liabilities, income, expenditure, affairs or other matters on a periodic basis.[41] To confirm the information submitted by banks, the regulator can carry out examinations of the operations and affairs of a bank[42] and may, without prior notice, carry out investigations or scrutiny into a specific matter or activity or office relating to the affairs of a bank.[43] The BoG may take custody of records, files and other documents considered relevant to an examination or investigation by an order in writing issued to the chief executive of the bank.[44] BoG may authorise its officials, a qualified auditor or other professional to verify any return, information or data furnished and report on its accuracy.[45] After an examination, the BoG will furnish the bank concerned with a copy of its examination report and require the bank concerned to give written explanations on the findings within a specified time.[46] After an examination and explanation from a bank, the BoG may take remedial action to which the bank must comply.[47] This includes the appointment of a competent person as advisor to the management of the bank for a stated period. The advisor is entitled to attend the meetings of the board of directors of the bank and the views of the advisor are to be recorded in the minutes of the meetings. An advisor is however not entitled to vote on a matter for determination by the meeting.[48]

In spite of the broad and potentially intrusive regulatory environment, some banks may still experience financial distress due to both internal and external factors. In that case, the law provides a path to the resolution of that distress. General company, restructuring and insolvency law rules are often the first port of call. The Companies Act 2019 has within it rules for the variation of class rights, schemes of arrangements, mergers, divisions and debt compromises which are relevant in a corporate reorganisation. As is the case with many jurisdictions, distress in banks is specially regulated under Ghana law. Directors and management of Ghanaian banks are also however subject to general corporate governance mechanisms under the Companies Act.[49] Indeed the CA 2019, passed post-crisis, is itself a significant overhaul of general corporate governance mechanisms under Ghanaian law. An assessment of the CA 2019 shows that it "places a greater reliance on specific rules while retaining the largely principles-based regulatory techniques adopted for regulating director conduct under [the old Companies legislation] and points to a firmer legislative view of the serious consequences of reckless director conduct."[50] The 2016 banking law however has a far more specific set of rules for regulating director, management and other insider conduct within banks. The CA 2019 was therefore relegated to the background in the responses used by the BoG during the financial sector crisis. In fact, where there is a conflict between the banking and the companies' legislation, the rules in the BSDIA 2016 prevail.[51]

There has also been a recent overhaul of Ghanaian restructuring and insolvency law with the passage of the Corporate Insolvency and Restructuring Act 2020 with the inclusion of administration and restructuring agreements between the distressed company and its creditors classes as tools for corporate restructuring or rescue[52]. The new insolvency law is, however, not applicable to banks and specialised deposit-taking institutions.[53] The legal framework for the resolution of a bank in financial distress is thus mainly regulated under BSDIA 2016. The next part discusses that framework.

The Legal Framework for the Resolution of Banks' Financial Distress in Ghana

The formal options for resolution of banks' financial distress under the BSDIA 2016 can be found within three sets of rules on a spectrum of possibilities: (1) early intervention mechanisms, (2) official administration and (3) liquidation interventions. The rules in the first category cover those rules that are applicable when it is possible to intervene to stop the bank from becoming irredeemably insolvent. The third set of rules are the mandatory rules for liquidation that apply when a bank has become irredeemably insolvent. Official administration[54] is a hybrid of the first and third set of rules. It is essentially the bridge that may transition a bank from an early intervention and rescue mechanism to the application of a mandatory liquidation intervention.

The early intervention mechanisms cover remedial measures against banks, directors and key management personnel and significant shareholders of banks and *prompt corrective actions* for adequately capitalised, undercapitalised and significantly undercapitalised banks. Liquidation interventions cover the mandatory revocation of an insolvent bank's licence, putting the insolvent bank into receivership and thereafter liquidation.

In respect of capitalisation, the BoG's *Capital Requirements Directive* issued in June 2018 and made pursuant to the Basel II Accords, prescribes a risk-based capital adequacy requirement measured as a percentage of the capital of the bank to the risk of its assets. This risk-based capital adequacy ratio (CAR) is calculated on a standalone or on a consolidated basis with all subsidiaries of that entity.[55] A bank is only adequately capitalised if all components of eligible regulatory capital under the directive "satisfies, in both form and substance, all applicable requirements prescribed for the capital tier to which it is to be included"[56] in compliance with the CAR set for the bank in light of its peculiar risks.

The principal publicly known pre-crisis informal process for resolution of financial distress of banks was BoG liquidity assistance to solvent but illiquid banks or to insolvent banks in an attempt to protect deposits in anticipation of the application of formal interventions. The provision by BoG of Intraday Liquidity Facility and Emergency Liquidity Assistance is now covered by the Bank of Ghana Liquidity Assistance Framework published in February 2021.[57]

The test of a bank's solvency is not defined within the 2016 banking law. section 156 of the Companies Act 2019 provides that " 'solvent' in relation to a body corporate means the ability to pay its debts as they fall due." The legality of dividend payments or other returns or distribution of corporate assets require compliance with a "distribution test" which in turn requires the company to be able to pay its debts as they fall due.[58] The more recent Corporate Insolvency Restructuring Act 2020 provides that "insolvent" means unable to pay debts as the debts fall due.[59] Within the Insolvency Act 2006, which is applicable to personal insolvencies, insolvent is defined to mean "unable to pay debts as they fall due."[60]

It appears that the statutory disposition favours a cash flow or commercial' insolvency test, determined as being unable to fulfil debt obligations as they fall due, in preference to a balance sheet or 'technical' insolvency test, where the value of the entity's liabilities exceed its assets taking into account, in both cases, contingent and prospective liabilities. It is far easier, on the whole, to establish the cash flow test.[61] In considering whether a winding-up order should be drawn in respect of a company which was alleged not to be able to pay its debts, Benin J. in *Billy v Kuwor* remarked that 'for it is my view that the court must look at the business realities of the situation and should avoid taking a narrow legalistic view that because the company is owing, it should be wound up.'[62] In considering an analogous cash flow insolvency test under the UK Insolvency Act 1986, Lord Walker in the UK Supreme Court in *BNY Corporate Trustees Services Ltd v Eurosail-UK 2007–3BL Plc,*[63] opined that the provision "does not treat proof of a single specific default by a company as conclusive of the general issue of its inability to pay its debts" and this "may open up for inquiry a much wider range of factual matters, on which there may be conflicting evidence."[64] There is currently a dearth of cases exploring the insolvency of companies by the Ghanaian courts and they ought to be additionally guided by these prescriptions in litigation in which the solvency of a bank is disputed.

Early Intervention Mechanisms

The early intervention mechanisms are a critical part of the rules that became available to the Central Bank after the passage of the BSDIA 2016 as part of its powers of supervision and control. There are five categories of these early intervention mechanisms:

1. Remedial measures for banks
2. Remedial measures for directors, key management personnel and significant shareholders
3. Prompt corrective action for adequately capitalised banks
4. Prompt corrective action for undercapitalised banks
5. Prompt corrective action for significantly undercapitalised banks

Due to the lack of publicity that surrounds the use of these formal early interventions, it is not clear how effectively the regulator deployed these tools between September 2016 until the first revocation of licences in August 2018. Early intervention and rescue mechanisms are often by way of private communication between the management of banks and the regulator and as such are not available to the public. Effective use of these tools should have revealed and corrected some of the more egregious violations that came to the fore following the collapse of some of the banks.[65] 'The undue regulatory forbearance of the BoG is taken as an indication of regulatory failure.'[66]

Remedial Measures Against Banks or Key Personnel of Banks

Where the effective exercise of the broad powers of supervision and control of banks by the BoG reveals that a bank has failed to comply with the law, is engaging in an unsafe or unsound practice, conducted its affairs in a manner detrimental to the interests of its depositors and creditors or has violated a condition or restriction attached to a licence, the regulator will take remedial measures against the bank.[67] These can include written warnings, specific remedial actions to be taken by the bank, to cease a violation or unsafe or unsound practice, take affirmative action that eliminates the grounds for an order, to conclude a written agreement with the bank's board to provide for a programme of remedial action, appoint an advisor or to revoke the bank's licence.[68] A bank may also be prohibited from receiving or renewing existing deposits, from further lending or taking further financial exposures. The bank can also be ordered to suspend an activity causing material loss, divest itself of a subsidiary, restrict transactions with affiliates, restrict payment of bonuses or "excessive compensation" to directors or key management personnel.[69]

Remedial measures may also be directed at directors, key management personnel[70], significant shareholders[71] and employees of banks.[72] In this option, the BoG can issue a mandatory order to a person, impose an administrative penalty, require reimbursement by a person to a bank for a loss caused by their breach, prohibit the individual from direct or indirect exercise of voting rights attached to shares of the bank or suspend the individual from office or declare that person as no longer a *fit and proper person*[73] to be involved in the affairs of a bank.[74] These interventions mirror closely procedures under the CA 2019 for disqualifying errant directors, restraining fraudulent persons from managing companies, to enforce directors' duties, manage conflicts of duty and interest, enforce civil liabilities for breach of duty, bring legal proceedings to enforce liabilities, and grounds for bringing derivative actions by corporate insiders.[75]

Where the BoG determines that the individual has repeatedly violated a provision of the BSDIA 2016, Regulations or directives issued following a written warning or has been engaged in an unsafe practice or has conducted the bank's affairs in a manner detrimental to the interests of its depositors and creditors, the BoG may take any of the following actions: the Bank can direct the dismissal of the person from the bank, prohibit the person from serving in or engaging in deposit-taking business for a stated period, impose an administrative penalty for the contravention or require the person to dispose of all or any part of the direct or indirect holding or interest in the bank.[76] If the individual is also charged with a criminal offence, the BoG may issue an order to temporarily suspend the person from the bank. A dismissal or acquittal on the merits will not preclude the BoG from taking further enforcement action in relation to the person.[77] A person who is the subject of a remedial directive or order by the Central Bank which has suspended that person from office or prohibited the exercise of voting rights in shares in a bank, is precluded from holding a position in an affiliate of the bank.[78]

Prompt Corrective Actions for Undercapitalised Banks

The BSDIA 2016 provides rules on capital and reserves by banks. The object of the rules are for banks to maintain unimpaired paid-up capital and maintain capital adequacy requirements based on the risks of the particular bank and the vulnerabilities of the financial system.[79] The BoG has power to require additional capital in respect of special risks and to determine a bank's capital adequacy requirements on a consolidated basis with its subsidiaries, a financial holding company or another subsidiary in a wider corporate group.[80]

Prompt corrective actions are called into play when the BoG determines a bank, although adequately capitalised has incurred material losses within a financial year, or when a bank is either undercapitalised or significantly undercapitalised. Where that bank is adequately capitalised at the time of a material loss within a financial year, the regulator can prohibit it from declaring and distributing dividends and BoG is required by law to conduct more frequent examination of that bank.[81] Key personnel of the bank may also be called on to provide written explanations detailing the causes of the losses and the measures to rectify the position and avert future losses.[82] The regulator is required to give notice to the Ghana Deposit Protection Corporation (GDPC), immediately it initiates a corrective action against a bank. The GDPC was set up by the Ghana Deposit Protection 2016 (Act 931) to manage an insured pay-out scheme to "support the development of a safe, sound, efficient and stable market-based financial system in Ghana by ensuring prompt pay outs to insured depositors on the occurrence of an insured event."[83]

Where the bank involved is undercapitalised, rules additional to those that apply for adequately capitalised banks which have incurred material losses in a financial year will apply. A bank is considered undercapitalised when its capital requirements fail to meet those prescribed by the regulator under the capital and reserves rules.[84] The capital and reserve rules include periodic prescriptions for minimum paid-up capital unimpaired by losses, a risk-based capital adequacy requirement measured as a percentage of capital of the bank, leverage or gearing ratios, eligible capital and risk assets, additional capital in respect of special risks, capital adequacy ratios on a consolidated basis within groups and a Reserve Fund into which are transferred thresholds out of net profits for each year.[85]

The undercapitalised bank is required under law to produce a *capital restoration plan* acceptable to BoG within 45 days to restore the bank to capital adequacy within 180 days.[86] The BoG can also prohibit a bank from awarding bonuses, salary increments and other benefits to directors and key management personnel of that bank. An advisor may also be appointed for the bank. The advisor is required to regularly report to the BoG on the progress of the capital restoration plan.[87] Where the bank is unable or refuses to implement a capital restoration plan or to add more capital, it will be prohibited from opening new branches, engaging in new business, restricted from growing assets or liabilities and the interest rate payable by the bank on all interest earning deposits will be restricted as the regulator will determine. BoG may direct the removal of the officers of the bank and take other actions to rectify the capital deficiency.[88]

Under the BSDIA 2016, a bank is significantly undercapitalised when it does not hold at least 50 percent of the capital requirements set under the capital and reserves rules.[89] By the time a bank becomes significantly undercapitalised, the host of prompt corrective actions that may be taken against an adequately capitalised bank facing material losses and against an undercapitalised bank will already apply to that significantly undercapitalised bank. Beyond these, far more intense salvage measures are required. The Bank of Ghana is required to enter into an agreement with the Board of directors of the bank to rectify the significant undercapitalisation within 180 days. In the meantime, the BoG may prohibit new "off-balance sheet" transactions by the bank.[90] If within the 180-day period, the financial position of the bank continues to deteriorate, the Bank of Ghana shall, without waiting for the expiry of the period, place the bank in official administration or revoke the bank's licence and initiate a receivership.[91]

Official Administration

Official administration is the bridge between the spectra of remedial measures aimed at rescue and the mandatory insolvency related interventions under the 2016 BSDIA. The object of the Administration process is to bring external managerial control into the bank to evaluate the bank's true financial position and to protect depositors and other creditors. This is especially where the initial formal and informal rescue mechanisms do not yield the desired results. The grounds for appointing an official administrator (OA) for a bank includes similar considerations for the use of remedial measures: namely, contravention of the banking laws, engagement in unsafe or unsound practices or activities that have or may seriously jeopardise the interest of depositors or have dissipated assets of the bank.[92] A bank may also be placed in official administration when it is significantly undercapitalised, or where BoG has reasonable cause to believe that the directors, key management personnel or significant shareholders have engaged in or are engaging in illegal activities that will jeopardise depositors interest or it has failed to co-operate with BoG in an examination, concealed data or records or failed to comply with remedial measures or prompt corrective measures directed at it or its officers and significant shareholders.[93] A bank by a resolution of its directors or shareholder can also request the appointment of an OA.[94]

After appointment, an OA must within 30 days prepare an inventory of the assets and liabilities of the bank by itemising assets according to their risk profiles and classifying non-performing loans. Within 90 days after appointment, the OA must also present a report on the financial condition and prospects of the bank.[95] After this preliminary process by the OA, four main options are available for the way forward. Depending on the extent of the loss, existing shareholders may be required to purchase additional shares to increase the bank's capital. The OA can invite other persons to purchase additional unsubscribed shares where the existing shareholders are unable to do so. The OA may also carry out a merger of the bank with another bank or to transfer the whole or part of the assets and liabilities of the bank. The transfer of assets and liabilities can be to a bridge institution, or an asset management vehicle established by the Government. The OA may also restructure the liabilities of the bank without the approval of creditors or shareholders concerned.[96] The OA may also remove any or all of the directors and key management personnel of the bank and appoint other *fit and proper* persons to replace them.[97] All these activities by OA are undertaken with the approval of the Bank of Ghana.

The official administration terminates at the expiry of the period stated in the appointment of the OA. Before the expiry of that period, the official administration may also terminate when the OA determines that the circumstances no longer justify their continuance in office, that the bank cannot be rehabilitated, or the circumstances require the liquidation of the bank.[98] Where there is no resolution of the financial distress via the official administration process, the Central Bank moves into the mandatory application of the liquidation interventions under the BSDIA.

Liquidation Interventions

Where the BoG determines that a bank is insolvent or is likely to become insolvent within sixty days, the only formal options are to revoke the licence of the bank and to immediately initiate receivership.[99] In light of the historical responses by the BoG, aided by the overall language of the provision, it is accurate to conclude that the regulatory view of insolvency that triggers the mandatory application of the liquidation interventions is not simply a failure to meet a cashflow test but rather serious balance sheet or technical insolvency. When financially distressed banks were also cashflow insolvent, as in Unibank's case, the BoG intervened with liquidity assistance. A receiver is appointed at the effective time of the mandatory revocation of the insolvent bank's licence.[100]

Receivership of a Bank

The receiver becomes the sole legal representative of the bank and assumes the rights and powers of the shareholders, the directors and the key management personnel of the bank.[101] A receiver may also instruct the shareholders, directors and key management personnel to exercise specific functions for the bank.[102] The receiver has unrestricted access to and control over the offices, books of accounts and other records and assets of the bank.[103] The most significant part of the receiver's tasks at the beginning of the receivership is to establish a new financial position for the bank based on a determination of the liquidation values of the assets.[104] The receiver may, within 30 days after appointment, repudiate non-performed or partially performed contracts where those contracts are considered burdensome for the bank to fulfil and repudiation will promote the orderly administration of the affairs of the bank.[105] Even more significantly, the OA may set aside pre-receivership transactions and recover an asset from a transferee or other beneficiary of the transaction.[106]

Liquidation of a Bank

There are provisions, within the BSDIA 2016, on the post-receivership procedures which will lead to the formal liquidation of an insolvent bank. There are detailed processes guiding the liquidation of other companies in the more recent CIRA 2020 and voluntary winding-up within the CA 2019 but these legislation are inapplicable to banks.[107] The relevant rules in the 2016 Act, read as a whole, show that the rules of the receivership process were conceived by the drafters of the legislation, as a continuum to the final liquidation of the assets of the bank and not two separate processes.

Under general Ghanaian company and insolvency law, official administration and receivership processes are distinct from the final step of the liquidation (of the assets) of a company, which is guided by separate rules. The view that within the banking law, "liquidation" is fused into the receivership process is confirmed by the provision that the receivership is only terminated after there has been a distribution of the proceeds of the sale of the assets of a bank and a submission of a final report to the BoG.[108]

The BoG has the power to prescribe the procedure for determining the validity and priority of claims and the liquidation of the assets of banks.[109] Apart from the rules contained in the BSDIA 2016, there has not been a supplementary directive by the regulator which provides further guidelines in a bank's involuntary or mandatory liquidation. In January 2021, BoG issued a new directive titled "*Voluntary Winding-Up Directive for Banks and Specialised Deposit-Taking Institutions*, 2021."[110] The rules in this directive are strikingly similar to the rules for voluntary winding-up in the CA2019 with slightly differing timelines for the constituent processes from receivership to liquidation. This therefore brings the voluntary winding-up process for banks close to the general law but does not do same for involuntary or mandatory liquidation.

Conclusions on Legal Framework

On the basis of the summary of the applicable rules, we take the view that the Bank of Ghana has more than adequate tools at its disposal to intervene in the management of banks to avoid detrimental risk-taking and unsafe practices. These wide powers of enquiry, which when added to enhanced current financial reporting standards of the financial activities of banks, accord with international best practice. The rules may even be characterised as potentially intrusive into the management affairs of banks. This part has set the tone for the main discussion within this chapter which advocates for the regulator to shift towards early intervention mechanisms for distressed banks rather than the belated resolution of banks through bailouts which will often come at far greater cost and produce increased instability within the banking sector. The regulatory responses to the crisis are specifically explored in section "The Actual Responses to the Financial Sector Crisis".

Towards Early Intervention in the Distress of Banks in Ghana

The summary of the regulatory framework available to Ghanaian regulators to prevent or manage the financial distress of banks in section "The Legal Framework for the Resolution of Banks' Financial Distress in Ghana" of this chapter concludes that the regulatory powers are wide and even potentially intrusive. It is a great wonder therefore, how despite these broad powers, the Central Bank looked on until the failure of the ten banks because of bad financial management and serious corporate governance breaches.

The regulation of banks is a complex business. The efficacy of banking supervision rules is affected as much by the nature and scope of the rules as the regulatory and political will to enforce them. Banks and bankers the world over have been known to get away with regulatory breaches that will not be permissible in other sectors of the economy. In spite of wide media coverage and public outcry from the revelations surrounding the collapse of some of the banks and other financial institutions, there is at yet no conclusion to any prosecution, nearly four years after the start of the so-called "financial sector clean up." It cannot be seriously argued that the use of early intervention mechanisms do not have more benefit to the integrity of the financial system as a whole than the resort to final insolvency procedures if banks are allowed to fail. Our task is therefore not to argue only in favour of early intervention but to diagnose what militated against early intervention in the distressed banks before and during the 2017–2019 period of turmoil.

Factors Militating Against Early Intervention, in Fact

We conceive of four main reasons that militate against the implementation of the host of early intervention mechanisms available within the banking supervision framework:

1. Potentially criminal behaviour
2. Politically exposed persons and powerful interests
3. Poor corporate governance and
4. Regulatory forbearance and complicity

Potentially Criminal Behaviour

Proper regulation should unearth breaches of prudential restrictions and unsafe or unsound practices. However, in territories such as the United States and Europe with some of the best regulatory resources, the management of banks and other financial entities have succeeded in getting away with reckless behaviour, the consequences of which has cost the taxpayer billions of dollars. This is the same for Ghana. The determination to conceal potentially criminal behaviour was clearly stronger than the regulatory will to ensure conformity with the banking rules. In the end, it became obvious that some of the persons behind the banks had been engaging in potentially criminal behaviour for years without consequences. Depositors' funds were consistently diverted to support affiliate businesses and large loans were made to related persons and businesses with little due diligence. Worryingly, it appeared that persons involved in some of the banks in near collapse were hurriedly using emergency liquidity assistance to their dying banks to outwit regulators as supporting capital for the grant of new banking licences.[111]

Politically Exposed Persons and the Challenges

A recurring theme in the instances of the failed banks are the number of shareholders and other key personnel and management who are politically exposed persons. Beyond politically exposed persons, there are also generally powerful interests and personalities who were in some way significantly connected to the banks' crisis. Two of the individuals who were connected to the failed Capital Bank as Board Chairperson and Chief Executive Officer when it collapsed, are the head pastors of two well-known Christian congregations in Ghana.[112] These pastors lead a large network of churches spread across southern Ghana. A large portion of the Ghanaian population is religious. Gauging from the connected social media commentary in 2019, the prosecution of the Board Chair especially in connection with some of the clearly negligent and potentially fraudulent allegations at Capital Bank will have been very poorly received by the public. It appears the political and regulatory inertia to fully investigate and perhaps prosecute some of the actors in the crisis accords with this wider social sentiment. The majority shareholder and CEO of Capital Bank are however being prosecuted.

A few of the indigenous banks had very powerful persons at the helm. A good example is Unibank Ghana Limited, which is part of a wider family-controlled business group, led by a former Governor of the Bank of Ghana who held office between July 1997 and September 2001. This former Governor and patriarch of the family was appointed Minister for Finance between February 2009 and January 2012. Unibank was established at a time when its promoter was Governor of the Central Bank and therefore regulator of banking business. At the time of the Unibank's placement in administration in March 2018, the bank, now led by the son of this former governor, had a Capital Adequacy Ratio of minus 24%.[113] Unibank is reported to have suffered persistent cash shortfalls and regularly fell below cash reserve requirements and thus had to rely extensively on liquidity support of GH¢ 2.2 billion (roughly US$ 498 million/GBP 356 million)[114] to meet its recurring liabilities in the two years before its collapse. Under law, emergency liquidity assistance should only properly be available to "illiquid but solvent" banks "that is facing temporary liquidity challenges."[115] BoG also accused Unibank of misreporting the state of its loan book.[116] The liquidity support to Unibank from the Central Bank, at the time, far outstripped the support to any other bank. The reasons for this are not hard to guess.

GN Bank was also controlled by Groupe Nduom, another family-controlled business conglomerate, whose patriarch had variously served as Minister for Energy, Minister for Public Sector Reforms and Chairperson of the National Development Planning Commission between 2001 and 2007 and thereafter as presidential candidate for the Convention People's Party and his own political party, the Progressive Peoples' Party in the 2008 and 2012 elections respectively. GN Bank had been reclassified in January 2019 to GN Savings and Loans following its inability to raise the new minimum capital for banks. Despite this, GN Savings and Loans was unable to resolve its acute liquidity challenges even after an advisor was appointed for it by the regulator. Its licence as a Savings and Loans company was also revoked in August 2019 when the BoG determined that its Capital Adequacy Ratio stood at minus 61%, making it technically insolvent.[117] The shareholders of both Unibank and GN Savings have been in the courts since 2019 challenging the revocation of their banks' licences.

Poor Corporate Governance Practices in the Banking Sector

All the threads of the causes of the banking sector crisis indicate a poor level of corporate governance in Ghana's banking sector. These were predominantly underpinned by several instances of unscrupulous related party activities.[118] Banahene characterises these as an "opulent display of incompetence, unethical behaviour, and sheer disregard of precise regulations and operational procedures."[119] Very similar sentiments have been repeated in numerous BoG press releases and media commentary on the subject. To highlight the extent of the problem, one example suffices:

> Shareholders, related and connected parties had taken amounts totaling GH¢3.7 billion which were neither granted through the normal credit delivery process nor reported as part of the bank's loan portfolio. In addition, amounts totalling GH¢1.6 billion had been granted to shareholders, related and connected parties in the form of loans and advances without due process and in breach of relevant provisions of Act 930. Altogether, shareholders, related and connected parties of Unibank had taken out an amount of GH¢5.3 billion from the bank, constituting 75 percent of total assets of the bank.[120]

Regulatory Forbearance and Complicity

The egregious violations of eligible capital and other asset requirements and very risky ventures by some of the newer banks point clearly to regulatory complicity. It is hard to imagine how the Central Bank especially starting from 2015 until 2017 continued to provide liquidity support to banks whose businesses had clearly reached a perilous state.

In the face of regulatory violations, the management of the Central Bank continued to provide liquidity support to distressed banks without due regard for its use. As has been asserted, it turns out that some of this liquidity support that was intended to secure payments to depositors was squandered.[121] Court records show that of GH¢620 million banking liquidity support facility granted to Capital Bank between June and November 2015, the majority shareholder transferred GH¢130 million of this liquidity support to a related company. Even more seriously, part of this sum was then used to secure the establishment of another bank, Sovereign Bank, in very serious violation of eligible capital rules.[122] The new leadership of the Central Bank in 2017 recognised that the banks which were licensed in 2016 and which commenced operations in 2017 "began to show signs of distress, primarily due to conditions under which they obtained their licences."[123] In a scathing criticism of the previous leadership of the BoG, the current leadership has described their response to the emerging crisis as a ' "do nothing" approach.'[124]

Awuah asserts that political ideology had a role to play in the 'regulatory forbearance' of the period between 2013 and 2016 and could be the result of the social democratic ideology of the government in the period.[125] Following the 2016 elections and the shift to a government that professes pro-market ideals, the regulatory posture thus changed. While the regulatory powers of the BoG were enhanced and clarified under the BSDIA 2016, the repealed Banking Act 2004 as amended[126] had analogous provisions for Capital and Reserves, Liquidity, Ownership and Control, Restrictions on Lending and Investments and examination and investigation powers which the BoG could have exercised pre-BSDIA had it wished to do so.

The Actual Responses to the Financial Sector Crisis

In this section, the responses to the financial sector crisis in Ghana by BoG in collaboration with the Government of Ghana are considered. This section also provides an assessment of the responses, sounds caution or provides alternatives where desirable.

"Purchase and Assumption": the "Absorption" of UT and Capital Banks into GCB Bank

The first step in the flurry of regulatory responses that began the "financial sector clean-up" was the BoG's approval for the 'purchase and assumption' of some assets of UT and Capital Banks in August 2017. The "purchase and assumption" order tool is provided for under the BSDIA 2016 and allows for part or the whole of the assets of a failed bank to be purchased and all or some of the liabilities assumed by an acquiring bank.[127]

The BoG took the view that GCB Bank, the largest indigenous bank, was the best bank to absorb the shock of the takeover of customer deposits and some of the more viable assets of UT and Capital banks. This also allowed the defunct banks' business to remain in Ghanaian shareholders' hands. The approach by the two other competitors with GCB Bank for the role of assuming bank involved a total impairment of the loan assets of the two banks.[128] The regulators did not accept this and hence the choice of GCB Bank. GCB Bank reported that after the "takeover," the collapsed banks' customer base had withdrawn their funds from GCB Bank in a panic by December 2017. GCB Bank lost cash reserves of almost GH¢1 billion In the four months between August and December 2017 and had to rely on short term liquidity support from the Bank of Ghana of about GH¢400 million to be able to meet the spate of the withdrawals.[129]

The announcement and implementation of the "purchase and assumption" was however a seamless one-day event. Customers woke to the announcement of the collapse of UT and Capital but with swift assurances from the regulator that depositors' funds were available for withdrawal under GCB Bank. GCB Bank had been on-standby and advertisement signs of UT and Capital Banks on major branches were taken off their buildings on the very same day and replaced with signage of GCB Bank. It helped that GCB Bank had a decades-long reputation of stability and nationwide presence, and this went to calm the nerves of customers of UT and Capital. This time, the Central Bank is to be congratulated for the handling of the affairs of UT and Capital Banks post-collapse.

Consolidation of Viable Assets: the New Consolidated Bank

The Bank of Ghana granted a universal banking licence to Consolidated Bank Ghana Limited (CBG), established by the Government of Ghana, on the same day it revoked the licences of Unibank, The Royal Bank, Beige Bank, Sovereign

Bank and Construction Bank in August 2018. Deposits of the five banks were transferred to Consolidated Bank and a Receiver appointed for the five banks. CBG was established as a bridge institution under section 127(10), BSDIA 2016 to assume the assets and liabilities of the five failed banks under a "Purchase and Assumption" Agreement.

As was the "purchase and assumption" of UT and Capital Bank assets by GCB Bank, the transfer of deposits to the new Consolidated Bank was a seamless process with far less glitch than would have been expected. It appears the confident switchover that was offered by the UT/Capital Bank "takeover" increased public confidence in the bridge institution. This confidence was bolstered by the fact that CBG was backed by the government.

This "consolidation" of the business of the five banks has proved a smooth process that avoided the potential loss of millions of depositors' funds. The Government issued a bond in the amount of GH¢5.76 billion (US$ 1.215 billion[130]) towards the acquisition of the assets of the five failed banks by CBG, effectively increasing Ghana's public debt by more than a billion US dollars.[131] Part of the problem with the need for a new bank was because the Deposit Protection Scheme (DPS) under Ghana Deposit Protection Act as amended[132] had not been operationalised to effectively cover losses by small depositors. The formation of a bridge institution in CBG and a guaranteed return of deposits provided a return of funds far superior to what perhaps the DPS could have paid out. Banks protested government plans in 2021 to introduce a levy of 5 percent on banks' gross profit to recover expenses of the financial sector bailout.[133] This levy is to be reviewed in 2024.[134] This is amid exigencies of COVID-19 pandemic for banks in Ghana. The well-run banks are essentially being forced to pay for the sins of the 'badly behaved' banks.

Guarantee of Deposits by Government

Following concerns about the ability of the assets of the collapsed banks to satisfy the savings and investments of their customers, the government through the BoG made a commitment to provide cash support to protect all customers deposits.[135] It appears that other creditors apart from customers were this entitled to the proceeds of the receivership process

In its Budget and Economic Statement for 2021, the Ghanaian government claims to have spent a little over GHc 21 billion (US$3.2 billion), representing 4.6 percent of GDP, in the financial sector clean up.[136] The precise details of this expenditure are unclear and it is not also publicly available how or indeed if the government intends to recover some of the pay outs to the receiver after liquidation of the assets of the defunct banks.

While this intervention comes at a heavy cost, without it, faith in the banking system would have been very severely eroded. Concurrent large losses in investments made by over a hundred thousand investors in financial institutions promising unusually high returns over very short periods have created widespread hardship since 2015, well before the banks' troubles of 2017–2019.

Victims of these "ponzi schemes" run by some of these financial institutions, mainly savings and loans and microfinance companies, have become wary of future use of formal financial services. The related loss of income has affected basic needs such as access to safe drinking water and education.[137] Customer deposits' growth slowed down between 2017 and 2018, compared to the period 2014–2016, largely the result of concerns with the stability of the financial sector.[138] The banking industry has since recovered with total asset growth of 22.8% and 15.7% year-on-year in 2019 and 2020 respectively premised significantly on customer deposits.[139]

The Flurry of Regulatory Output

On account of the regulator's diagnoses of the sector's problems, it has since 2018 set out a comparatively extraordinary output of new directives that, among other things, tackle banks' capital adequacy, management appointments and corporate governance issues. BoG has effectively called on its directive making power.[140] It allows public input on some of the proposed directives by publishing exposure drafts for industry and wider public input before finalisation.[141] Recent directives directly related to issues of the crises include:

1. Capital Requirements Directive, June 2018
2. Financial Holding Companies Directive, July 2018 (Exposure Draft)
3. Cyber and Information Security Directive, October 2018
4. Mergers and Acquisition Directive, July 2018 (Exposure Draft)
5. Corporate Governance Directive, December 2018
6. Explanatory Notes on the Revised Corporate Governance Directive, December 2018
7. Fit and Proper Persons Directive, 2019
8. Fit and Proper Persons Directive Explanatory Notes
9. Directive for Voluntary Winding-Up, January 2021
10. Liquidity Assistance Framework, February 2021
11. Risk Management Directive, June 2021 (Exposure Draft)
12. Mergers and Acquisitions Directive, August 2021
13. Explanatory Notes on the Revised Mergers and Acquisitions Directive, August 2021

The directives provide regulatory clarity and offer an implementing backdrop to the rules within the BSDIA 2016. The BoG is to be congratulated for its efforts in this respect since 2018.

Changes within the Bank of Ghana

There is a tacit recognition by the current BoG leadership that the BoG had a role to play in the collapse of the banks by turning a blind eye to some of the occurrences and also by active engagement by its own officials in unethical conduct. Beyond the changes in the top management of the Central Bank between 2017 and 2018, another change at the Central Bank stands out. There is now an Office of Ethics and Internal Investigations within BoG. By BoG's own account, this new Office is intended 'to strengthen good governance within the Bank and to promote the highest standards of ethical conduct commensurate with the Bank's mandate. The Office will investigate all allegations of misconduct by staff including any role in respect of the collapse of the defunct banks. Staff found culpable will be dealt with in accordance with our Human Resource policies, and referred to law enforcement agencies, if necessary.'[142]

The Ghana Amalgamated Trust: Current Fix or Future Trouble

With the steep rise in the new minimum capital requirement set by the BoG, a number of solvent local banks found themselves unable to meet the new minimum capital requirements. Banks with foreign ownership quickly fulfilled the minimum capital requirements by the deadline of December 2018. This created a situation in which the Ghanaian banking landscape would have been bereft of significant local participation or ownership.

Government therefore announced the incorporation of the Ghana Amalgamated Trust Co (GAT), a public limited liability company in December 2018. GAT is a special purpose investment vehicle primarily set up to raise funds to recapitalise selected indigenous Ghanaian banks that needed assistance to meet the new minimum capital requirements and to help transform these banks to become more competitive in the industry.[143] In 2019, GAT raised initial bridge capitalization of GH¢800 million and successfully recapitalised the following banks under its programme:

1. Agricultural Development Bank Limited (ADB)
2. OmniBSIC Bank Limited (OmniBSIC) following the merger of OmniBank and Sahel Sahara BSIC Bank
3. Prudential Bank Limited (PBL)
4. Universal Merchant Bank Limited (UMB)

GAT reports that it is raising funds to recapitalize National Investment Bank Limited (NIB), the fifth bank under the programme. GAT has significant equity stakes and representation on the boards of directors of the entities it invests in to formalize its mandate to help transform the selected indigenous banks to become more competitive.[144] GAT's initial funds come mainly from pension funds and other investors.[145] Government originally tried to bolster initial investments in GAT through the instrument of a government and sovereign guarantee. The choice of this structure however received a legal challenge. This was abandoned in favour of initial bridge capitalisation of GH¢800 million backed by a Put Call Option Agreement (PCOA) from the government.[146]

The curious part about the strategy of using GAT as the vehicle for bank support is that, of the five banks that have received support, the government through the BoG and the Ministry of Finance is a major shareholder in ADB and NIB. Perhaps, the Government as shareholder could have directly increased its shareholding in those banks to meet the new capital requirements to avoid the costs of the interposition of GAT. While the use of GAT to maintain local ownership of some banks may sound like a good plan, the Ghanaian public ought to be wary. The heavy investments by pension funds into institutions like GAT only goes to increase the exposure that pension funds will have to future banking crises. In a country where there are little social protection avenues after retirement, risky adventures for pension funds is a firm exercise in national self-destruction.

Recommendations

Now that we have considered what was done in response to the financial crises, we present a number of recommendations to support the theme of early intervention in the distress of banks. But a change in the regulatory attitude towards early intervention alone will not suffice. A few other changes are necessary to promote the viability of the Ghanaian banking sector.

Prosecutions and Recovery of Dissipated Funds

There has been slow prosecution of the people involved in potentially criminal behaviour across the banks that collapsed. There have been a few civil suits by the Receivers and some of the persons connected to the collapsed banks. The slow pace and small number of prosecutions in the wake of the egregious examples of corporate misbehaviour creates a wrong impression of the ability to get away with potentially criminal conduct. Only a handful of persons related to the banks' collapse have been charged with crimes. In one of the more interesting episodes of the banking failures, three persons have been charged with stealing in connection with alleged board complicity in the reckless use of customer funds and Central Bank liquidity support. That criminal case remains unresolved in early 2022 after filing of criminal charges in 2019 for events that are alleged to have occurred between October and November 2015.[147] A former deputy governor of the BoG has been charged with the offence of wilfully causing financial loss to the state in connection with the Unibank collapse. It remains to be seen, if we see it at all, how that case will reveal regulatory complicity in how potentially criminal behaviour was allowed to continue and to cause the failures witnessed between 2017 and 2019. Successful prosecutions and civil suits to recover dissipated and diverted funds will send the right signal of the potential personal consequences of similar behaviour to current management, shareholders and directors of banks. A clearer national response, in this respect, is urgently required.

Addressing Regulatory Inertia in Relation to Politically Exposed Persons

The Companies Act 2019 regulates beneficial ownership of company shares by politically exposed persons. In an application for incorporation, the documents delivered to the Registrar of Companies must indicate whether any shares are beneficially owned by politically exposed persons. Politically exposed persons are defined within CA 2019 to include:

(a) a person who is or has been entrusted with a prominent public function in this country, a foreign country or an international organisation including

(i) senior political party official, government, judicial or military official;
(ii) a person who is or has been an executive of a State owned company;
(iii) a senior political party official in a foreign country; and

(b) an immediate family member or close associate of a person referred to in paragraph (a)[148]

Banks are subject to the rules on the declaration of beneficial ownership. BoG should take a stricter view of the declaration of the beneficial ownership of bank shares to be able to anticipate how powerful interests may use the medium of banks to raise money in relatively risk-free ways to support themselves while impairing depositors' funds and putting the wider financial system at risk.

A Frequent Reconsideration of Currently Operational BoG Directives

The recent flurry of regulatory output has helped bring clarity to the broad legislative framework under the BSDIA 2016 and the Bank of Ghana Act 2002. We urge the BoG to frequently reconsider the operationalisation of existing and future regulatory directives to avoid loopholes that may be exploited by ever cunning banks' management and their well-paid and determined advisors.

Impartial Enforcement of Relevant Rules

The BoG should, impartially, enforce all relevant rules relating to banks. In 2019, the board of the Agricultural Development Bank (ADB) was composed of at least three persons connected to the collapsed UT Bank as former members of UT's Board.[149] That historical association does not, of itself, invalidate their membership of the ADB Board. The circumstances of UT's collapse and the language of the Fit and Proper Persons Directive 2019 relating to the suitability of a person who has "been a director of, or directly involved in the management of, any company or institution: which has had its licence revoked."[150] raises questions about the impartial enforcement of the relevant regulatory rules in relation to persons whom the regulators view favourably. While this particular example may not present problems, where necessary the rules should be applied without fear or favour and in line with regulatory objectives.

Full Operationalisation and Widening of the Cover of the Deposit Protection Scheme

The Deposit Protection Scheme (DPS) should be fully operationalised to provide an avenue for additional relief in the face of a bank insolvency that requires additional support in the repayment of depositors' funds. Currently the DPS is tailored only for 'small depositors.' The sums currently insured are wholly inadequate for any meaningful recoveries in the event of banks' financial distress and should be revisited. This should significantly reduce the use of borrowed government funds in the return of depositors' funds in future sector crises.

Divesting GAT of Continuing Government Influence

As soon as is practicable, GAT should divest itself of its equity investments in the identified indigenous banks, preferably by ordinary trading on the stock exchange and not by negotiated private placement to new shareholders. This should avoid the very real possibility of GAT being used as a vehicle to redirect bank shareholding to favoured persons. This anxiety is not unfounded in view of the corruption perception of government financial dealings in Ghana. These recommendations should, in our view, restore sanity for a longer period of time in the Ghanaian banking industry.

Disclosure

The author was involved in litigation between 2019 and 2020 as supporting counsel on behalf of one of the eight failed banks for the restoration of its licences. All information reproduced and discussed in this chapter is information freely available to the public.

Notes

1 Bank of Ghana, 'Annual Report' (2019) 4.1, 26.
2 ibid.
3 GN Bank was first reclassified as a Savings and Loans Company in 2018 and thereafter its licence as a Savings and Loans Company revoked in August 2019.
4 At the end of 2008, a total of 26 banks, were operating in Ghana. See Bank of Ghana, 'Annual Report' (2008) 26.
5 Bank of Ghana, 'Annual Report' (2020) 4.4, 26.
6 Bank of Ghana, 'Press Statement – Restoring Confidence and Building a Resilient Banking System for Ghana' (undated) <www.bog.gov.gh/wp-content/uploads/2019/07/Restoring-Confidence-and-Building-a-Resilient-Banking-System-for-Ghana.pdf > accessed 11 April 2022.
7 Bank of Ghana, 'Annual Report' (2017) Section 4.3.1, 19.
8 World Bank, 'Population, Total – Ghana' <https://data.worldbank.org/indicator/SP.POP.TOTL?locations=GH> accessed 10 April 2022.
9 Comprising 21 commercial banks, five (5) merchant banks and one (1) non-interest bank with a combined total of 5,450 bank branches at the end of 2016.
10 Central Bank of Nigeria, 'Annual Report' (2017) 4.1.1, 109.
11 World Bank (n 8).

12 At the average September 2017 exchange rates.
13 Bank of Ghana (n 7) Section 4.2, 19; Bank of Ghana, 'Notice to the Banks and the General Public' (Notice BG/GOV/SEC/2017/19, New Minimum Paid Up Capital, 11 September 2017) <www.bog.gov.gh/wp-content/uploads/2019/09/Notice-on-New-Minimum-Paid-Up-Capital.pdf> accessed 29 April 2022.
14 Maxwell Akalaare Adombila, 'BoG Raises Minimum Capital to GHc400 Million' (*Graphic Online*, 8 September 2017) <www.graphic.com.gh/news/general-news/bog-raises-minimum-capital-to-gh-400-million.html> accessed 10 April 2022; Bank of Ghana (n 5).
15 Bank of Ghana (n 6).
16 Capital Bank Limited and UT Bank Limited.
17 GCB Bank Limited.
18 Banks and Specialised Deposit-Taking Institutions Act 2016 (Act 930) (hereafter BSDIA 2016), s. 156: 'purchase and assumption' means an agreement in which a part or the whole of the assets of the failed bank are purchased and all or some of the liabilities are assumed by an acquiring bank.
19 Construction Bank, Sovereign Bank, The Beige Bank, The Royal Bank and Unibank Ghana Ltd.
20 Capital Bank, UT Bank, Unibank Ghana Limited, Construction Bank, Sovereign Bank, Royal Bank and The Beige Bank. GN Bank had been reclassified to a savings and loans company in 2018 and its licence as a savings and loans company revoked in August 2019. As at April 2022, Unibank and GN Savings and Loans were still contesting the revocation of their licences in the Ghanaian courts.
21 Bank of Ghana, 'Annual Report' (2018) Section 4.1.1, 19.
22 Bank of Ghana (n 7) Section 4.3, 19.
23 Bank of Ghana (n 1). Bank of Ghana Bank of Baroda, an Indian Government- owned bank 'exited the Ghanaian banking space on strategic reasons' – see Bank of Ghana (n21), section 4.2, 15. The Bank of Ghana approved 3 mergers between OmniBank and Sahel Sahara Bank; Energy Bank and First Atlantic Bank; and First National Bank (FNB) and GHL Bank Limited. Consolidated Bank Ghana Limited (CBG) was incorporated to take over some of the viable assets of the five failed banks in August 2018.
24 Bank of Ghana, 'Banks' <www.bog.gov.gh/supervision-regulation/registered-institutions/banks/> accessed 30 April 2022.
25 Construction Bank, Sovereign Bank, Royal Bank, The Beige Bank and Unibank Ghana Limited in August 2018 and thereafter Heritage Bank and Premium Bank in January 2019.
26 Bank of Ghana (n 21).
27 Government of Ghana, 'The Budget Statement and Economic Policy of the Government of Ghana for the 2021 Financial Year' (12 March 2021) para. 263; Ekow Dontoh, 'Ghana Banking Cleanup Cost Risks Surging to $3.5 Billion' (*Bloomberg*, 17 January 2022) <www.bloomberg.com/news/articles/2020-01-17/ghana-finance-sector-cleanup-cost-risks-surging-to-3–5-billion> accessed 11 April 2022.
28 Government of Ghana, 'The Budget Statement and Economic Policy of the Government of Ghana for the 2022 Financial Year' (17 November 2021) paras. 1146, 46.
29 ibid para 109.
30 Festival Godwin Boateng and others, 'Collapsing Microfinance Institutions in Ghana: An Account of How Four Expanded and Imploded in the Ashanti Region' [2016] IJAD 37.
31 ibid.
32 Bank of Ghana (n 1) 20.
33 Kenneth Ghartey, 'Regulating Related Party Activities in Ghanaian Banking' (2020) Ghana Law J 128–29.
34 Non-Bank Financial Institutions 2008 (Act 774), s. 2, 4, First Schedule.
35 Bank of Ghana Act 2002 (Act 612) as amended by the Bank of Ghana (Amendment) Act 2016 (Act 918) (hereafter BOG Act 2002), s. 2.

36 BSDIA 2016, s 3(1).
37 ibid s 91(1).
38 ibid ss 91–106.
39 ibid s. 92(1).
40 ibid s 92(2).
41 ibid s 93(1).
42 ibid s 94(1).
43 ibid s 95(1).
44 ibid s 97(1).
45 ibid s 98(1).
46 ibid s 99(1).
47 ibid s 100(1).
48 ibid s 101(1)(4)(5).
49 Act 992 (hereafter CA 2019).
50 Kenneth NO Ghartey, 'Directors' Duties Under the 2019 Companies Act of Ghana' (2020) 46 (2) CLB 249.
51 BSDIA 2016, s 2(2).
52 Act 1015, passed and assented to in April 2020, hereafter CIRA 2020.
53 Corporate Insolvency and Restructuring Act 2020 (Act 1015) (hereafter CIRA 2020), s 1(3).
54 BSDIA 2016, s 107–22.
55 Bank of Ghana, 'Capital Requirements Directive' (27 June 2018) paras. 2, 15; BSDIA 2016, s. 31.
56 ibid para. 15.
57 Bank of Ghana, 'Liquidity Assistance Framework' (February 2021) <www.bog.gov.gh/wp-content/uploads/2021/02/Bank-of-Ghana-Liquidity-Assistance-Framework-February-2021.pdf> accessed 28 April 2022.
58 CA 2019, s 156.
59 CIRA 2020, s 169.
60 Insolvency Act, 2006 (Act 708) (hereafter IA 2006), s. 77.
61 Kubi Udofia, 'Establishing Corporate Insolvency: The Balance Sheet Insolvency Test' <https://papers.ssrn.com/sol3/papers.cfm?abstract_id=3355248> accessed 28 April 2022.
62 [1991] 1 GLR 522, 529.
63 [2013] UKSC 28, Lord Walker, para 25.
64 ibid para 25.
65 Of the eight failed banks, three of the banks: Royal Bank, Sovereign Bank and Construction Bank were relatively new and therefore had a small customer base and had not transacted business for a long time. The Beige Bank, although also a 'new' bank at the time of its resolution had conducted business for many years as a savings and loans company as Beige Capital and a member of the Beige Group.
66 George Baffour Awuah, 'Bank of Ghana's Regulatory Forbearance: A Political Economy Analysis' [June 2020] Res Gate 3 <http://dx.doi.org/10.13140/RG.2.2.13758.10560>.
67 BSDIA 2016, s 102(1).
68 ibid s 102(2).
69 ibid s 102(3).
70 Includes the 'chief executive, deputy chief executive, chief operating officer, chief finance officer, board secretary, treasurer, chief internal auditor, the chief risk officer, the head of compliance, the anti-money laundering reporting officer, the head of internal control functions, the chief legal officer, the manager of a significant business unit of the bank . . . or any person with similar responsibilities' – BSDIA 2016, s 156.
71 A shareholder who has a direct or indirect holding which represents 5% or more of the capital or of the voting rights. – BSDIA 2016, s 156.
72 ibid s 103.
73 Bank of Ghana, 'Fit and Proper Persons Directive' (July 2019) reg 4: 'Fit and Proper person' means a person who is suitable to hold the particular position which that

persons holds or is to hold as regards: (a) the probity, competence and sounds of judgment of the person for purposes of fulfilling the responsibilities of that person; (b) the diligence with which that person fulfils or is likely to fulfil those responsibilities; (c) whether the interests of depositors or potential depositors of the entity are threatened, or a likely to be, in any way threatened by the person holding that position; and (d) that the integrity of the person is established and the qualifications and experience of the person are appropriate for the position in the light of the business plan and activities of the entity of the entity which he serves, or is likely to serve, taking into account the size, nature and complexity of the institution.'

74 BSDIA 2016, s 103(1).
75 CA 2019. Ss. 173, 176–78, 190–95, 199–201.
76 BSDIA 2016, s 103(2).
77 ibid s 103(4).
78 ibid s 103(5).
79 ibid ss 28–29.
80 ibid ss 30–31.
81 ibid s 104(1).
82 ibid s 104(2).
83 Ghana Deposit Protection Act 2016 (Act 931) as amended, s 3.
84 BSDIA 2016, s 105(1).
85 ibid ss 28–35.
86 ibid s 105(2)(b).
87 ibid s 105(2–5).
88 ibid s 105(6).
89 ibid s 106(4).
90 'Off balance sheet transaction' includes contingent assets, contingent liabilities in the form of letters of credit, guarantees, bids, bonds and indemnities, BSDIA 2016, s 153.
91 BSDIA 2016, s 106(3–4).
92 ibid s 107(1)(a).
93 ibid s 107(1)(b-f).
94 ibid s 107(1)(g).
95 ibid s 114(1–3).
96 ibid s 118(1).
97 ibid s 119(1).
98 ibid s 122.
99 BSDIA 2016, s 123(4).
100 ibid s 123(2).
101 ibid s 127(1).
102 ibid s 127(2).
103 ibid s 129(1).
104 ibid s 130.
105 ibid s 131.
106 ibid s 132.
107 ibid s 138.
108 ibid s 136(1); ss 123–29 – titled '*Receivership and Liquidation.*'
109 ibid s 133(1).
110 Bank of Ghana, 'Voluntary Winding-Up Directive for Banks and Specialised Deposit-Taking Institutions, 2021' (January 2021) <www.bog.gov.gh/wp-content/uploads/2021/01/Voluntary-Winding-Up-Directive-FINAL-PUBLICATION-1.pdf> accessed 23 April 2022.
111 Bank of Ghana, 'Press Release – Government Establishes New Indigenous Bank; Bank of Ghana Revokes Licences of Five Banks and Appoints Receiver in Respect of Their Assets and Liabilities' (1 August 2018) <www.bog.gov.gh/wp-content/uploads/2019/07/PRESS-RELEASE-Grand-Final-August-2018.pdf> accessed 27 April 2022.

112 Magdalene Teiko Larnyoh, 'Capital Bank Board Misused GHC 610 Million from BoG' – Report (*Pulse*, 8 August 2018) <www.pulse.com.gh/ece-frontpage/bank-collapse-capital-bank-board-misused-ghc-610-million-from-bog-report/c6k9xey> accessed 26 April 2022.
113 Deza Mones, 'Bank of Ghana Places uniBank in Administration' (*S&P Global Market Intelligence*, 21 March 2018)<www.spglobal.com/marketintelligence/en/news-insights/trending/j1qzh33wtjks3kbvojcdzq2> accessed 27 April 2022.
114 At the then prevailing average exchange rate of US$ 1= 4.4165 cedis and GBP 1 = 6.1796.
115 Bank of Ghana Act 2002 (Act 612), s. 46A as inserted by Bank of Ghana (Amendment) Act 2016 (Act 918), s 18.
116 Kwasi Kpodo, 'UPDATE 2 – Ghana Central Bank Places Unibank in Administration' (*Reuters*, 20 March 2018, <www.reuters.com/article/ghana-bank/update-2-ghana-central-bank-places-unibank-in-administration-idUSL8N1R2692>, accessed 27 April 2022.
117 3news.com, 'Why Bank of Ghana Revoked GN Savings & Loans Licence' (*3news*, 16 August 2019), <https://3news.com/why-bank-of-ghana-revoked-gn-savings-loans-license/> accessed 27 April 2022.
118 Ghartey (n 33) 128.
119 Kwabena Owusu Banahene, 'Ghana Banking System Failure: The Need for Restoration of Public Trust and Confidence' (2020) 8(10) Int J Bus Syst Res 1.
120 Bank of Ghana (n 111).
121 Larnyoh (n 112).
122 Ghanaweb.com, 'Otabil, 15 Others Sued Over GHc748m Capital Bank Cash' (*Ghanaweb.com*, 6 November 2018) <www.ghanaweb.com/GhanaHomePage/NewsArchive/Otabil-15-others-sued-over-GH-748m-Capital-Bank-cash-698336> accessed 26 April 2022.
123 Bank of Ghana (n 111) 1.
124 Bank of Ghana, 'Press Release – Response to Former Deputy Governor Dr. Johnson P. Asiama's Interview on Joy FM' (23 August 2019) <www.bog.gov.gh/notice/response-to-former-deputy-governor-dr-johnson-p-asiamas-interview-on-joy-fm/> accessed 19 April 2022.
125 Awuah (n 66) 22.
126 Banking Act 2004 (Act 673) as amended by Banking (Amendment) Act 2007 (Act 738), Parts III-VIII, ss 23–69.
127 BSDIA 2016, ss 127, 156.
128 Bank of Ghana (n 124).
129 Emmanuel Bruce, 'GCB Bank Lost GH¢1bn in 4 Months After Absorbing UT, Capital Banks' (*Graphic Online*, 28 May 2019) <www.graphic.com.gh/business/business-news/ghana-news-gcb-bank-lost-gh-1bn-in-4-months-after-absorbing-ut-capital-banks.html> accessed 27 April 2022.
130 At average exchange rate of US$ 1 = GHS 4.7402 in August 2018.
131 Ministry of Finance, 'Press Statement by the Minister for Finance, Ken Ofori-Atta, in Relation to Government Support for Strengthening Ghana's Banking Sector' (1 August 2018) <https://mofep.gov.gh/news-and-events/2018-08-01/press-statement-by-the-minister-for-finance-ken-ofori-atta-in-relation-to-government-support-for-strengthening-ghana-banking-sector> accessed 30 April 2022.
132 Ghana Deposit Protection Act 2016 (Act 931) as amended by the Ghana Deposit Protection Act 2018 (Act 968).
133 Maxwell Akalaare Adombila, 'Banks Protest 5% Tax on Gross Profits' (*Graphic Online*, 16 March 2021) <www.graphic.com.gh/business/business-news/bankers-protest-5-tax-on-gross-profits.html> accessed 30 April 2022.
134 Government of Ghana (n 28) para 263.
135 Bank of Ghana (n 124).
136 Government of Ghana (n 28) para 26.

137 Edmond Ofori, 'The Effects of Ponzi Schemes and Revocation of Licences of Some Financial Institutions on Financial Threat in Ghana' (2020) J Fin Crime <https://doi.org/10.1108/JFC-01-2020-0003> accessed 13 April 2022.
138 Oxford Business Group, 'Ghana's Banking Sector Clean-Up Has Created a More Sustainable Industry, <https://oxfordbusinessgroup.com/overview/restoring-confidence-sector-clean-led-regulators-has-resulted-smaller-more-sustainable-industry> accessed 27 April 2022.
139 Bank of Ghana (n 1) 4.4, 21; Bank of Ghana (n 5) 4.4, 26.
140 BSDIA 2016, s 92.
141 Bank of Ghana, 'Procedures for Issuance of Directives to Banking Industry' (December 2020) <www.bog.gov.gh/wp-content/uploads/2020/12/BOG-Procedures-for-Issuing-Directives.pdf> accessed 30 April 2022.
142 Bank of Ghana, 'Press Release – Bank of Ghana Established Ethics and Internal Investigations Unit to Strengthen Good Governance Within the Bank' (15 August 2018) <www.bog.gov.gh/wp-content/uploads/2019/07/PRESS-RELEASE-Ethics-and-Internal-Investigations-Unit.pdf> accessed 31 January 2022.
143 Ghana Amalgamated Trust Plc, 'Our Background' <https://gatplc.com/> accessed 21 April 2022.
144 Ghana Amalgamated Trust Plc, 'Company Overview' <https://gatplc.com/pages/about-us#company-overview> accessed 21 April 2022.
145 Ministry of Finance, 'Press Release – Support for Solvent Indigenous Banks to Meet New Minimum Capital Requirement' (5 January 2019) <www.mofep.gov.gh/sites/default/files/news/Ghana-Amalgamated-Trust-Press-Release-20180105.pdf> accessed 28 April 2022.
146 Ghana News Agency, 'Government Needs GH₵800 Million Initial Capitalisation for the Ghana Amalgamated Trust' (*NewsGhana*, 14 November 2019) <https://newsghana.com.gh/government-needs-gh%E2%82%B5800-million-initial-capitalisation-for-the-ghana-amalgamated-trust/> accessed 28 April 2022.
147 Graphic.com, 'Ato Essien, Three Others Charged Over Capital Bank Collapse' (*Graphic Online*, 9 October 2019) <www.graphic.com.gh/news/general-news/ato-essien-three-others-charged-over-capital-bank-collapse.html> accessed 27 April 2022.
148 CA 2019, First Schedule: Definitions.
149 Emmanuel Bruce, 'ADB Shouldn't Be Part of GAT – Isaac Adongo' (*Graphic Online*, 5 March 2019) <www.graphic.com.gh/business/business-news/ghananews-adb-shouldn-t-be-part-of-gat-isaac-adongo.html> accessed 28 April 2022; Agricultural Development Bank, 'Board of Directors' <www.agricbank.com/about-us/board-of-directors> accessed 28 April 2022.
150 Bank of Ghana (n 73).

5 Deposit Protection Schemes in Effective Bank Resolution Regimes

Kenya's Experience

Joy Malala

Introduction

Kenya's banking system has been characterised as 'shallow and fragile'.[1] This is reflected in low lending levels, high interest rate spreads which can be attributed to as Ngugi states 'interest rate spread increase because of yet-to-be gained efficiency and high intermediation costs'[2] in addition to high levels of non-performing loans because of very poor business environments and distress borrowing as well as several bank failures. The banking system is equally segmented by size and ownership factors (foreign owned banks, government owned banks, large private owned banks, and small private owned banks). There have been three cycles of bank failures which have swept Kenya's history since 1986. Between 1986 and 1997, Kenya had experienced a total of 37 bank failures which precipitated an attempt at strengthening the regulatory framework. As a result, the preceding decade showed some stability until 2016 when three commercial banks failed. Although these failures were not systemic, they unearthed the overwhelming lack of confidence in the banking system and a sense of panic among depositors in small banks leading to a run on at least one of the banks. The discourse on banks in distress has been prevalent in the last several years with discussions that focused on the causes of distress in banks and how best to 'wind down' financial institutions, including banks.[3] The GFC[4] has revealed the true extent of the role of the regulator in crisis management particularly in the management of commercial banks and not solely financial institutions. This is, in part, due to historical bank failures, which had focused on banking instability and not necessarily the appropriate role of government policy through regulation, much less laws.[5]

The GFC which began in the US markets and promptly reached Europe with its own property bubble[6] as well as equally engaging in excessive deficit spending, continued deregulation coupled with increased credit, the policy responses and resolution regimes for countries such as Germany and France were very similar and largely ineffective. However, after the bubble burst,[7] leading to the crises, it became clear that these policies and resolution regimes needed reform. The emergence of special resolution regimes has become prevalent due to the special nature of banks. Banks classically hold deposits which should be repayable on demand without the possibility of triggering distress. They hold long-term loans,

DOI: 10.4324/9781003173984-6

on the asset side which become difficult to dispose of or borrow against at short notice. Usually, the variance of maturity should not cause challenges as loans will be held until maturity and repaid at face value. A well-capitalised bank should be able to cover the risk of loan loss. It should also ensure that it is able to cover withdrawals without destabilising the public's confidence. The inability to meet these obligations threatens its solvency. Their special nature is also evidenced in the fact that they are fundamental to the functioning of an economy. They extend credit, take deposits and process payments. They therefore remain the primary source of liquidity through capital mobilisation. Banks also provide the channel for monetary policy that is linked to the economy. Therefore, the justification for a special resolution regime when banks become insolvent is to ensure that their functions are intact and that the process minimises systemic risks, protect consumers, limit moral hazard, and promote market efficiency which are all public interest considerations.[8] These frequent themes of financial stability, systemic risk and taxpayers' exposure to losses are not trivial. The argument can be made, however, as to what extent a special resolution regime for banks can add to the enhancement of the financial system through limiting systemic risk. This chapter seeks to explore these possible *ex ante* incentives that a (recovery and) resolution regime may provide for controlling systemic risk and preventing bank insolvency.

This chapter will discuss the recent bank crises in Kenya and attempts to chart a 'resolution regime'[9] that is in the interest of the public[10] rather than strictly market economics and insolvency laws. The failures of Imperial Bank Kenya Ltd (Imperial Bank),[11] Dubai Bank Kenya Ltd (Dubai Bank)[12] and Chase Bank Kenya Ltd (Chase Bank) provided opportunities for a new resolution regime that seeks, through early intervention, to avoid the disruptive nature of financial instability.[13] This chapter will also discuss the mandate under the Central Bank Act[14] of the Central Bank of Kenya as well as its roles as the apex regulator of the financial system. Both the Central Bank of Kenya, as the Lender of Last Resort,[15] and the Kenya Deposit Insurance Corporation (KDIC) form part of the mechanisms that manage banks in distress. It will further discuss the current resolution regime considering the recent bank failures as well as an appropriate resolution regime in the management of banks in crises. In this context, this chapter discusses issues of macro-prudential supervision and proposes that more should be done to ensure that these actors (the Central Bank of Kenya and the Kenya Deposit Insurance Corporation) operate with autonomy, accountability, transparency, and integrity.[16] It will argue that while financial stability is at the core, issues of public interest[17] are critical in designing an appropriate resolution regime that goes beyond market economics. Additionally, the chapter will address to what extent a special resolution regime for banks and financial institutions can contribute to the enhancement of a financial system's stability and can limit systemic risk. It also discusses the possible *ex ante* incentives that a recovery and resolution regime may provide for controlling systemic risk. The final part is the *ex-post* remedies for the curtailment of systemic risk.

The increase of regulation of banks is due to their fragility and vulnerability to failure.[18] These weaknesses are increased by the fact that the inter-bank market is made up of a systemic network of large unsecured creditor-debtor relationships, where the failure of one bank could lead to the collapse of others if confidence in the market is undermined in some way and the trust in them becomes eroded then it becomes the perfect set up for failure.[19] Indeed, holding a significant asset reserve and a large proportion of illiquid assets in the form of loans are conditions that contribute to the distress in banks. It is largely expected that Central Banks or any higher regulatory authority would institute safety nets that would ensure that the effects of bank failures and the management of banks in crises are carried out in the least disruptive way, after all, their main functions is to manage the distribution of savings and loans which is essential for an economy to operate effectively as well as being the central vehicle for the exercise of a state's monetary policy. The purpose of this chapter is, therefore, to examine recent problems of bank failures in Kenya and attempt to chart a resolution mechanism that is effective and is able to intervene early, which is an effective tool in managing distressed banks.[20] While this chapter recognises the facts that *ex ante* regulation, which is aimed at preventing bank failure, may be appropriate it will focus on *ex post* regulation and guidance that is aimed at responding to that failure.

While trust and confidence are critical to sustaining financial stability in perfect market conditions, particularly where there is unequivocal deposit insurance and effective bank crisis management, central bank actions, sound business and financial practices as well as prudential supervision help to mitigate the severe consequences of banks in crises. However, it is widely appreciated that banks may eventually fail.[21] It is this inevitability that, Kindelberger described in his historical analysis of financial crises as manias, panics, and crashes[22] and Reinhart and Roggoff also reiterated the fact that crises occur regularly[23] and that an effective resolution regime should be at the forefront of regulation particularly in Kenya's very short history of bank failures which suggests that more should be done if lessons have been learned.[24] Moreover, the three failed banks brought to the fore, at least to the public's consciousness, the role of the agencies tasked with resolving distressed banks. The role of the Kenya Deposit Insurance Corporation (KDIC) instituted by the Kenya Deposit Insurance Act, in the management in crisis times is also a necessary element of the discussion. The KDIC, instituted by the Kenya Deposit Insurance Act[25] has imbued public awareness of the financial system. Furthermore, while the management of bank crises has not been scrutinised or at least not much attention has been paid in the way Kenyan banks are rescued or resolved, the causes have extensively been examined.[26] There is, however, a regulatory mandate by the Central Bank to place under statutory management banks in distress or bound to fail.[27] Various explanations may be put forward about the lack of attention and, perhaps, the lack of scrutiny as there seems to be recurring crises with no lessons learned. It has been stated that failure and crises are inevitable for banks due to their systemic nature. Their risk exposure and profiles make them inherent to distress either through panic or the consequences of contagion which may lead to losses.[28] These lessons have, to an extent, not been able to guide future directions and therefore have left banks susceptible to future exposures. This is because, usually after banks in Kenya have been placed under statutory management, very few of those banks have been restructured positively and most have ended in liquidation. Resolving troubled banks or at least identifying a way in which banks in distress may be salvaged is important as it ensures that severe systemic disruption is avoided. The disruption would eventually expose depositors and by extension taxpayers, through government guarantees.[29] Therefore, it becomes important as a public interest objective to protect depositors through having a mechanism that makes it necessary for shareholders, unsecured and uninsured creditors to avoid losses in a way that adheres to the hierarchy of claims in an insolvency process.[30] These can essentially affect any financial system and challenge public authorities particularly the regulators. It also shows that even in times that are free of crises there needs to be a continued effort to strengthen financial stability and that it should not stagnate. This chapter will, consequently, discuss the causes of the recent bank crises, as well as the recent resolution regime aptly named the *failure regime*. It will then try to assess the current financial safety net that highlights the roles of the Central Bank as the Lender of Last Resort as well as the Kenya Deposit Insurance Corporation which both act as agents in the management of banks in crisis. It will then aim to discuss an effective regime that would mitigate the resultant effects of distressed banks.

Why Are Banks S*till* Special?

The interconnectedness of banks and their complexity can be attributed to their increase in size and arguably the start of universal banking.[31] This has often led to blurred lines because of the intertwining of the global economy leading to a *Too Big to Fail* phenomenon. Stern and Feldman reflected extensively on this phenomenon when they stated that 'banks fail'.[32] Such a label may be attributable to the bank's large size and significant role in the financial system. The failure of a large bank could result in an unwelcome knock-on effect on other institutions, the financial system and, indeed, the wider economy. Thus policymakers would typically react to this by, *inter alia*, protecting depositors and other uninsured creditors of banks. These too big to fail banks are also, at least conventionally, recipients of discretionary government support. This support is to the extent that creditors of such banks expect government protection, and as a result reduce their vigilance in monitoring and responding to these banks activities. When creditors exert less of this type of market discipline the banks tend to take excessive risks.[33]

The engagement of banks in sophisticated products and services such as derivatives trading, and securitisation go beyond the traditional business of banking which only included taking deposits and extending credit and their critical element of payment systems. This all means that: (1) the business of these banks are inherently riskier; and (2) their failure could have significant systemic implications. To this end, it is debatable that conventional insolvency proceedings might not be best suited to resolve pecuniary challenges of distressed banks. Banks play a special role in society due to their impact on distributions of profit and loss associated with commercial activities in society. Their failure therefore means significant implications, they need and deserve a special approach when in distress or are likely to be in distress. Thus, bank failure merits a *lex specialis*. Hüpkes has stated that, 'banks play a special role in a country's economy in that, collectively, their functions are so important as to constitute a type of public service'.[34] She goes on to state that, what really makes banks special is their vulnerability to the loss of public confidence and bank runs which requires swift action to prevent contagion and loss of value when a bank encounters financial difficulty.[35]

Hüpkes argues that in one part, an insolvent bank that can no longer conduct the business of a bank seizes being a bank and should consequently be treated like any other bankrupt corporation. The other part is that banks are already the subject of special regulation which determines the condition of their operation, it is therefore only the bank supervisor – and not a bankruptcy judge or a meeting of creditors – who is able to determine whether a bank is viable. Thus, the bank supervisor must have a voice in the insolvency procedure.[36] She further points out that financial assets, as opposed to material assets such as merchandise, can be dissipated secretly and very quickly. For this reason alone, she argues that the bank supervisor needs to be able to intervene rapidly to prevent losses to depositors. Hüpkes also remarks that the unitary decision-making process under [bank] regulatory law appears faster and more efficient than the negotiated process under ordinary insolvency laws. This is because, given the special challenges involved in dealing with the failure of a bank as special institution in the financial system and economy, the bank regulator needs to be able to swiftly act in an emergency without being hamstrung by pre-compliance with various procedural requirements as would apply in terms of ordinary insolvency rules.[37] Additionally, bank insolvency differs from ordinary insolvency procedures by pace but also by objectives. Ordinary insolvency procedures have always tended to maximise proceeds and not leave creditors in a worse off position, but bank insolvency additionally aims to preserve financial stability.[38]

With this, it is clear that public interest considerations are at the forefront of bank insolvency regimes which is a departure from the *pari passu*[39] principle that posits the equal treatment of all creditors a tenet of insolvency law. However, and although this rule is mandatory, it may in many circumstances only apply to unsecured creditors leaving many stakeholders in the proceedings. For instance, depositors and small creditors may be paid out in full while larger creditors are forced into a renegotiation of their claims. This sentiment that normal corporate insolvency procedures are insufficient to deal with bank failure is echoed by Randell who observes that the task of resolving even quite a small bank swiftly, and without allowing contagion to spread to other parts of the financial system, can be impossible if the authorities only have corporate insolvency procedures at their disposal.[40]

The exigencies of bank failure are often costly and complex and require either radical or innovative measures to be applied. Further, the rescue of financially distressed banks is increasingly difficult as it is. As a result, viable parts of banks are saved whilst the other vestiges are *allowed* to fail. This is somehow now an approach to resolution.[41] The wake of the crisis also highlighted a near end to the *Too Big to Fail* and evidenced a decisive move from the culture of 'bail-out'[42] that was prevalent in the pre-GFC landscape and during the GFC, to a more controlled culture of 'bail-in'[43] post GFC. This approach constitutes drastic rethinking over who should bear the operational, monitoring and financial burdens of the financial system. With this approach, therefore, substantial onus is placed on bank (inside) stakeholders to maintain appropriate levels of governance oversight and market controls if they are to avoid the financial costs that come with bail-in. Therefore, the post GFC regulatory regime has taken the shape of pre-emptive and remedial stance and detailed and elaborate ex ante interventions by international standard setting bodies such as the Basel Committee on Banking Supervision that issued Basel III.[44] This provides a pre-emptive intervention framework aimed at preventing bank distress and failure by strengthening prudential regulation and the ability of banks to be more resilient in the face of adverse economic circumstances and other events. Basel III seeks to achieve this objective through imposing more stringent capital reserve requirements, enhanced risk coverage, reducing pro-cyclicality[45] and promoting countercyclical buffers. There was also renewed emphasis on the need for effective deposit insurance systems[46] designed to mitigate moral hazard and promote market discipline through the imposition of risk-based premiums on member banks.[47] The resolution regimes post-GFC have hence attempted to have an order in resolving failing banks which according to Randell, are the

> special arrangements for the winding-up or restructuring of a failing bank by virtue of powers that go beyond the general powers conferred by the normal insolvency law applying to companies. These powers may exist within insolvency legislation or by adaptation of insolvency processes, but often they take the form of special administrative powers that can be exercised by the authorities without, or alongside, normal insolvency proceedings.[48]

With reference to the Barings insolvency in the UK, not much has changed.[49]

At the time of the GFC most countries had frameworks for dealing with failing banks, but these frameworks were generally pegged on non-integrated resolution options that were limited in scope and scale and consisted of narrow bank rescue procedures and of a liquidation process for banks that could not be saved. Following the GFC, with the added impetus of the insolvency of Lehman Brothers in September 2008,[50] the G20 and other international leaders acknowledged that an effective resolution framework for financial institutions was essential to secure financial stability and limit moral hazard. It was also recognised that such a framework should be accompanied by robust cross-border coordination mechanisms as the financial services sector became increasingly interconnected and global over time. The G20 consequently called for a review of resolution regimes and insolvency laws.[51]

In April 2009, the Financial Stability Forum (the Financial Stability Board's predecessor) published 'Principles for cross-border cooperation on crisis management', requiring that national authorities develop cooperation strategies and measures for information sharing between themselves. In this document they also strongly encouraged financial institutions to maintain contingency plans.[52] The BCBS also worked on a report and recommendations for the resolution of cross-border financial institutions following the recognition that prudential measures such as capital requirements alone cannot limit moral hazard without instituting a viable resolution process for cross-border financial institutions. Haentjens observes that the realisation had dawned that 'in order to prevent financial institutions from relying on public lenders of last resort, a credible resolution framework should be put in place'.[53] The BCBS concluded that national authorities should have the tools to effectuate the orderly resolution of all types of financial institutions, and thus contribute to the minimization of risk, consumer protection, limitation of moral hazard and promotion of market efficiency.[54] At the domestic or national level, deposit taking institutions have been the focus of regulation particularly in relation to bank insolvency.[55] Cross-border institutions were not at the fore, however, under an enhanced mandate, cooperating authorities could share the burden of funding failed banks and agree on taking resolution actions with cross-border effects. In 2004 UNCITRAL published Parts 1 and 2 of its 'Legislative Guide to Insolvency Law' in respect of domestic commercial insolvency regimes.[56] In the wake of the GFC Part 3 of the UNCITRAL Guide was published in 2010 and addressed the treatment of enterprise groups in insolvency, nationally and internationally.[57] The international best practice benchmark for orderly resolution frameworks was conceptualised by the Financial Stability Board (FSB) that issued its *Key Attributes of Effective Resolution Regimes for Financial Institutions* (the Kas) in 2011 (updated in 2014) as a blueprint for reform to facilitate the orderly recovery and resolution of distressed financial institutions.[58] Although the core text of UNCITRAL does not specifically relate to banks, arguably, its interpretation into domestic laws could be examined as well as to what extent these standards can be complied with at the domestic level.[59]

The Recent Kenyan Bank Failures

Bank failures in developing countries have focused on mainly macroeconomic factors.[60] Credit expansion[61], non-performing loans, lack of adequate corporate governance, insider lending, the ability of banks to accumulate interest on non-performing loans (NPLs) and the revaluation of assets to hide capital inadequacies are also contributory factors to bank insolvencies. The Kenyan banking system has been said to be shallow, inefficient, and fragile and one of the main outcomes of this is the high level of non-performing loans.[62] Despite the fact that it is impossible to define a single measurable dependent variable that has continually caused the failure of banks. High non-performing loans, high interest rate spreads and high levels of bank failures could all be considered a symptom of the fragility and consequently dependent variables, which seems to suggest that shallowness and fragility are interlinked.[63] Corporate governance is essentially crucial particularly in banks.[64] This coupled with strong prudential regulation and supervision an appropriate savings deposit protection system and sound resolution regimes. Corporate governance in banks pertains to the culmination of the systems infrastructures and information utilised for directing and overseeing the management of an organisation.[65] It also refers to the practices and processes of a bank are managed so as to permit positive dealings and the application of power in the 'management of assets and resources with an aim of advancing shareholders' value and shareholders' satisfaction together with improved accountability, resource use, and transparent administration'[66] Without a doubt the relationship between internal governance and risk management is undisputed and the poorer the bank's corporate governance, the riskier the bank. It is left for discussion as to whether more robust regulation is the panacea of resolving failing banks or more targeted supervision. This is since targeted supervision may complement the effective corporate governance of the banking system. Corporate governance is essential in the management of banks as it fosters transparency in its capacity and corporate function as well as its capability to protect investors. It is also accepted that it involves the manner in which the business and affairs of individual institutions are governed by their directors, which, through perhaps the stakeholder theory, consider the interest of its stakeholders which also perhaps is of public interest. It also concerns the alignment of its activities and to operate in a safe and sound manner. Furthermore, the dominance of banks and their role in Kenya where issues of integrity and ethics are called into question, does not exclude the fundamental importance of corporate governance. This is since banking supervision cannot exist where corporate governance lacks. The OECD Corporate Governance Principles[67] and the Basel Principles provide international perspectives on the issue of corporate governance. The CBK corporate governance guidelines[68] which was to establish 'best practice' in corporate governance even though it may be difficult to identify what these corporate governance practices may be. To maintain a safe and sound bank through the examination of corporate governance, it is essential to scrutinise the actions of directors of banks as an indication of whether best practices are employed. This is since bank failures may be led by the actions of the directors either through determining the separation of ownership and management, an issue that Imperial Bank faced, with its board of directors.[69]

Several reasons have been posited for the failures, including weak corporate governance practices, poor risk management strategies, weaknesses in regulatory and supervisory systems, and conflicts of interest. More specifically this chapter will focus on the recent failures, Dubai Bank, Imperial Bank and Chase Bank as a result of corporate governance failures. However, as a general point, bank specific factors that lead to distress are always attributed to capital adequacy measures, assets, management capability, earnings, liquidity, and sensitivity to market risk.[70] Although no harmonised discourse can be accurately accorded to which indicators are at the core of evaluating the safety and soundness of banks, building effective early intervention mechanisms may aid in managing distressed banks. There are some indicators that regulators are able to utilise *ex ant*e in order to intervene such as looking at capital reserves.[71] This is due to the fact that good indicators of distress may be attributed to the proportionality of the ratio of loan loss reserves to capital and the resultant growth in loans.[72] Therefore a theoretical understanding of the causes of bank crises in Kenya is still scant, however this paper will discuss the very specific insider lending as well as weak corporate governance issues that seemed to have been the direct cause of the recent bank failures. Kenya had not however experienced significant banking failures since the 90s and when Euro Bank[73] collapsed in 2003. Similarly, it was not in the consideration of most bank customers that three banks in crises with large customer bases would be in distress. This all changed in the period between 2015 and 2016. Towards the end of 2015 and the beginning of 2016, the new Central Bank of Kenya Governor[74] instituted tough policy directives on banks that were in crises. Imperial Bank, Dubai Bank and Chase Bank were facing liquidity issues, and had tried to access lender of last resort assistance.[75]

The available literature on bank failure has tended to focus on the 1980s and 1990s in which various banks were undermined by the political landscape at the time, either through the withdrawal of parastatal funds, which made up a large percentage of deposits or through intimidation through establishment of regime banks.[76] This was done by the said political and or regime banks who sourced deposits cheaply and through their ability to circumvent regulations in particular on capital regulations influenced their lending decisions. This eventually amplified the prevalence of insider lending to directors, which usually leads to high levels of non-performing loans.[77] Furthermore the causes of bank failures in Kenya have also been exacerbated by the lacunae in the regulatory framework. Such lacunae had included the ability of banks to continue accruing interest on non-performing loans and the revaluation of assets to hide capital shortfalls have also been identified as causes of bank failures.[78] Despite these lacunae being closed there remains uncertainty over the supervisory capacity of the CBK in how the CBK should intercede in the case of a failing bank through a resolution regime or how they should be managed when in crisis times.[79] Insider lending is worth mentioning here, as it almost always attracts an 'atmosphere of abuse, corruption, and unethical, if not illegal, behaviour.'[80] However, insider lending is always connected to the ownership of the bank and therefore these concepts are always intertwined.[81] This is precisely why literature is awash with discussions on the separation of ownership and management to reduce the instances of insider lending. The verdict has always been skewed as some systems with very high capital ratios seem to suggest that insider lending may not be detrimental.[82] Therefore insider lending can be said to have a dual effect on bank performance. In Kenya, insider lending has always negatively affected bank performance in Kenya, for instance Trust Bank that closed in 1998, originally had a total loan portfolio of over Kshs. 10. billion. Of this about 5 billion (52%) was nonperforming. In addition, there existed an additional 2.6 billion (25%) of non-performing insider loans. Although the CBK guidelines now control insider lending. The guidelines forbid unsecured insider lending. These issues have not been addressed from a regulatory perspective and Kenya's company law is insufficient in acting as a frontline tool to dealing with these corporate governance failings.

The Central Bank of Kenya announced that due to the interests of the depositors and creditors, it had placed Dubai Bank under receivership.[83] This was after close monitoring of its daily cash reserve ratio when the bank had begun to breach its daily cash reserve ratio requirements.[84] The Central bank was made cognizant of the non-compliance of the bank and as a result Dubai bank had attracted penalties. This was made possible due to Sections 43(1), 43(2) and 53(1) of the Kenya Deposit Insurance Act.[85] Among the many causes of Dubai Bank's demise was the failure of Dubai Bank to honour its financial obligations when they fell due which exposed its liquidity issues.[86] This capital requirements failure and liquidity ratio as well as its provisions for non-performing loans and weak corporate governance structures contributed to the concern of CBK. The KDIC in the end saw that liquidation was the only feasible option for the bank.[87] Consequently, it was decided that only insured deposits of Sh100, 000 would recover their deposits and other creditors' claims would be paid equitably as and when the liquidator accumulates enough funds from the liquidation process. Dubai Bank Kenya was established in 1982. As of December 2013, the bank's total assets were valued at about US$34.4 million (KES 2.92 billion. In August 2015, the bank was placed under receivership by the Central Bank of Kenya (CBK) which appointed Kenya Deposit Insurance Corporation (KDIC) as the receiver of Dubai bank. As reported by the CBK, the main contributory factors leading to the collapse of the Dubai bank were capital deficiencies and liquidity. The bank had been breaching its daily cash reserve ratio (CRR) requirement of 5.25 per cent (CBK, 2016). The bank had failed to honour some of its financial obligations, such as paying off KES 48 million which it owed to the Bank of Africa Kenya. Despite the troubled bank being penalised by the CBK for non-compliance, the situation was not rectified.[88] Penalties are issued by CBK directives on various aspects. The Prompt Corrective Actions.[89] This guideline stipulates those actions have to be taken by banking institutions to prevent their failure and instability generally in the banking sector. On 24 August 2015, KDIC published a report on the financial conditions of Dubai bank. The report recommended the bank's liquidation due to its parlous financial position.

The Central Bank placed Imperial Bank under receivership after learning that 'unsafe and unsound business conditions to transact business' existed in the bank.[90] As a result, the board of directors of Imperial Bank brought to the attention of the regulator their inappropriate banking practices in a bid to salvage the bank through self-reporting.[91] This move was viewed as highly contentious as one of the directors of Imperial Bank was deceased and it therefore brought the discourse on bank ownership and corporate governance issues as interlinked. This self-reporting moreover highlighted the attention of the CBK and the inappropriate banking practices that Imperial Bank was engaged in. It also warranted the immediate remedial action in order to safeguard the interest of both depositors and creditors. Chase Bank, which had established itself as the 'jewel among small and medium sized enterprise lenders in the market and attracted funding from international investors, became distressed.'[92] The run on the branches of Chase Bank commenced on 7 April, as the public had heard speculations about its difficulties. This became the first time in a very long time that a Kenyan bank had experienced a run on its deposits and despite public assurances by their managing director, the run increased in intensity, particularly on their online platforms.

By 8 April 2016 the situation had become so dramatic that Chase Bank, had to shut down all its branches as well as its online banking options due to increased public panic controversially attributed to social media[93] and the Central Bank Governor, had to intervene by placing Chase Bank under receivership. Although Chase Bank attempted to revert the blame to the accounting surrounding the bank's Islamic Banking assets,[94] the implications were directed towards insider lending as well as weak internal controls. These loans were particularly disbursed to its directors as well as to its staff members. Chase Bank Kenya Ltd is a privately owned commercial bank with a long history. As of December 2015, it had an estimated asset valuation of KES 142 bn (US$1.428 bn).8 On 7 April 2017, Chase Bank was placed under receivership by the CBK, which appointed the KDIC as the receiver. The CBK reported the reasons for the move to receivership as liquidity difficulties following inaccurate social media reports and the stepping aside of two of its directors. Despite the inability to meet its financial obligations, the CBK and KDIC considered Chase Bank a viable option and in response, appointed KCB as 'the Manager', which granted customers immediate access to their deposits up to a maximum of KES 1m. The KDIC called for investors to present an expression of interest in acquiring an equity stake in the bank which was offered by SBM Holdings Limited (SBM). SBM is a financial services group and the third largest company listed on the Stock Exchange of Mauritius, with a growing international presence currently extending to Madagascar, India and Kenya. On 5 January 2018, the CBK and KDIC announced the acceptance of a binding offer from SBM; a few months later, announced the signing of an agreement between SBM and KDIC. The agreement provided for a transfer of 75% of the value of deposits and the transfer of most staff and branches and only 25% of the value of deposits remained with Chase Bank. On 20 August 2018, the CBK announced the completion of the acquisition and assumption process. Depositors were granted structured access to their remaining balances and 50 branches opened their doors and carried out the full range of banking transactions.

The Kenyan Bank Resolution Framework

At the crux of it, bank insolvency should provide 'an alternative self-standing procedure with the primary objective of protecting eligible depositors'.[95] Therefore, any bank insolvency regime ought to have regard for protecting depositors at its core. Insolvency Law in Kenya is derivative of its colonial history. This colonial legacy is evidenced through English Law and concepts which are still applicable in Kenya, with slight deviations in local contexts as provided in for instance section 3 of the Judicature Act Cap 8 of 1967. This transplantation of English laws was through either, the adoption of entire colonial legislations, re-enactments of reception clauses and local ordinances for many years after Kenya gained independence. It is only until after 50 years that calls for reforms and reviews of these transplanted laws have begun to take shape. There are two instruments that govern distressed banks and financial institutions in Kenya, the Central Bank Act as well as the Banking Act as well as the Kenya Deposit Insurance Act. It is arguable on how effective these three instruments have been particularly during the failing of the three banks between 2015 and 2016. This, in my opinion, presents a very convoluted and fragmented framework for bank resolution.

The Central Bank of Kenya supervises the banking sector, through the Central Bank of Kenya Act (CBK)1966 which is further emboldened by the Constitution of Kenya under art 231.[96] S4 and 4A of the Act outline its key mandates with Pt VII on the inspection and control of institutions providing rules and procedures that should be followed during bank insolvencies. When Kenya enacted the CBK Act 1966 and the Banking Act 1968, it adopted the functional approach of financial supervision under which banks are supervised by the CBK. Subsequently, Kenya enacted statutes for the supervision of other financial institutions in the insurance, securities, pensions and retirement, microfinance, and savings-cooperative sectors by functional regulators. Since universal banking facilitates the provision of financial services in more than two sectors, the functional supervisory structure may however not be effective in the supervision of financial conglomerates on a consolidated basis. Nevertheless it could be argued that Kenya has strengthened its regulatory structure and financial safety net when compared to the initial provisions of the Banking Act 1968.[97] Thus, Kenya's financial safety net consisting of the Ministry of Finance and the CBK under the Banking Act 1968,[98] was strengthened by the introduction of Deposit Protection Fund Board (DPFB) in 1985 to provide explicit deposit insurance, and reformed in 2006 by restricting the Minister's powers to exempt licenced institutions from the provisions of the Act.[99] In addition, the National Treasury has recently published Draft Bills to establish a Financial Services Authority (published in 2016) and a Financial Conduct of Business Authority (published in 2018) to strengthen Kenya's supervisory and safety net structures. One of the main objectives of the Central Bank of Kenya is to support and enhance the stability of the Kenyan financial system.[100] A key aspect of this is supported by prudential regulation and supervision, which promotes the safety and soundness of financial firms, among other objectives.[101] The regulatory system in Kenya is not designed to ensure that no firm ever fails, it would be an impossible task to ensure that no financial institution fails. While the Central Bank of Kenya (CBK) is Kenya's resolution authority for banks, building societies, central counterparties, and certain investment firms. The role of the Central Bank of Kenya in this new regulatory landscape, with reference to its function as lender of last resort is to ensure that banks in distress are managed appropriately. This is since bank insolvency essentially leads to liquidation because of the receivership procedures whose main goals are to preserve and protect the interests of creditors.[102] Therefore, in times of distress in banks the CBK is seen as the Lender of Last Resort. The CBK's intention is not to prevent illiquid but solvent banks from failing despite its obligation and discharge are discretionary and not mandatory. This is because the distinction between illiquidity and insolvency is not always clear and needs to be clarified at least in practice.[103] The ambiguity stems from the inconclusive indicators. The fact that illiquidity may mean being unable to fulfil credit obligations on an ongoing basis, as an institution can be cash flow solvent and balance sheet insolvent. This role is rarely contested, as its justification lies at the apex of instability.[104] The Central Bank of Kenya has however not provided liquidity for any of the three failed banks but rather directed the Kenya Deposit Insurance Corporation (KDIC) to place them under receivership which provides the mechanism for Kenya's *ex ante* resolution regime which is an alternative to insolvency and often bailout of distressed banks.

The Kenya Deposit Insurance Act, No. 10 of 2012 (KDI Act) is an Act of Parliament that provides for the establishment of a deposit insurance system and the receivership and liquidation of deposit taking institutions; and that also provides for the establishment of the Kenya Deposit Insurance Corporation.[105] Under section 20, the KDI Act establishes the Deposit Insurance Fund (the Fund)[106] which provides insurance protection to depositors against potential loss of their deposits in the event of failure of a member financial institution. The Fund is managed by the Kenya Deposit Insurance Corporation (KDIC), which is also established under the KDI Act, under section 4.[107] Membership is compulsory for all institutions licenced to carry on deposit taking business such as commercial banks, financial institutions, mortgage finance companies, building societies and micro finance institutions.[108] The Banking Act (Cap. 488) also empowers CBK to intervene in the management of a bank or other financial institution by among other things, appointing KDIC to administer or liquidate any institution if it is established that its assets are less than its liabilities to its creditors. This is further echoed under section 43(1) of the KDI Act, which states that 'The Central Bank shall . . . whenever the circumstances require, appoint the Corporation (KDIC) to be the sole and exclusive receiver of any institution'.[109]

Unlike in ordinary corporate insolvencies which almost always protect company assets from creditors, the KDIC, prioritises depositors. This depositor preferences assures depositors of reimbursement of their deposits. Although, like corporate insolvencies, there exists a creditor hierarchy that ranks depositors among unsecured and thus concurrent, creditors who may only recover funds if there are residual assets remaining after its liquidation. Through the KDI Act which established the KDIC as a receiver for distressed banks. Therefore, the KDI Act provides for a Special Resolution Regime (SRR) for insolvent banks. Previously, receivers were appointed under the Companies Act, to liquidate assets, managers were appointed to continue the company's business. Receiverships, in this light were replaced by administration when the Companies Act was repealed and its insolvency provisions enacted in the Insolvency Act of 2015 which consequently replaced receivers and managers with administrators, the KDI Act has, as yet not been amended to reflect this change and therefore still refers to the KDIC as receiver of institutions.

Between 2015 and 2016, Kenya has had three banks collapse and placed under receivership by the Central Bank of Kenya (CBK). First, in August 2015, Dubai Bank[110] was placed under receivership by CBK and appointed Kenya Deposit Insurance Corporation (KDIC) as the receiver[111]. As reported by the CBK, the main contributory factors leading to the collapse of the Dubai bank were capital deficiencies and liquidity.[112] The bank had been breaching its daily cash reserve ratio (CRR) requirement of 5.25 per cent (CBK, 2016). The bank had failed to honour some of its financial obligations, such as paying off KES 48 million which it owed to the Bank of Africa Kenya. Despite the troubled bank being penalised by the CBK for non-compliance, the situation was not corrected.[113] KDIC made a report to the CBK on August 24, 2015, concerning the financial conditions of Dubai bank. The report indicated that the bank could not be salvaged and went on to recommend the bank's liquidation.[114] According to KDIC's report, liquidation was the only feasible option due to the Dubai Bank Kenya Limited's magnitude of weaknesses.[115] Second, in October 2015 the CBK put Imperial Bank[116] under statutory management. The main reasons for receivership were unsafe and unsound business conditions and practices of transacting business in the bank. At the time the bank was taken over by KDIC the bank had about 53,000 customers with deposits estimated at KES 58 billion. On 21 June 2016, NIC Bank was appointed as asset and liabilities consultant for Imperial Bank (in receivership) by the Central Bank of Kenya. As such, NIC Bank became responsible for returning funds to the failed bank's deposit customers. NIC was also allowed to acquire some of the assets, deposits, and liabilities of Imperial Bank as soon as its receiver-manager, the KDIC, started liquidating the bank. As of December 2021, following a press release by CBK, Imperial Bank Limited (in receivership), is under liquidation.[117] Third, on 7 April 2016, CBK appointed KDIC as receiver for Chase Bank Limited, after the bank was unable to meet its financial obligation. The major causes for placement were associated with failure to meet the statutory banking ratios and under-reporting of insider loans. The insider loans stood at 13.62 billion Kenya shillings compared to the 5.72 billion Kenya shillings it reported.[118] The main issue at Chase bank was governance problems. The bank made large amounts of loan to its directors of about 13.62 billion Kenya shillings.[119] On 20 April 2016, KDIC appointed KCB Bank Kenya Limited (KCB) as Manager of Chase Bank Limited (In-Receivership) (CBLIR), with the concurrence and approval of CBK. This was intended to ensure the continued operations of CBLIR, leveraging on KCB's credentials as a strong bank with a solid brand, adequate human resources, and wide experience in the country.[120] Consequently, CBLIR resumed limited banking operations in accordance with the Banking Act on 27 April 2016, under KCB's management. This enabled CBLIR customers to have immediate access to their deposits to a maximum of Kshs.1 million. On this basis, 162,970 deposit accounts equivalent to 97 per cent of the depositors' accessed their funds in full.[121] On 7 April 2021, KDIC submitted the Receiver's Report to CBK recommending that CBLIR be liquidated. The report indicates that considering the weak status of CBLIR's financial position, liquidation is the only feasible option.[122] As it stands, KDIC is expected to release information about the liquidation of CBLIR and payment of depositors.[123]

Deposit insurance is a core feature in banking systems.[124] It provides bank creditors, especially those providing retail deposits, with a credible guarantee that in the event of a bank's insolvency their deposits, up to a certain limit, will be protected. To an extent, it reduces a bank's liquidity risk.[125] However, this provision creates a moral hazard thus affecting supervisory authorities as discussed it encourages risk taking where banks hold less capital or hold riskier asset portfolios.[126] Nevertheless, it is argued, the existence of such guarantees creates a moral hazard affecting banks (and, indeed, supervisory authorities): it can encourage increased risk-taking where banks hold less capital or hold riskier asset portfolios. Equivocally, the introduction of explicit forms of deposit protection may in certain instances, reduce risk taking.[127] However, the success would depend on the design and particularly the extent of the explicit government support provided. The Kenya Deposit Insurance Act by the Central Bank of Kenya instituted the Kenya Deposit Insurance Corporation, which was previously the Kenya Deposit Protection fund. This legal framework is heavily borrowed from the US Federal Deposit Insurance Corporation.[128] and it is where the various mechanisms to resolve bank crises are derived from. This is termed legal transplantation,[129] shaping their legislation by adapting the legal frameworks of developed countries,[130] either through the continuation of post-colonial legal frameworks or through transplantation from elsewhere in this case the US model of deposit protection. However, such transplantation must reflect the KDIC's regulatory capacity, which is the ability of the KDIC to implement its statutory mandate, with respect to resolving crisis banks.

Kenya established a Deposit Protection Fund Board which was emboldened by the Kenya Deposit Insurance Act 2012 (KDIA) which was enacted which provided for the establishment of the Kenya Deposit Insurance Corporation (KDIC) to replace the DPFB which manages the scheme as well as the receivership and liquidation of failed deposit-taking institutions. The Authority is now an independent department of the CBK. As a matter of bank insolvency law on a national level, the KDIC provides the most comprehensive resolution regime. The CBK initially had the power to liquidate any failed banking institutions.[131] These powers have been relayed to the KDIC as set out in Pt VI of the KDIA 2012 which only offers two proceedings, liquidation, or receivership. Section 43(1) mandates the CBK to appoint the KDIC as the receiver of an institution in certain circumstances, set out in s43(2). Section 53(2) mandates the KDIC to confirm that the institution has complied with all requirements or recommend that the institution be liquidated. Where the KDIC recommends liquidation, s54(1) states that the CBK will appoint the KDIC as the liquidator. Where an institution is unlikely to be viable, s44(1) grants the KDIC the power to require the institution to implement any actions considered necessary, stop carrying on any of its businesses, or restructure the whole or part of its business.

Recovery and resolution regimes are at the nexus of prudential regulation and supervision on the one hand and corporate insolvency law and reorganisation on the other, spilling over into both areas. The main objective of the recovery and resolution framework is to maintain financial stability in a crisis and to minimise losses for society without the need to rely on taxpayer intervention.[132] The pre-crisis Insolvency framework for banks and financial institutions had various deficiencies. The Crisis, unearthed the grave limitations of insolvency law in managing distressed financial institutions, including vulnerability to losses of confidence, unsuitability for performing critical functions and inability to ensure prompt pay-out of insured deposits and client's assets. Collectively, they led to an evident loss of confidence in the financial system resulting in wholesale and depositor bank runs, contagion, and loss of access to capital markets. In Kenya particularly, an appeal for reform in the aftermath of the three (Chase, Dubai and Imperial) bank failures underlined the need to review existing insolvency proceedings and restructuring measures and to introduce a modified resolution regime. Resolution suggests the restructuring of a financial institution to maintain its critical functions. The IMF describes insolvency proceedings as all types of official action involving removal of management and or the imposition of limits on or suspension of the rights of shareholders and the assumption of direct control by a banking authority or other officially appointed person over a bank that has crossed a threshold for the commencement of insolvency proceedings. Under this definition insolvency proceedings constitute an umbrella term encompassing both the application of resolution tools and powers and the application of standard insolvency law. It describes the process of liquidating a financial institution to repay its insolvency creditors. However, after the 2007 financial crisis a new perspective emerged, the consideration of deposit-taking institutions which provide liquidity to the real economy was regarded as a priority. It was also noted that financial institutions need not be rescued in their entirety to safeguard financial stability. In this regard, resolution represents a compromise and a pragmatic solution to insolvency laws inability to manage distressed banks. Resolution is an administrative, non-judicial procedure empowering a resolution authority to restructure without interfering with creditor and shareholder rights. This framework should isolate systemically relevant functions of financial institutions and safeguard their continuity while ensuring that functions and services deemed irrelevant can be subject to ordinary or modified insolvency proceedings. According to the Bank Resolution Regime Directive, (BRRD) that forms part of the European Resolution Framework, resolution seeks to replicate the effects of insolvency.[133] Although the BRRD observes the accepted principles of insolvency law, its overriding objective is to safeguard financial institutions and safeguard their continuity while ensuring that functions and services deemed irrelevant can be subject to ordinary or modified insolvency proceedings. To protect financial stability, the application of insolvency proceedings to any remaining institution, requires that the objectives must be realigned with that of resolution.[134] Deposit Insurance and resolution are therefore closely linked. It is even described as a risk minimizer mandate.[135] The protection of depositors from banks in distress was stressed during the GFC and several countries strengthened their deposit protection schemes.[136] Kenya, through the KDI Act, strengthened its institutional structure and mandates. This in turn provided a more effective resolution regime through the KDIC.[137] The Act authorises KDIC to own property and hire its own staff.[138] The KDI Act further repealed sections of the Banking Act relating to the powers of the DPFB and those relating to the CBK's powers over the liquidation of financial institutions.[139] The CBK's powers to intervene in bank management by appointing the KDIC as a manager for financial institutions in distress were retained in the Banking Act.[140] Therefore it is worth examining whether such a design adequately addressed the gaps in the system that operated under the DPFB and whether it adequately implemented the IADI Core principles to curb moral hazard ex ante and the FSB Key attributes in mitigating the effects of bank moral hazard ex post.[141] The Act prescribes the mandate for the KDIC as a resolution regime for insolvent institutions.[142] They are also able to levy administer and apply funds in accordance with the Act[143] as well as to promote sound risk management by institutions to maintain the stability of the financial system.[144] The Corporation is further required to provide incentives to promote sound risk management by member institutions, and to promote financial system stability.[145] To carry out these functions, the Corporation is empowered to, *inter alia*, invest the contributions and enter into transactions that enhance the management of the Fund,[146] reimburse insured depositors of failed banks[147] and to avert risk to member institutions, the financial system or loss to the Corporation, through acquisition of assets of the insolvent institution.[148] The Corporation is also empowered to advance loans to financial institutions through open bank assistance,[149] or the acquisition of the assets and capital instruments of failed institutions.[150] Additionally as the use of public funds to avert risk to member institutions or the financial system involves bailout of the failed institutions and creates the moral hazard dilemma the KDI Act requires KDIC to exercise the powers to avert systemic risk only with the approval of the Treasury Secretary.[151] Which means that, the KDIC implements the broadest mandate of 'risk minimiser' through the authority to 'avert risk to member institutions and the financial system'.[152] Additionally, it releases the 'loss minimiser' mandate through the adoption of the least costly resolution strategy for insolvent institutions.[153] Consequently, the Corporation combines the 'risk minimiser' mandate in administering the 'loss minimiser' role in conducting resolution as receiver and liquidator which enables KDIC to participate in the safety net provision.[154] Depositor preference in bank insolvencies unlike ordinary corporate insolvencies that mainly seeks to protect the asset of the insolvent company from a free for all pursuit of recovery by individual creditors and the KDIC through its explicit nature allows this.[155] Through creditor hierarchy depositors among unsecured and thus concurrent, creditors who may only recover funds if there are residual assets remaining after paying secured creditors. Usually, corporate insolvency adapts creditor hierarchy laws that rank depositors among unsecured and thus concurrent, creditors who may only recover funds if there are residual assets remaining after paying secured creditors.[156] This assures depositors that their funds would be reimbursed. This is important because depositors are the largest group of creditors of banks.

Conclusion

In summary, the effectiveness of banks' internal governance arrangements have a bearing on precluding and resolving bank insolvencies. Many bank insolvencies, controlling for macroeconomic factors, might be precipitated by poor risk management within the bank itself, poor governance and the capital reserves not meeting acceptable ratios. Additionally, poor risk management is ultimately a failure of internal governance.[157] Kenya has a long way to go in this regard, the simple adoption of US models may not always work because the country specific factors are highly contextual. Nevertheless, the 'failure resolution' are specifically designed to address systemic risks caused by bank failure in order to avoid contagion, while freeing the public authorities from the recurrent dilemma of having to use public funds to bail out all of a bank's creditors.[158] In doing so, they submit to the benefits that a resolution would have in a financial system not only at the point of use but also more generally through their effect on the behaviour of banks and their creditors.[159] Additionally, loss allocation among creditors is usually a tenet of insolvency laws. Similarly in resolutions, the allocation of the costs or the absorption of those losses is the most important aspect of an effective resolution regime. Therefore, the success of any resolution regime will be assessed on the basis of how effectively they would have stabilised a failing institution. The post-GFC bank insolvency law has evolved into an important branch of law that overlays other divisions of law with imposition within its fundamental values which remains challenging for practitioners and academics.

Notes

1 Radha Upadhyaya, 'Analysing the Sources and Impact of Segmentation in the Banking Sector: A Case Study of Kenya' (PhD thesis, University of London, 2011).

2 N Ndung'u and RW Ngugi, *Banking Sector Interest Rate Spreads in Kenya* (Kenya Institute for Public Policy Research and Analysis Discussion Paper, No. 5, 2000).

3 Eva Hupkes, 'Insolvency – Why a Special Regime for Banks?' in *Curriculum Development Monetary Finance Law* (vol 3, International Monetary Fund, forthcoming) 471–513.

4 The Global Financial Crisis in 2007/2008 as defined in John R LaBrosse, Rodrigo Olivares-Caminal and Dalvinder Singh (eds), *Financial Crisis Containment and Government Guarantees* (Edward Elgar, 2013).

5 David C Wheelock and Paul W Wilson, 'Explaining Bank Failures: Deposit Insurance, Regulation, and Efficiency' (1995) 77 Rev Econ Stat 689.

6 The is a swathe of literature on the Global Financial Crises and the causes, See Gary Gorton, *Slapped by the Invisible Hand* (OUP, 2010).

7 The discussion on the housing bubble in the US between the period of 1998–2008 which was due to the availability of subprime mortgages during this period while arguably increasing consumption levels and home ownership rates resulted in the bubble. Major Coleman, Michael LaCour-Little and Kerry D Vandell, 'Subprime Lending and the Housing Bubble: Tail Wags Dog?' (2008) 17 J Hous Econ 272.

8 See, generally, B Wessels and M Haentjens, 'Three Paradigm Shifts in Recent Bank Insolvency Law' (2016) 31 J Int Bus Law Rev 396–400.

9 This term is largely used in the UK after its prescription into the UK Banking Act of 2009. See e.g., Financial Stability Board, <www.fsb.org/wp-content/uploads/r_111104cc.pdfaccessed> which monitors and assesses the vulnerabilities affecting the global financial system. accessed 2 October 2021.

10 Mike Feintuck, 'Regulatory Rationales Beyond the Economic: In Search of the Public Interest' in Robert Baldwin, Martin Cave and Martin Lodge (eds), *The Oxford Handbook of Regulation* (OUP, 2013).

11 Imperial Bank Kenya Limited was a Kenyan bank founded in 1992, which was placed under statutory management on 15 October 2015 by the Central Bank of Kenya.

12 Dubai Bank Kenya Limited was placed under receivership by the Central Bank of Kenya on the 14th of August of 2015. Bankelele, 'Kenya Bank Rankings 2013 Part I' (*Bankelele*, WordPress, 28 April 2014) <http://bankelele.co.ke/2014/04/

kenya-bank-rankings-2013-part-i.html> accessed 30 January 2022; Standard Reporter, 'CBK Orders Liquidation of Dubai Bank Kenya Following Cash Flow Problems' *The Standard* (Nairobi, 24 August 2015) <www.standardmedia.co.ke/business/article/2000174000/cbk-orders-liquidation-of-dubai-bank-kenya-following-cash-flow-problems> accessed 30 January 2022.

13 John B Taylor, *The Financial Crisis and the Policy Responses: An Empirical Analysis of What Went Wrong* (National Bureau of Economic Research Working Paper 14631, 2009).

14 Central Bank Act Chapter 491.

15 Lender of Last Resort was elaborated by Goodhart and Gerhard, in Charles A Goodhart and Gerhard Illing (eds), *Financial Crises, Contagion, and the Lender of Last Resort: A Reader* (OUP, 2003).

16 Dalvinder Singh and John R LaBrosse, 'Developing a Framework for Effective Financial Crisis Management' (2011) OECD J Fin Mark Tr 125 <www.oecd.org/finance/financial-markets/49191776.pdf> accessed 2 August 2016. (Please amend access date to this year).

17 John McEldowney, 'Defining the Public Interest: Public Law Perspectives on Regulating the Financial Crisis' in John R LaBrosse, Rodrigo Olivares-Caminal and Dalvinder Singh (eds), *Financial Crisis Management and Bank Resolution* (Informa Law, 2009) and see further Andrew D Crockett, 'Why Is Financial Stability a Goal of Public Policy?' (1997) 82 Econ Rev 5.

18 Radha Upadhyaya in her thesis, discusses the fragility and segmentation of the banking industry as characterised by low lending levels, high interest rate spreads, high levels of non-performing loans and several bank failures where she aimed to understand the sources of its shallowness and fragility. Upadhyaya (n 2).

19 A discussion on the decline in trust during the Global Financial Crisis and that banking trust is contagious. Markus Knell and Helmut Stix, *Trust in Banks? Evidence from Normal Times and from Times of Crises* (Oesterreichische Nationalbank (Austrian Central Bank) Working Paper 158, 2009).

20 Early Intervention has been encouraged in many EU states as an effective crisis management tool for banks in distress see Joe Peek and Eric S Rosengren, 'Will Legislated Early Intervention Prevent the Next Banking Crisis?' (1997) 64 South Econ J 268.

21 The inevitability of bank failure as discussed in, Iman Anabtawi and Steven L Schwarcz, 'Regulating Ex Post: How Law Can Address the Inevitability of Financial Failure' (2013) 92 Tex Law Rev 75.

22 See generally, Charles P Kindleberger and Robert Z Aliber, *Manias, Panics, and Crashes: A History of Financial Crises* (7th edn, Palgrave Macmillan Ltd, 2015).

23 Carmen M Reinhart and Kenneth S Rogoff, 'The Aftermath of Financial Crises' (2009) 99 Am Econ Rev 466.

24 Martin Brownbridge, 'Financial Distress in Local Banks in Kenya, Nigeria, Uganda and Zambia: Causes and Implications for Regulatory Policy' (1998) 16 Development Policy Review 173.

25 ibid.

26 See generally, Nelson M Waweru and Victor M Kalani, 'Commercial Banking Crises in Kenya: Causes and Remedies' (2009) 4 Afr J Acc Econ Fin Bank Res 23 12, where an extensive discussion on the causes of bank crises.

27 ibid.

28 Steven L Schwarcz, 'Systemic Risk' (2008) 97 Georgetown Law J 193.

29 Fabio Panetta and others, *An Assessment of Financial Sector Rescue Programmes* (Banca D'Italia Occasional Papers No. 47, 2009).

30 FSB, 'Key Attributes of Effective Resolution Regimes for Financial Institutions' (2011) <www.fsb.org/wp-content/uploads/r_111104cc.pdf?page_moved=1> accessed 30 January 2022.

31 Helen A Garten, 'Universal Banking and Financial Stability' (1993) 19 Brooklyn J Intl Law 159; Jonathan R Macey, 'The Inevitability of Universal Banking' (1993) 19 Brooklyn J Intl Law 203; George J Benston, 'Universal Banking' (1994) 8 J Econ Pers 121.

32 Frederic S Mishkin, 'How Big a Problem Is Too Big to Fail? A Review of Gary Stern and Ron Feldman's Too Big to Fail: The Hazards of Bank Bailouts' (2006) 44 J Econ Lit 988.

33 ibid; Michael C Munger and Richard Salsman, 'The Implications of Bailouts: Is "Too Big to Fail" Too Big?' (2013) 11 Georgetown J Law Pub Pol 433. See also Chen Zhou, 'Are Banks Too Big to Fail? Measuring Systemic Importance of Financial Institutions' (2010) 6 Intl J Cent Bank 205.

34 Eva Hüpkes 'Insolvency – Why a Special Regime for Banks?' in *Current Developments in Monetary and Financial Law* (vol 3, International Monetary Fund, 2005) 3.

35 ibid.

36 ibid 8.

37 ibid 12.

38 Günter Franke, Jan P Krahnen and Thomas von Lupke, *Effective Resolution of Banks: Problems and Solutions* (Sustainable Architecture for Finance in Europe ("SAFE") Working Paper Series No. 19, 2014), 2.

39 Rodrigo Olivares-Caminal, *The Pari Passu Clause in Sovereign Debt Instruments: Developments in Recent Litigation* (BIS Papers No. 72, 2013) <www.bis.org/publ/bppdf/bispap72u.pdf> accessed 30 January 2022.

40 Charles Randell, *Legal Aspects of Bank Resolution: Designing the Powers and Solutions* (Operational Aspects of Bank Resolution and Restructuring Conference, European Bank for Reconstruction and Development, 19 March 2012) 1.

41 Joseph E Stiglitz, 'Lessons from the Global Financial Crisis of 2008' (2010) Seoul J Econ 321.

42 Simon Brodie, *Bank Resolution: Key Issues and Local Perspectives* (INSOL International, 2019).

43 Emilios Avgouleas and Charles Goodhart, 'An Anatomy of Bank Bail-Ins: Why the Eurozone Needs a Fiscal Backstop for the Banking Sector' (2016) 2016 Euro Econ – Bank Reg Real Sect 75.

44 Basel Committee on Banking Supervision, *Basel III: A Global Regulatory Framework for More Resilient Banks and Banking Systems -Revised Version June 2011* (BIS, 2011) <www.bis.org/publ/bcbs189.pdf> accessed 11 December 2021. The Basel III Accord was issued in December 2010 and revised in June 2011.

45 L Landau, *Procyclicality – What It Means and What Could Be Done* (The Bank of Spain's Conference on Procyclicality and the Role of Financial Regulation; Madrid, 4 May 2009) <www.bis.org/review/r090805d.pdf> accessed 11April 2021.

46 International Association of Deposit Insurers, 'IADI Core Principles for Effective Deposit Insurance Systems' (2014) <www.iadi.org/en/assets/File/Core%20Principles/cprevised2014nov.pdf> accessed 11 December 2021. See also V Micajkova, 'Deposit Insurance in Times of Financial Crisis' [2013] South-Eastern Euro J Econ 165; J Kerlin 'Development of Deposit Insurance Systems in the World' [2015] J Manag Fin Sci 33.

47 ibid.

48 Randell (n 41) 4.

49 United Nations, Commission on International Trade Law, Working Group V (Insolvency Law), 'Insolvency of Large and Complex Financial Institutions, Note by the Secretariat' (24 September 2012) 3 <https://undocs.org/en/A/CN.9/WG.V/WP.109> accessed 17 August 2020.

50 For more detail on the failure of Lehman Brothers see Frederic S Mishkin, 'Over the Cliff: From the Subprime to the Global Financial Crisis' [2011] J Econ Pers 49 and

also R Swedberg, 'The Structure of Confidence and the Collapse of Lehman Brothers' [2010] Mark Trial Econ Sociol US Fin Crisis Part A 71.

51 IMF, 'Resolution of Cross-Border Banks – A Proposed Framework for Enhanced Coordination' (2010) 5 <www.imf.org/external/np/pp/eng/2010/061110.pdf> accessed 17 August 2020; Matthias Haentjens, 'Bank Recovery and Resolution: An Overview of Institutional Initiatives' (2014) 5 Intl Insol Law Rev 255.

52 Financial Stability Forum, 'FSF Principles for Cross-Border Cooperation on Crisis Management' (2009) <www.fsb.org/wp-content/uploads/r_0904c.pdf> accessed 1 August 2020; Haentjens (n 52) 255.

53 Basel Committee on Banking Supervision Consultative Document Report and Recommendations of the Cross-Border Bank Resolution Group (2014) 3 <www.bis.org/publ/bcbs162.pdf?noframes=1> accessed 18 May 2020; Haentjens (n 52) 255.

54 ibid 5 and 16 et seq.; Haentjens (n 52) 255.

55 Sean Hagan and Christopher Towe, 'International Monetary Fund and the World Bank an Overview of the Legal, Institutional, and Regulatory Framework for Bank Insolvency' (2009) <www.imf.org/external/np/pp/eng/2009/041709.pdf> accessed 18 May 2022.

56 United Nations, Commission on International Trade Law, *Legislative Guide on Insolvency Law* (part 1–2, United Nations, 2004) <https://uncitral.un.org/sites/uncitral.un.org/files/media-documents/uncitral/en/05-80722_ebook.pdf> accessed 30 January 2022; Haentjens (n 52) 255.

57 B Wessels, *International Insolvency Law* (3rd edn, Sweet & Maxwell, 2012) para. 10425; Haentjens (n 52) 255. Given the overlap between the issues addressed in Part 3 of the UNCITRAL Guide and the issues addressed by the BCBS in its work on cross-border banking groups, the BCBS recommended that the UNCITRAL Guide should also be used for banking group insolvencies. Consequently, the UNCITRAL Working Group V (Insolvency Law) referred the development of rules regarding the recognition of foreign resolution actions and cross-border cooperation in the context of large and complex financial institutions insolvencies to the FSB.

58 Financial Stability Board 'Key Attributes of Effective Resolution Regimes for Financial Institutions' (2014) <www.fsb.org/wp-content/uploads/r_141015.pdf> accessed 7 June 2020.

59 See also the discussions in ch 8.

60 Brownbridge (n 25) 173.

61 Jecinta Waitherero Waititu, 'Relationship Between Strategy Implementation and Performance in Commercial Banks in Nairobi County Kenya' (2016) 11 Intl J Bus Manag 230.

62 ibid 30.

63 Non-Performing Loans have been the most Jianbo Lou, *China's Troubled Bank Loans: Workout and Prevention* (Kluwer Law International, 2001).

64 TG Arun and JD Turner, 'Corporate Governance of Banks in Developing Economies: Concepts and Issues' (2004) 12 Corp Gov 371; Yunis Hamad, 'Corporate Governance for Banks' in Simon Archer and Rifaat Ahmed Abdel Karim (eds), *Islamic Finance: The Regulatory Challenge* (John Wiley & Sons, 2007).

65 ibid.

66 ibid 54.

67 The OECD Principles of Corporate Governance states have been designated as the 12 key standards for sound financial systems.

68 These were introduced in 2000 and referred to as '2000 CBK guidelines and the Prudential Guidelines of the same year.

69 The regulation stipulates that a shareholder who has 5% cannot hold an executive position.

70 Sloan Swindle, 'Using CAMEL Ratings to Evaluate Regulator Effectiveness at Commercial Banks' (1995) 9 J Fin Ser Res 123.
71 Graciela Laura Kaminsky, *Currency and Banking Crises: The Early Warnings of Distress* (IMF Working Papers 1, IMF, 1999) 99.
72 Anwer S Ahmed, Carolyn Takeda and Shawn Thomas, 'Bank Loan Loss Provisions: A Reexamination of Capital Management, Earnings Management and Signalling Effects' (1999) 28 J Acc Econ 1.
73 Euro Bank Kenya Ltd was placed under statutory management but however did not survive and was eventually liquidated.
74 Dr. Patrick Njoroge was appointed the new Central Bank Governor on the 18th of June 2015.
75 Rosa Maria Lastra, 'Lender of Last Resort, an International Perspective' (1999) 48 Intl Comp Law Q 340.
76 Anne W. Kamau, *Capital Requirements and Bank Behaviour in Kenya: Empirical Evidence* (No. 36. Kenya Institute for Public Policy Research and Analysis, 2004).
77 Hippolyte Fofack, *Nonperforming Loans in Sub-Saharan Africa: Causal Analysis and Macroeconomic Implications* (World Bank Policy Research Working Paper 3769, 2005).
78 Ahmed, Takeda and Thomas (n 73) 1.
79 Gabriel Jiménez and others, 'Credit Supply Versus Demand: Bank and Firm Balance-Sheet Channels in Good and Crisis Times' [2012] SSRN Electronic Journal <https://ideas.repec.org/p/tiu/tiucen/a0842b60-0c4b-438b-a405-abcc91848425.html>.
80 Naomi R Lamoreaux and National Bureau of Economic Research, *Insider Lending: Banks, Personal Connections and Economic Development in Industrial New England* (CUP, 1994). Naomi R. Lamoreaux discusses how historically, insider lending enabled banks to finance economic development.
81 Luc Laeven, 'Insider Lending and Bank Ownership: The Case of Russia' (2001) 29 J Comp Econ 207.
82 Noel Maurer and Stephen H Haber, 'Related Lending and Economic Performance: Evidence from Mexico' [2004] SSRN Electronic Journal 551.
83 <www.centralbank.go.ke//images/docs/media/2015/DubaiBankpressrelease.pdf> accessed 30 January 2022.
84 ibid.
85 Kenya Deposit Insurance Corporation Act 2012.
86 Douglas W Diamond and Raghuram G Rajan, 'Liquidity Risk, Liquidity Creation, and Financial Fragility: A Theory of Banking' (2001) 109 J Pol Econ 287.
87 ibid 49.
88 This account will be found in RN Gathaiya, 'Analysis of Issues Affecting Collapsed Banks in Kenya From Year 2015 to 2016' [July–Sept 2017] Int J Manag Bus Stud 9.
89 Sections 33 and 34 of the Banking Act, Prudential Guidelines, Guideline on Prompt Corrective Action, CBK PG 21 p. 467.
90 <www.centralbank.go.ke//images/docs/media/Press> accessed 30 January 2022.
91 For a discussion on value of self-reporting strategy, see Louis Kaplow and Steven Shavell, 'Optimal Law Enforcement with Self-Reporting of Behavior' (1994) 102 J Pol Econ 583.
92 John Gitau, 'Is Weak Governance to Blame for Bank Collapses in Kenya?' (25 April 2016) <https://cfi-blog.org/2016/04/25/is-weak-governance-to-blame-for-bank-collapses-in-kenya/> accessed 30 January 2022.
93 Nanjira Sambili, 'Chase Bank Is in Receivership Because of Chase Bank and Not Social Media' (*Nation News Paper*) <www.nation.co.ke/oped/blogs/chase-bank-receivership-social-media/620-3151826-q3twewz/index.html> accessed 30 January 2022.
94 Diana Ngila, 'Directors Blame Audit Firm Deloitte for Chase Bank's Fall' (*Business Daily*, 9 June 2016) <www.businessdailyafrica.com/Directors-blame-audit-firm-Deloitte-for-Chase-Bank-s-fall/539546-3242452-pry2nez/index.html> accessed 30 January 2022.

95 Michael Schillig, *Resolution and Insolvency of Banks and Financial Institutions* (OUP, 2016) 444.
96 Constitution of Kenya, Art 231.
97 Banking Act Chapter 488 Laws of Kenya.
98 Central Bank of Kenya Act Chapter 491 Laws of Kenya.
99 ibid.
100 See <www.centralbank.go.ke/index.php/bank-supervision> accessed 6 August 2021.
101 ibid.
102 Companies Act cap 486 sections 212 and 228.
103 See *BNY Corporate Trustees Services Ltd v Eurosail-UK 2007–3BL plc* [2013] UKSC 28.
104 Charles M Kahn and João AC Santos, 'Allocating Bank Regulatory Powers: Lender of Last Resort, Deposit Insurance and Supervision' (2005) 49(8) Eur Econ Rev 2107–36.
105 Preamble, The Kenya Deposit Insurance Act, No. 10 of 2012.
106 Section 20(1), The Kenya Deposit Insurance Act, No. 10 of 2012.
107 Section 4(1), The Kenya Deposit Insurance Act, No. 10 of 2012.
108 Section 24(1), The Kenya Deposit Insurance Act, No. 10 of 2012.
109 Section 43(1), The Kenya Deposit Insurance Act, No. 10 of 2012.
110 Dubai Bank Kenya was established in 1982. As of December 2013, the bank's total assets were valued at about US$34.4 million (KES 2.92 billion).
111 Press Release, 'Dubai Bank Kenya Ltd (in Receivership)' (Central Bank of Kenya, August 2015) <www.centralbank.go.ke/images/docs/media/2015/KDICPRESSRELEASE.pdf> accessed 19 August 2021.
112 Gathaiya (n 89).
113 ibid.
114 ibid.
115 Business Daily, 'Receiver KDIC Says Dubai Bank Kenya Should Be Wound Up' (*Business Daily*, August 2015) <www.businessdailyafrica.com/Central-Bank-appoints-liquidator-for-Dubai-Bank/539546-2844218-mp6icd/index.html> accessed 30 January 2022.
116 Imperial Bank Limited was established as a Finance and Securities Company in 1992. In 1996, the bank commenced commercial banking services, after it was issued with a banking licence by the Central Bank of Kenya. The bank's stock is privately held. The bank is a medium-sized retail bank that caters to both individuals as well as corporate clients. As of December 2013, its total asset base was valued at about US$498 million (KES 43 billion), with shareholders' equity of approximately US$66.2 million (KES 5.719 billion). At that time, the bank was ranked the 19th largest Kenyan commercial bank, by assets, out of forty-three licenced banks in the country (CBK, 2016).
117 <www.centralbank.go.ke/uploads/press_releases/1065588915_Press%20Release%20-%20Imperial%20Bank%20%20Liquidation-December%202021.pdf> accessed 30 January 2022.
118 ibid.
119 ibid.
120 Press Release, 'Liquidation of Chase Bank Limited (in Receivership)' (Central Bank of Kenya, April 2021) <www.centralbank.go.ke/uploads/press_releases/706595395_Press%20Release%20-%20Chase%20Bank%20-%20Liquidation.pdf> accessed 30 November 2021.
121 ibid.
122 ibid.
123 ibid.
124 Deniz Anginer and Asli Demirgüç-Kunt, 'Bank Runs and Moral Hazard: A Review of Deposit Insurance' in Allen Berger and others (eds), *The Oxford Handbook of Banking* (3rd edn, OUP, 2019).

125 Charles Calomiris and Matthew Jaremski, *Deposit Insurance: Theories and Facts* (Columbia Business School Research Paper No. 16–35, 2016).
126 Reint Gropp and Jukka Vesala, *Deposit Insurance and Moral Hazard: Does the Counterfactual Matter?* (ECB Working Paper No. 47, 2001).
127 Regulation and the Global Financial Crisis (Routledge Research in Finance and Banking Law, p. 144).
128 'Open Bank Assistance' <www.fdic.gov/bank/historical/managing/history1-05.pdf> accessed 5 September 2021.
129 Scholar Alan Watson to indicate the moving of a rule coined the term legal transplant or a system of law from one country to another as maintained by Watson, transplantation is the most fertile source of legal development. Alan Watson, *Legal Transplants: An Approach to Comparative Law* (Lightning Source UK Ltd, 2013); Alan Watson, *Legal Transplants: An Approach to Comparative Law* (2nd edn, UGA Press, 1993).
130 There is no established convention for the designation of 'developed' and 'developing' countries or areas in the United Nations system. United Nations, 'Composition of Macro Geographical (Continental) Region' (2013) <http://unstats.un.org/unsd/methods/m49/m49regin.htm#ftnc> accessed 3 September 2021. The designations 'developed' and 'developing' are intended for statistical convenience and do not necessarily express a judgment about the stage reached by a particular country or area in the development process also see, United Nations, 'United Nations Statistics Division: Standard Country and Area Codes Classifications (M49)' (2012) <http://unstats.un.org/unsd/methods/m49/m49.htm> accessed 3 September 2016.
131 S 35 Banking Act 1968.
132 Proposal for a Directive of the European Parliament and the Council establishing a framework for the recovery and resolution of credit institutions and investment firms COM (2012) 280 final.
133 Bank Recovery and Resolution Directive <https://ec.europa.eu/info/business-economy-euro/banking-and-finance/financial-supervision-and-risk-management/managing-risks-banks-and-financial-institutions/bank-recovery-and-resolution_en> accessed 30 August 2021.
134 Shilling (n 96) 15.
135 FSB, 'Thematic Review on Deposit Insurance Systems-Peer Review Report' (2012) <www.fsb.org/wp-content/uploads/r_120208.pdf> accessed 30 December 2021.
136 A Demirguc-Kunt, EJ Kane and L Laeven, 'Deport Insurance Around the World' (2015) J Fin Stab 155.
137 S 5 of the KDI Act.
138 S 4(2)(b) of the KDI Act and S 11 of the KDI Act.
139 S 35(10) of the Banking Act.
140 s 34(1) and 34(2)(b), (c), (d), (e), (f), (g) and (h) of the Banking Act.
141 IADI Core principles 10.
142 S 5(1) of the KDI Act.
143 S 5(2) of the KDI Act.
144 S 6(b) of the KDI Act.
145 S 5(2) of the KDI Act.
146 S 6(a) of the KDI Act.
147 S 23 of the KDI Act.
148 S 6(b)(i) of the KDI Act.
149 S 6(b)(ii) of the KDI Act.
150 S 6(b)(iii) of the KDI Act.
151 Proviso to s 6(b) of the KDI Act.
152 S 6(b) of the KDI Act.
153 S 50(7)(a) of the KDI Act.
154 Kahn and Santos (n 105) 3.

155 V Finch, *Corporate Insolvency Law: Perspectives and Principles* (2nd edn, CUP, 2009).
156 Hupkes (n 4) 3.
157 Martin S Feldstein, *Economic and Financial Crises in Emerging Market Economies* (UC Press, 2003).
158 Douglas W Diamond and Philip H Dybvig, 'Bank Runs, Deposit Insurance, and Liquidity' (1983) 91 J Pol Econ 401–19.
159 ibid.

Part II

Bank Insolvency Law

Selected Cross-Border Paradigms

6 Institutional Development of the Dubai International Financial Centre and the Qatar Financial Centre

The Insolvency Law Framework

Horace Yeung and Saleh Al-Barashdi

Introduction

This chapter seeks to appraise, through a comparative perspective, the unique institutional and regulatory model adopted and practised by the Dubai International Financial Centre (DIFC) and the Qatar Financial Centre (QFC), with respect to insolvency law. The key institutional innovation of these two financial centres is their transplanting and operation of laws based on common law and international best practices, independent of their national legal systems (continental civil law systems, heavily influenced by Islamic tradition). The DIFC was established in 2004, as the pioneer in introducing this ground-breaking institutional model. The QFC quickly followed suit in 2005. This institutional model has also been subsequently adopted elsewhere such as the Abu Dhabi Global Market (ADGM) also in the United Arab Emirates (UAE), as well as more recently the Astana International Financial Centre (AIFC) in Kazakhstan.[1]

On the face of it, the implementation of a legal regime based on common law to regulate the legal relationships between market participants sits well with the twofold belief that: firstly, under the law and finance scholarship that legal institution is essential in financial development; and secondly the common law systems are capable of providing superior investor protection. To assess the institutional advantages of the DIFC and QFC, a comparative law approach will be adopted by this chapter. There are essentially three dimensions of comparison: (1) comparing the centres' rules and regulations with their UK counterparts to reveal the degree of legal transplantation; (2) comparing the centres' rules and regulations with their domestic counterparts to explore a potential regulatory gap between the two systems; and (3) comparing the regimes of the DIFC and QFC to reveal their potentially different experience in transplanting (insolvency) law from the UK (and/or elsewhere).

This edited volume has the objective to investigate bank insolvencies in developing economies. In the view of Cranston and colleagues, most jurisdictions in the world have developed and adopted a range of specialist tools for addressing bank distress, both in the form of liquidity support and in the form of insolvency mechanisms.[2] The former is largely dealt with by banking law,

DOI: 10.4324/9781003173984-8

whereas the latter by insolvency law, which is also the focus of this chapter. There can be two general regulatory models to deal with the insolvencies of banks.[3] One is a specialised standalone bank insolvency regime; another one is based on the general corporate insolvency framework, with adjustments (if applicable). From the investigation of this chapter, both the UAE and Qatar (as well as their Financial Centres), despite being some of the wealthiest economies in the world, have clearly not reached the point of enacting a bespoke bank insolvency regime. That is why the focus of this chapter will be on a generic corporate insolvency regime, which applies to all companies, including banks and non-banks; but also with the important task of pinpointing any bank-specific provisions currently in their systems. Meanwhile, it is worth highlighting that at least the DIFC has been conscious of the need to enhance its recovery and resolution system for banks.[4]

This chapter is structured as follows. The next section will give an overview of Dubai and Qatar, as well as their financial centres. Afterwards, the question of whether the DIFC and QFC possess different (and potentially better/worse) laws than their national/federal counterparts in general will be considered, before a specific and substantive comparison of their insolvency law frameworks. Given that it is virtually impossible to compare every single element of a typical set of insolvency law, the selected scope of comparison will include the varieties of insolvency procedures, the personal liabilities of directors in a distressed/insolvent company, the possibility to avoid certain dubious transactions, as well as the presence of any bank-specific provisions. In line with the three dimensions of comparison mentioned earlier, the specific and substantive comparison will entail discussion of the laws of the DIFC and QFC with reference to their national/federal frameworks, as well as the law of the UK. The final part will conclude. Given the scarcity of academic literature in English language on the insolvency law of jurisdictions like those in the Middle East, we believe that this chapter will form an original and significant contribution to the topic, especially in relation to the emergence of distinct common law commercial/financial zones in civil law systems.

An Overview of Dubai and Qatar and Their Financial Centres

Dubai and Qatar share a number of similarities. Both are located in the Middle East, and in close proximity to one another. Dubai is not a country by itself but one of the seven Emirates of the UAE, situated in the southeast of the Arabian Peninsula, bordering Oman and Saudi Arabia. Qatar is a country situated opposite to the UAE on the west coast of the Persian Gulf, bordering Saudi Arabia only. Both are Islamic countries. About 76 per cent of the population in the UAE is Muslim, whereas in Qatar it is 67.7 per cent.[5] Accordingly, both countries are considered as having a mixed legal system of Islamic (sharia) law and civil law.[6] As a federation of seven Emirates, the legal structure in the UAE runs in two essentially parallel systems: the Federal Judiciary presided by the Federal Supreme Court as the highest judicial authority in the country and the local judicial departments at the Emirati level.[7] Dubai has chosen to maintain their own independent judicial system.[8] Both Dubai and Qatar have had a period of colonial history associated with the British Empire. The Trucial States, which became the UAE in 1971 had previously signed trade and protection agreements with the British government.[9] Quite similarly, Qatar had had its own period of history as a British Protectorate, before going fully independent since 1971.[10]

Economically, both the UAE and Qatar have traditionally relied on oil and natural gas resources as the countries' main economic engine and government revenue source, but have worked successfully to migrate away from that. According to the World Economic Forum, among the UAE's two most successful emirates, Abu Dhabi still relies on oil for much of its wealth today; but for Dubai, less than 1 per cent of its GDP is from oil now when at one time it was over half.[11] Indeed, it has been pretty much the same story in Qatar. At one point in 1974, oil used to account for over 80 per cent of the country's GDP; but now at 16 per cent.[12] It is fair to say the two economies are now well diversified. According to data from the Dubai government, the three major economic pillars there are: wholesale and retail trade, transport and storage, as well as finance and insurance.[13] In Qatar, the three most important sectors (as a percentage of GDP) are energy, construction, as well as finance and insurance.[14] It can be seen that both economies have placed a great deal of focus on their financial sector. One major initiative has been arguably the establishment of their financial centres: the DIFC and the QFC.

The DIFC is a geographic and legal jurisdiction within the emirate of Dubai, part of the federation of the UAE. In 2004 the UAE constitution was amended to allow an emirate to establish a 'financial free zone', a separate legal, geographic and judicial jurisdiction.[15] Federal Law (No. 8 of 2004) of the UAE allows a free zone to be established by Federal Decree. The zone shall be subject to all Federal laws, with the exception of Federal civil and commercial laws.[16] This on the one hand empowered the DIFC to create its own legal and regulatory framework for all civil and commercial matters. On the other hand, it confirmed the application of Federal criminal laws in the zone, including the Federal laws on anti-money laundering.[17] Federal Decree (No. 35 of 2004) officially created the DIFC as a financial free zone in Dubai with accompanying cabinet resolution setting out the geographic boundaries of the DIFC. Furthermore, the Dubai Law (No. 9 of 2004) acknowledged and confirmed the creation of the DIFC by recognising its financial and administrative independence, and creating essential regulatory bodies, which include the DIFC Authority[18], Dubai Financial Services Authority[19] (DFSA), and DIFC Courts[20].

The DIFC Authority is responsible to oversee the strategic development, operational management and planning of the centre. It is also responsible for the development and administration of laws and regulations other than those related to financial services firms. The DFSA is an independent regulator of financial and related services conducted in or from the centre. The DFSA also supervises regulated companies and monitors their compliance with the applicable laws and regulations. The DIFC Courts are the designated legal fora for resolving all civil and commercial laws disputes.

As for the QFC, the Qatari Law (No. 7 of 2005) became effective on 1 May 2005. Although the country's first constitution had been issued in 2004, it did not actually come into effect until after the establishment of the QFC.[21] However, the 2005 Law did make brief reference to its predecessor, the Amended Provisional Constitution 1972. The 2005 Law sets out the structure of the QFC and establishes the independent bodies necessary for its operation. These include the QFC Authority, the QFC Regulatory Authority, the Civil and Commercial Court (first instance and appellate divisions), and the QFC Regulatory Tribunal. The functions of the first three bodies are broadly similar to their Dubai counterparts and require no additional explanation. But it is worth noting that the QFC Regulatory Tribunal is established as a specialist appeals body to hear complaints raised by individuals and corporate bodies against decisions of the QFC Authority, Regulatory Authority and other QFC institutions.[22] The Appellate Circuit of the Civil and Commercial Court shall have the jurisdiction to hear appeals against decisions of the First Instance Circuit, as well as appeals against decisions of the Regulatory Tribunal.[23] Except criminal law, the QFC laws and regulations shall apply to the contracts, transactions and arrangements conducted by the entities established in, or operating from the QFC.[24]

As of 2019, the DIFC was home to 2,437 companies, including world leading banks, law firms, insurance companies and asset managers, with over 25,000 people working in the special zone.[25] The DIFC estimated that the value from DIFC activities amounted to US$700 billion. The size of the QFC was comparatively modest. In 2018, there were 492 companies, with over 12,000 people working in the zone.[26] The QFC estimated that QFC companies held over US$20 billion of assets and created almost US$3 billion of revenues.

The Oxford Business Group particularly acknowledges the UAE's banking industry as the biggest in the region, accounting for nearly one-third of the Gulf Cooperation Council (GCC) countries' banking assets.[27] According to the investigation by Forbes, half of the top 10 banks in the Middle East are from either the UAE or Qatar; with the rest from Saudi Arabia and Kuwait.[28] The largest bank, QNB, is based in Qatar, whereas Emirates NBD (fourth largest) and Dubai Islamic Bank (tenth largest) are based in Dubai.

Are the Two Zones Providing a Bespoke Legal Framework?

The headline feature of the two Financial Centres is their 'unique legal and regulatory framework is based on international standards and principles of common law'.[29] The idea of a special financial zone with bespoke regulations based on common law, which is independent of its national legal system based on civil law, is theoretically sound. Institutional economics, which has existed for nearly a century, is a branch of scholarship which explores the role of institutions in economic activities and growth. Different types of institutions have been reviewed by scholars, including but not limited to finance, law, politics, trade, culture, technology, education, colonial origin, etc.[30] For the relationship between law, finance and growth, the explanation can be that law helps deepen the financial markets, thereby facilitating economic growth.[31] The 'Law and Finance' scholarship seeks to explore the correlations between law and financial development.[32] La Porta and colleagues examined legal rules covering the protection of corporate shareholders and creditors, the origin of these rules and the quality of their enforcement in 49 countries.[33] They alleged that the legal environment, including both legal rules and their enforcement, matters for the size and extent of a country's capital market. It is because a good legal environment protects the potential financiers against expropriation by entrepreneurs. Investors are willing to surrender funds in exchange for securities and therefore expand the scope of capital markets. Based on their findings, they claimed that civil law countries with weaker investor protection, have smaller and narrower capital markets.[34] La Porta and colleagues' research has been thought-provoking though at the same time controversial. It has received criticism from various scholars.[35]

Despite the controversial nature of 'Law and Finance', La Porta and colleagues have certainly raised the awareness of the role of legal institutions in financial development. The close link between investor protection and financial development is in principle widely accepted by policymakers and scholars. For example, the importance of legal institutions in fostering a good business environment is underlined by the World Bank's Doing Business project.[36] This project provides objective measures of business regulations and their enforcement across 190 economies and selected cities at the subnational and regional level. The first Doing Business report, published in 2003, covered five indicator sets and 133 economies. The most recent report in 2020 covers 12 areas of business regulation and 190 economies.

By referring to the Doing Business report, it can be seen that the overall ease of doing business in Qatar has been ranked 77th out of 190 economies, and the UAE[37] has outperformed Qatar by being placed at 16th in the same ranking. In the context of this chapter, the 'Resolving Insolvency' indicator of the report is perhaps the most relevant. In this regard, the rankings for Qatar and the UAE are 123th and 80th respectively. Comparing this performance with their overall ease of doing business rankings, it can be seen that insolvency law may not be the strength of their legal systems. Since both the DIFC and the QFC have, to a large degree, looked to the English legal system as a learning model, it may be a good idea to see how the UK has fared in the rankings. The UK has indeed performed very well by being placed at 8th in the overall ranking and 14th with respect to 'resolving insolvency'. A summary of these has been provided in Table 6.1. If the findings from the World Bank are robust, it can be seen that the two economies will still have plenty to learn from the English system.

It should be worth noting that in their 'Resolving Insolvency' indicator, the World Bank seeks to measure the time, cost and outcome of insolvency proceedings involving domestic entities, as well as the strength of the legal framework applicable to judicial liquidation and reorganisation proceedings.[38] Whilst time

Table 6.1 Performance of Qatar and the UAE in the Doing Business Ranking (Using the UK as a Benchmark)

Countries	*Overall Ease of Doing Business*	*Resolving Insolvency*
Qatar	77th	123th
UAE	16th	80th
UK	8th	14th

Source: World Bank, 'Doing Business 2020' (2020)

and cost as a parameter should not be difficult to understand, the term 'outcome' is understood in terms of recovery rate. The recovery rate is recorded as cents on the dollar recovered by secured creditors through judicial reorganisation, liquidation or debt enforcement (foreclosure or receivership) proceedings. Meanwhile, the strength of insolvency framework index is based on four other indices: commencement of proceedings index, management of debtor's assets index, reorganisation proceedings index and creditor participation index.[39] A supplementary dataset that may be useful in assessing the strength of their insolvency law framework, but with a bank-specific context, will be the ratio of non-performing loans across different countries.[40] The relevant data in the UAE and Qatar were 7.7 (2009–2020) and 2.0 (2000–2015) per cent respectively, which were apparently higher than, for example, the US (1.6; 1985–2020) and the UK (1.2; 2008–2020). This might suggest that the financial institutions in the latter countries have been more readily to claw back their lending from their insolvent debtor clients. And in this context, Qatar might have been doing better than the UAE according to the data.

As indicated before, both the DIFC and QFC have their own bespoke regulations, and national legislations are in principle not applied in the two financial free zones. Federal Law (No. 9 of 2016) is the primary legislation governing insolvency and restructuring proceedings in the UAE (but not the financial free zones like the DIFC and ADGM). Until this law came into force, the UAE had no single source of law governing insolvency procedures. The insolvency regime was spread across multiple sources, was rarely used, and did not reflect the growing trends toward restructuring.[41] Meanwhile, the DIFC Insolvency Law (DIFC Law No. 1 of 2019) sets out the procedures that result in the reorganisation or liquidation of an insolvent company within the DIFC. Its predecessor was the DIFC Law (No.7 of 2004). It shows that a comprehensive set of insolvency law and procedures has long existed in the DIFC, more than a decade earlier than its national/federal counterpart.

For Qatar, there is not a separate, dedicated set of insolvency law at the moment.[42] This matter is addressed in their Commercial Companies Law (Law No. 11 of 2015) for corporate entities. According to the Commercial Companies Law, a company may be dissolved and subsequently liquidated for a variety of reasons, including its inability to pay its debts as they come due.[43] Meanwhile, the QFC Insolvency Regulations 2005, revised in 2013, govern the insolvency of companies within the

QFC and are 'reasonably comprehensive', providing for administration and either voluntary or compulsory winding up.[44]

Although a more substantive comparison of these laws is to be carried out later in this chapter, at first glance, both the DIFC and the QFC have managed to introduce specialised regulations to address corporate insolvency issues, even at the time when these did not receive much attention at the national/federal level. In the context of this edited volume, the focus is particularly on the insolvency regimes for banks. There is a need to differentiate both regimes because the objective of maximising value for creditors is common to corporate insolvency and bank insolvency, but the latter regime often includes depositor protection as an additional, and sometimes explicit, statutory objective.[45] In the view of Armour and colleagues, bank insolvency is different from that of other companies for three reasons.[46] First, the risk of insolvency can escalate very quickly once doubts are raised about its financial viability. This risk is commonly known as a 'bank run'. Second, the typical mechanics of bankruptcy may not be well suited to a bank. Third, the collapse of one single bank can potentially drag down the entire banking system or even the whole economy. It is commonly known as 'systemic risk'. As a result, on top of bespoke insolvency procedures, there are also other bank resolution strategies to help banks turn things around.[47]

With specific regard to bank insolvencies, it is observed that there are two essential features which can help categorise regimes into different types.[48] First, a bank insolvency regime can be either bespoke, or based on general insolvency laws but with modifications. Second, the regime can be either predominantly administrative, or court-based. In the former case, the insolvency proceeding is managed by an administrative authority with little or no role for judicial authorities, whereas in the latter case, the process is predominantly driven by a liquidator who is an officer of the court. Under this categorisation, comparing both sides of the Atlantic, it is observed that the UK has a modified bank insolvency regime, which is court-based; whereas, the US has a free-standing bank insolvency regime, which is administrative.[49]

The shape of a bank insolvency regime is normally determined by the banking law. For example, in the UK, the relevant legislation is the Banking Act 2009. In terms of banking law, in the UAE, the key legislations are the *Federal Law (No. 14 of 2018) regarding the Central Bank & Organisation of Financial Institutions and Activities*, as well as the Islamic Bank Law of 1985. The prudential regulator is the Central Bank of the UAE. The new law of 2018 replaces the old law of 1980. According to commentators, the new law can help ensure the stability of the UAE's financial system by empowering the Central Bank to issue regulations regarding the protection of deposits held at local financial institutions and the rights of depositors, as well as regulations on minimum capital requirements and other risk based requirements, amongst numerous other new measures introduced.[50] As for the DIFC, the DFSA is the competent regulator of financial services conducted in or from DIFC (as opposed to the Central Bank of the UAE). According to Khan and Walker, the DFSA has adopted a regulatory approach modelled, at least in part, on the then Financial Services Authority in the UK.[51]

The DFSA does not grant banking licences *per se*; instead it authorises financial service providers to undertake specific financial services. As opposed to the DIFC Insolvency Law, in which there is a set of laws labelled as such, there is not a 'DIFC Banking Law'. Instead, many of the core elements in a banking law are seen in the DFSA Rulebook Modules.[52]

In Qatar, *Law (No. 13 of 2012) on the Issuance of the Qatar Central Bank Law and Regulation of Financial Institutions* is the key banking legislation. This law updated the previous law of 2006. Quite different from Dubai and the UAE, the Qatar Central Bank (QCB) has been empowered by the new law to develop and follow up on the implementation of policies in respect of financial services, business and other activities undertaken in the QFC.[53] This may represent a potential overlapping role between the QCB and the Qatar Financial Centre Regulatory Authority (QFCRA). An additional noteworthy change in the new law is the introduction of a possible bank resolution regime.[54] When the QCB is of the opinion that a financial institution is faced with problems affecting its financial standing, then the QCB may issue a decision to merge that financial institution with another, stronger, financial institution.[55] Also, the new law provides for temporary management of a financial institution if it is in danger of insolvency.[56] As for the QFC, similar to the DIFC, there is not a set of laws labelled as the 'QFC Banking Regulations' *per se*, but elements of banking law can be seen in the QFC Financial Services Regulations, as well as the QFCRA Banking Business Prudential Rules 2014.

Given that both economies and financial centres have yet to develop a highly specialised bank resolution and insolvency regime, later sections will focus on the general insolvency law framework to reveal the extent to which the bespoke laws from the two financial free zones are different from (or superior/inferior to) their national counterparts. However, in light of the overarching objective of this edited volume, there will also be a part pinpointing any bank-specific provisions currently present in the systems. For example, as indicated earlier, the Qatari national banking law did seemingly introduce such an element into the law almost a decade ago, while the UAE's move is relatively recent and extensive.

Substantive Comparison of Their Insolvency Law Framework

There are different theoretical underpinnings of the aims and objectives of insolvency law.[57] One point of the debate apparently hinges on whether the law should serve the interests of creditors only, or those of a broad range of different constituents. In a functional set of insolvency law, there should be robust legal strategies to protect creditors.[58] For examples, liabilities can be imposed on wrongdoing/negligent directors.[59] Also, dodgy transactions can be set aside to maximise the proceeds which can be duly returned to the creditors.[60] Furthermore, there should be a variety of procedures that may come into play when a company is in trouble;[61] some of them may be tailored just for banks.

These legal strategies will provide a framework of comparison to appraise the insolvency law in the DIFC and QFC respectively, with reference to their national/federal counterparts, as well as the law of the UK.

Choices of Insolvency Procedures

In the DIFC, the DIFC Insolvency Law has provided for five ways to help a distressed company out, namely company voluntary arrangements (CVA); rehabilitation; administration; receivership; and winding up.

Companies in distress may be able to negotiate settlements on a variety of terms and such agreements may operate within a statutory format or informally and contractually.[62] The Law has provided the statutory procedures for CVA to take place. Under which, the directors will appoint a DIFC registered insolvency practitioner as 'nominee' to act in relation to the CVA and supervise its implementation.[63] In the view of Finch and Milman, small and medium-sized companies may find a CVA useful, since it is generally less complex, time-consuming and costly than alternative procedures.[64]

Rehabilitation is not a terminology seen in the UK. It is a new addition to the 2019 law, alongside administration. In other words, previously there were only three statutory solvency procedures available in the DIFC. According to commentators, rehabilitation is a new concept which mirrors the 'debtor-in-possession' (DIP) regime of Chapter 11 bankruptcy in the US. The term refers to a debtor that keeps possession and control of its assets while undergoing a reorganisation under Chapter 11, without the appointment of a case trustee.[65] A debtor will remain a DIP until the debtor's plan of reorganisation is confirmed. Section 1107 of the US Bankruptcy Code places the debtor-in-possession in the position of a fiduciary, with the rights and powers of a Chapter 11 trustee, and it requires the debtor to perform all but the investigative functions and duties of a trustee. The DIP regime illustrates a fundamental difference in US and UK insolvency law.[66] In general, the UK law is manager-displacing when the US law allows existing management to remain in control of the ailing company during the reorganisation process.[67]

Similar to rehabilitation, administration is a new addition to the regime. The main objective of administration is to introduce a corporate rescue culture as opposed to liquidating the company. However, as opposed to the regime in the UK, where there are three methods by which an administrator can be appointed,[68] there is less flexibility in invoking the administration process in the DIFC. An application for the appointment of an administrator (who must be an insolvency practitioner) can only be made by one or more creditors where an application for Rehabilitation has been made and there is evidence of misconduct.[69] Also, the role of administrator differs. In the UK, the administrator will have more discretion in deciding between 'rescuing the company as a going concern', or 'achieving a better result for the company's creditors as a whole' to wind the company up.[70] In the DIFC, by comparison, the administrator will have a more rigid mission to 'manage the affairs, business and property of the company in accordance with' any Rehabilitation Plan or CVAs agreed.[71] In other words, administration is intertwined with other insolvency procedures provided by the DIFC Insolvency Law.

As for administrative receivership, in the UK, the Enterprise Act 2002 has largely made it redundant.[72] However, it apparently still retains a role in the DIFC. In brief, as opposed to the company as a whole, an administrative receiver is normally appointed to represent the interests of specific creditors.[73]

Winding up, also called liquidation, is normally considered as a procedure of last resort.[74] It involves a liquidator being appointed to take control of the company and to collect, realise and distribute its assets to creditors according to their legal priority. In the UK, there are two routes to liquidating an insolvent company: a creditors' voluntary liquidation and a compulsory liquidation.[75] The two are different in a number of ways.[76] In the latter, the powers of directors are terminated and they are removed from their office immediately, whereas in the former, they will retain their office for a short time, though their powers will be severely restricted. In a voluntary liquidation, creditors are in control as opposed to the court; liquidators can exercise their powers more freely without the sanction of the court. Also, a compulsory liquidation will in principle lead to an automatic stay of all proceedings against the company. In the case of a voluntary liquidation, the liquidator will need to apply for a stay. Such a dichotomy of voluntary and compulsory winding up is followed by the DIFC.[77]

In the view of Philips and Rolls, the QFC's legal framework in this regard is derived from English law.[78] In a QFC case regarding application for a winding up order, their Civil and Commercial Court acknowledged that their insolvency rules derive 'from concepts that formed part of the law of England and other common law countries' and they will provide 'useful guides to the interpretation of the Qatari legislation.'[79] The QFC insolvency procedures include administration, winding up, and company arrangements.[80] Comparing the QFC framework with the aforementioned DIFC and UK frameworks, it is worth noting that the QFC has more faithfully followed the UK approach, while the DIFC has also drawn on the US experience. Meanwhile, the QFC has not followed the UK approach wholesale. For example, administrative receivership, which is arguably redundant in the UK, is not seen in the QFC framework.

After looking at the two financial free zones, it is time to turn to their national/federal counterparts. As mentioned before, the UAE had had no single source of law governing bankruptcy procedures until the UAE Bankruptcy Law came into force on 29 December 2016. It shows that the DIFC Insolvency Law could be considered as pioneering in the country for around a decade before 2016 during a period when the country did not have a proper set of law in the area. In line with other forms of UAE legislations historically, the insolvency law has been influenced by French civil law traditions.[81] At the same time, it seeks to incorporate best practice concepts found in German, English and US insolvency legislations.[82] Under the 2016 law, the regime offers two court procedures.[83] First, a court-based distressed company-led process which can be used by a company that is in financial difficulties but is not yet technically insolvent, known as a Protective Composition Procedure (PCP). Second, a formal bankruptcy that is split into a rescue process (similar to the PCP) or liquidation. The PCP allows a company in financial difficulties to reach a binding agreement with its creditors as an alternative to filing for bankruptcy. The PCP follows the French *sauvegarde* model, where a debtor experiencing financial difficulties but is not yet insolvent, or has been in a state of over-indebtedness, or has ceased making payments for fewer than 30 consecutive business days, proposes a compromise with its creditors. A PCP application can only be made by the debtor or the court; it cannot be made by creditors. The PCP, in addition to French law, seeks to build upon useful features of US bankruptcy law as well.[84] Firstly, debtor-in-possession priority funding is permitted which may be secured or unsecured. Secondly, *ipso-facto* provisions exist to prevent contractual counterparties from using insolvency-linked termination provisions provided the debtor complies with its obligations under the plan. Thirdly, a supervisory creditor committee may be appointed.

As for Qatar, the matters of corporate insolvency are dealt with by the company law. The relevant part is contained in Part 11 of the Qatari company law[85] and is relatively brief. It essentially only provides for liquidation, which can be effected voluntarily (e.g., by agreement of the shareholders) or involuntarily (e.g., by court order).[86] It can be seen that the Qatari regulation is arguably the least developed in this area, in comparison to other regimes discussed earlier.[87] For example, as observed by Boast and Martyndale-Howard, with the exception of Qatar and Kuwait, all other GCC countries have now introduced new insolvency and bankruptcy laws, amidst a recent wave of these laws introduced in the region.[88] This perhaps coincides with the Doing Business rankings discussed earlier that Qatar did not do so well in resolving insolvency. It is also observed that, during the writing of this chapter by the authors, the Qatari situation is the least documented, making the research of it particularly difficult.

Directors' Liabilities

When a company is still a going concern, directors owe their fiduciary duties to the company as a whole.[89] During this time, in the UK for example, a director is subject to seven statutory duties.[90] However, in their survey of seven major jurisdictions, Armour and colleagues observe that directors may also be held personally liable to creditors resulting from the board's negligence or fraud to creditors when the company is, or is nearly insolvent.[91] In this context and in the UK, there are personal liabilities for the directors in the cases of fraudulent trading and wrongful trading.[92] There are several key differences between the two.[93] First, the former involves fraud or dishonesty and the latter involves negligence. Further, the scope of the former is broader than the latter in a sense that only directors can be proceeded against for wrongful trading, but any person knowingly a party to the carrying on of the business to defraud creditors or for any fraudulent purpose can be liable. Third, wrongful trading entails civil liability only, whereas fraudulent trading is criminal.

The DIFC Company Law (No. 5 of 2018) has transplanted in entirety the seven director duties from the UK Companies Act 2006.[94] Likewise, the DIFC

Insolvency Law includes both fraudulent trading and wrongful trading. But the problem will be, the criminal liability of fraudulent trading in the UK is provided by Section 993 of the Companies Act 2006 which runs in parallel with Section 213 of the Insolvency Act 1986. It is provided under Section 993 that a person guilty of fraudulent trading is liable to imprisonment for a term up to ten years and/or a fine. Nonetheless, the DIFC as a jurisdiction does not deal with criminal matters, although it is possible to impose administrative fines.[95] The DIFC Insolvency Law does provide for the remedy of fraudulent trading and wrongful trading, which is largely civil and compensatory in nature. A fine is not mentioned in either the DIFC Company Law or Insolvency Law in relation to fraudulent trading, let alone imprisonment.

In contrast to the DIFC where there is a rather wholesale transplant of the UK's directors' duties, the list of five directors' duties at the QFC is framed differently. There is a general duty to ask directors to 'act honestly and in good faith with a view to the best interests of the company.'[96] The duty to act in accordance with the company's constitution and to exercise independent judgement is combined into one, as opposed to two separate duties as in the DIFC and the UK.[97] The duty of care, skills and diligence is apparently the same one with the DIFC and the UK and a dual subjective and objective test will be used.[98] The fourth and fifth duties are concerned with conflicts of interests and the wordings are different from the comparable duties as in the DIFC and the UK.[99] In contrast, as for fraudulent and wrongful trading, the approach in the QFC is almost the same.[100] Similar to the DIFC, the QFC does not deal with criminal matters, but the authorities have the power to impose financial penalties.[101]

After looking at the two financial free zones, once again it is time to turn to their national/federal counterparts. In the UAE, the criminal liabilities of members of the board of directors, and the managers of the company are stipulated in Article 198 of the UAE Insolvency Law. A sliding scale of punitive measures (again including potential prison sentences and substantial fines) is included for other mismanagement or wrongful conduct which the Court finds has precipitated the failure of the company and caused losses to creditors.[102] It is worth noting that there is an obligation for the directors to contribute to the losses of the company in whole or in part if creditors make less than 20 per cent recovery, when their respective liability for the losses of the company is established pursuant to the provisions of the UAE Commercial Companies Law.[103] However, in the UAE, the duties of directors as provided in the company law are quite brief.[104]

As for Qatar, Slawotsky and Truby believe that the Qatari company law provides two basic duties for directors: duties of loyalty and due care.[105] In relation to the former, the law prohibits directors from engaging in conduct that raises questions regarding loyalty such as participating in competing businesses, engaging in self-interested transactions, obtaining cash loans from the company, or exploiting insider information.[106] As for the latter, the law provides that the directors are jointly responsible for managerial mistakes.[107] Slawotsky and Truby criticise that the duty of care in Qatar is rather 'open-ended and undefined'.[108] In the insolvency of a company, if the directors are fraudulently involved, they are liable to imprisonment and/or a fine.[109] If the directors are negligent, they are jointly liable for the obligations of the company.[110]

Avoidance of Transactions

In addition to pursuing claims against directors who may be liable to the company for breach of their duties or any other wrongdoings, a liquidator will seek to 'claw back' assets which the company should not have disposed of, in order to maximise the return to those entitled to the assets on a winding up.[111] The mode of adjustment to these vulnerable/problematic transactions takes a variety of forms.[112] In some cases, the transaction can be automatically rendered void.[113] In other cases, the liquidation is given the right to apply for an order reversing its effect. A third type is that the transaction may be set aside or varied.[114] In the UK, there are provisions in the Insolvency Act 1986, which deal with transactions at an undervalue, and preferences.[115] The former is aimed at improper reduction of the company's net asset value and is conceptually linked to the common law anti-deprivation rule, while the latter is linked to the common law *pari passu* principle and addresses unfair advantage towards specific creditors.[116] In either case, transactions are reversible at the discretion of the court on the application of the liquidator.

The law on antecedent transactions in the DIFC is set out in Articles 132 to 135 of the DIFC Insolvency Law. It is predominantly focused on three key areas: (a) transactions entered into at an undervalue; (b) preferences given to a creditor of the company or a guarantor of the company's liabilities; and (c) invalid security interests granted in favour of a person connected with the company.[117] It can be seen that the regime is seemingly a reproduction of the one in the UK. As for the national/federal regime, Article 168 of the UAE Insolvency law sets out five categories of transactions which are vulnerable to be set aside.[118] Although the arrangement looks slightly different, these five categories do not go much beyond the two limbs of transactions at an undervalue and preferences.

As for the QFC, the framework is almost the same one as seen in the DIFC. There are four articles in 'Section 5: Antecedent Transactions'. Three of them deal with transactions at an undervalue[119], preferences[120], and invalid security interests[121] respectively. The remaining article deals with the relevant time of the vulnerable transactions.[122] In the case of a transaction involving a connected person, the relevant time period will be two years before the commencement of liquidation or administration; and in a normal case, transactions within a period of six months will be covered. This illustrates a difference in approach across these jurisdictions on how they define 'relevant time'. The QFC approach in distinguishing a connected transaction is also seen for the regulation of preferences under the DIFC and UK laws. Meanwhile, in the DIFC and UK, the period for transactions at an undervalue is in all cases two years. Under the UAE law, the relevant period for both transactions at an undervalue and preferences is two years.

As for the national regime in Qatar, it is alleged that the court may go back two years from the commencement of bankruptcy to claw back preferences.[123]

However, as opposed to a very clear avoidance provision, there is seemingly one vague section in their company law to that effect.[124] One difficulty associated with Qatar is, as aforementioned, there is no dedicated insolvency law. Even if there are provisions dealing with insolvency in their company law, they are brief. More problematically, according to empirical evidence, Qatar has reported very low usage of their insolvency systems.[125] It is fair to say that their existing system has been both underdeveloped and untested.

Bank-Specific Provisions

As discussed towards the beginning of this chapter, there are two broad models addressing the insolvency of banks: bespoke; or based on general insolvency laws but with modifications, normally by banking law. The UAE and Qatar (as well as their Financial Centres) have clearly not yet reached a stage of having a bespoke bank insolvency law. Therefore, it is fair to suggest that they have followed the latter model, which is practised by, for example, the UK. As demonstrated earlier, the DIFC and the QFC have frequently transplanted/borrowed from the UK system in their regimes. In this part, the discussion will therefore start from briefly examining the UK system before moving on to the UAE and Qatar (and their Financial Centres).

In the UK, a special bank resolution regime was enabled by Parts 1–3 of the Banking Act 2009. Cranston and colleagues observe that this regime differ from general corporate insolvency procedures in a number of ways, including in: (i) the triggers for enlivening their operation; (ii) the choice of forum for their exercise, and the choice of decision-maker (or, resolution authority) and its powers; and (iii) the scope for intervention and challenge by disaffected stakeholders.[126] In relation to the first element of differences, early intervention is desirable as opposed to action after the actual point of balance sheet insolvency. As a consequence, bank resolution regimes will likely permit the commencement of proceedings on a range of pre-insolvency grounds.[127] In relation to the second element, there is a wider range of actions that can potentially be taken by a bank regulator.[128] These include transfer of all or part of the business of the bank to a commercial purchaser; transfer to a bridge entity controlled by the Bank of England; transfer of all or part of the business of the bank (or bridge bank) to an asset management vehicle controlled by the Bank of England, for eventual sale or orderly wind down; the bail-in tool; and transfer to temporary public sector ownership. The third element can be reflected in a 'no creditor worse off' principle, under which that creditors should not be left worse off than they would have been in an ordinary liquidation.[129] Disgruntled creditors may challenge in a court to the decisions/actions of a regulatory/resolution authority.

For Qatar, as discussed earlier, their Banking Law of 2012 has already introduced some of these elements into their national regime. Their bank resolution regime notably includes merging or interim administration.[130] According to Article 173 of the 2012 Law, if a financial institution experiences financial difficulties that have a material effect on its financial position, the QCB may 'issue a resolution that it be merged with another financial institution, with the approval of the financial institution that is to be merged with.' Article 176 of the same law also stipulates that, if a bank becomes threatened with insolvency financially, or upon its request, the QCB is granted the authority by means of resolution, for a specified period of time, to place the institution under interim administration. The pre-insolvency triggers include:[131]

1) If it stops paying its financial obligations as they become due
2) If it loses half of shareholders' equity rights or does not maintain the capital adequacy ratio set by the Bank, unless there is a plan to cover the required amount of the deficit within the period specified by the Bank
3) If the financial institution in the host country is exposed to the risk of bankruptcy or insolvency, at the discretion of the Bank

As discussed earlier, considering that the regulatory competence of the QCB will indeed extend to activities and entities within the QFC, it is expected that the same provisions will also apply there.

As to the UAE, their new Banking Law of 2018 provides a set of broad principles on which a recovery and resolution action or liquidation of a deposit-taking licenced financial institution can take place.[132] Meanwhile, the law has left the actual substantive formulation of a recovery and resolution regime to the regulators at the Emirati/financial zone level.[133] As a result of a consultation in January 2020, a new recovery and resolution regime for DIFC banks and certain other authorised financial institutions which experience financial difficulty came into force in April 2021. This new regime is set forth in the Regulatory Law (DIFC Law No.1 of 2004) (as amended by Regulatory Law Amendment Law, DIFC Law No. 1 of 2021) and a new Recovery and Resolution (RAR) Module of the DFSA Rulebook. According to commentators, the regime is based on international best practices and draws on the Financial Stability Board's 'Key Attributes on Effective Resolution Regimes for Financial Institutions' and the Basel Committee on Banking Supervision's Guidelines for identifying and dealing with weak banks.[134]

The Regulatory Law now grants the DFSA early intervention powers allowing the regulator to direct the bank or institution to take certain actions (such as drawing up a corrective plan and/or call a shareholders' meeting), where its liquidity or solvency is impaired, or may soon be impaired unless action is taken.[135] Furthermore, the DFSA, now designated as the resolution authority for banks, has new powers.[136] The RAR Module sets out more detailed rules covering application and interpretation, recovery and resolution planning, resolution, and miscellaneous (Management Information Systems). The general insolvency law will still apply, unless it is inconsistent with the bank-specific provisions.[137]

Conclusion

According to a 2011 World Bank policy research paper, the very first line was a rather powerful statement, 'The insolvency systems in the MENA region are by and large underdeveloped'.[138] Needless to say, much has changed in this past decade and it is unfair to apply this observation to nowadays. For example, the UAE introduced its insolvency law in 2016, alongside development around GCC countries such as Oman, where a change within the regime has been witnessed very recently with the introduction of a bespoke Bankruptcy Law which repealed the regime originally contained in its Civil Transactions Law (Commercial Code).[139] In light of the fact that the UAE Insolvency law is relatively new, and Qatar has yet to have a dedicated set of insolvency law, it is fair to say the two financial free zones, at least for a long period of time, have had more sophisticated laws in this area, relative to their national counterparts, to entice entrepreneurs, traders and investors. The fact that they have transplanted common law, as well as English legal principles should be welcome by international investors. According to empirical evidence, English law is arguably the most common choice of governing law in international commercial transactions.[140]

Needless to say, the idea of a distinct common law commercial/financial zone is in principle appealing which prompted the ADGM and the AIFC to follow in the footsteps of the DIFC and the QFC. According to commentators, 'Middle Eastern financial centres, particularly Qatar and Dubai, are set to become major regional financial locations'.[141]

As seen from the investigation in this chapter, the DIFC and the QFC have in general quite faithfully followed and transplanted relevant English and/or international legal principles into their jurisdictions. Terms like administration, wrongful trading and transactions at an undervalue should hardly be unknown to English lawyers. However, it is also worth noting that the two financial centres have not only learnt from the UK. The newly added Rehabilitation arrangement in the DIFC is a resemblance to the US Chapter 11 'debtor-in-possession' regime. Also, one more addition in the 2019 law, which was not discussed in this chapter, is the incorporation of the *UNCITRAL Model Law on Cross-Border Insolvency* to more effectively address cross-border insolvency proceedings.[142]

With specific regards to a bank resolution and recovery regime, in both countries and their respective Financial Centres, general insolvency law still largely applies but with modifications enabled by their respective banking law. Qatar clearly had taken action earlier than the UAE in developing their regime in this regard, but the UAE caught up very recently as seen by their more detailed rules introduced under a reform within the DIFC in April 2021.

Notes

1 For the development of the AIFC, see Horace Yeung and others, 'Institutional Development and the Astana International Financial Centre in Kazakhstan' (2020) 19 Wash Uni Glo Stud Law Rev 53.
2 Ross Cranston and others, *Principles of Banking Law* (3rd edn, OUP, 2017) 171.
3 Sophie Buckingham and others, *Study on the Differences Between Bank Insolvency Laws and on Their Potential Harmonisation* (European Commission, 2019) 13.

4 DIFC, *Early Intervention, Recovery and Resolution on the DIFC* (DFSA Consultation Paper No. 131, 2020) <https://dfsaen.thomsonreuters.com/sites/default/files/net_file_store/CP131_Recovery_&_Resolution.pdf> accessed 25 April 2021. The result of this consultation was the introduction of a new recovery and resolution regime in April 2021 for DIFC banks and certain other authorised financial institutions which experience financial difficulty.

5 CIA, 'The World Factbook' (2021) <www.cia.gov/the-world-factbook/> accessed 25 April 2021.

6 For example, Article 7 of the UAE Constitution provides for the position of sharia law within the Union.

7 UAE Government, 'Structure of the Judicial System' (2020) <https://u.ae/en/about-the-uae/the-uae-government/the-federal-judiciary/structure-of-the-judicial-system> accessed 25 April 2021.

8 Also the case for Abu Dhabi and Ras Al Khaimah. Meanwhile, the emirates of Sharjah, Ajman Fujairah and Umm Al Quwain follow the federal judicial system.

9 National Archives, 'Trucial States in 1914' (2021) <https://livelb.nationalarchives.gov.uk/first-world-war/a-global-view/the-middle-east/trucial-states/> accessed 25 April 2021.

10 Britannica, 'History of Qatar' (2021) <www.britannica.com/place/Qatar/History> accessed 25 April 2021.

11 World Economic Forum, 'From Fishing Village to Futuristic Metropolis: Dubai's Remarkable Transformation' (2019) <www.weforum.org/agenda/2019/11/dubai-uae-transformation/> accessed 25 April 2021.

12 World Bank, 'Oil Rents (% of GDP) – Qatar' (2021) <https://data.worldbank.org/indicator/NY.GDP.PETR.RT.ZS?locations=QA> accessed 25 April 2021.

13 Dubai Government, 'Department of Economic Development Brochure' (2019) <https://dubaided.gov.ae//ded_files/Files/StudiesAndResearch/DED-Brochure.pdf> accessed 25 April 2021.

14 Planning and Statistics Authority of Qatar, 'Window on Economic Statistics of Qatar' (2021) <www.psa.gov.qa/en/statistics/Statistical%20Releases/Economic/GeneralEconomicStatistics/windowonstatistics/2020/Q3/WinEconomicStat_34th_Issue_Q3_2020_AE.pdf> accessed 25 April 2021.

15 See Article 121 of the UAE Constitution, which deals with the division of powers between Federal and Emirati authorities.

16 Federal Law No. 8 of 2004 of the UAE, art 3(2).

17 ibid art 3(1).

18 Dubai Law No. 9 of 2004, art 6.

19 ibid art 7.

20 ibid art 8.

21 Al Jazeera, 'Qatar to Adopt First Constitution' (8 June 2005) <www.aljazeera.com/news/2005/6/8/qatar-to-adopt-first-constitution> last accessed 25 April 2021. Before that, a provisional constitution was enacted in 1970, subsequently amended in 1972.

22 Qatari Law No. 7 of 2005, art 8(2).

23 ibid art 8(3).

24 ibid art 18.

25 DIFC, 'DIFC Reports Record Growth in 2019' (2020) <www.difc.ae/newsroom/news/difc-reports-record-growth-2019/> accessed 25 April 2021.

26 QFC, 'The Economic Impact of Qatar Financial Centre in 2018' (2020) <www.qfc.qa/-/media/project/qfc/qfcwebsite/documents/insights/publications/research–insights-2020/eia_english_digital.pdf> last accessed 25 April 2021.

27 Oxford Business Group, 'The Report: UAE: Dubai 2020' (2021) <https://oxfordbusinessgroup.com/uae-dubai-2020/banking> accessed 25 April 2021.

28 Forbes, 'Top 50 Banks in the Middle East 2019' (2021) <www.forbesmiddleeast.com/list/top-50-banks-in-the-middle-east-2019> accessed 25 April 2021.
29 This quote is taken from the website of the DIFC. That of the QFC is along the same line.
30 For a comprehensive review of the scholarship in this area, see Flora Huang and Horace Yeung, *Institutions and Economic Growth in Asia* (Routledge, 2018) 7–36.
31 See for example, Ross Levine, 'Law, Finance, and Economic Growth' (1999) 8 J Fin Intermed 8.
32 Mathias Siems, 'Legal Origins: Reconciling Law & Finance and Comparative Law' (2007) 52 McGill Law J 55, 57.
33 Rafael La Porta and others, 'Legal Determinants of External Finance' (1997) 52 J Fin 1131.
34 ibid.
35 Spamann was of the opinion that many of the initial results from La Porta and colleagues are not robust to the correction of coding errors. Holger Spamann, 'The "Antidirector Rights Index" Revisited' (2010) 23 Rev Fin Stud 467. By building on La Porta and colleagues' research design, John Armour and colleagues, despite finding no evidence of a positive impact of legal changes on stock market development, agreed that common law systems are more protective of shareholder interests than civil law ones. See John Armour and others, 'Shareholder Protection and Stock Market Development: An Empirical Test of the Legal Origins Hypothesis' (2009) 6 J Emp Leg Stud 343.
36 World Bank, 'Doing Business 2020' (2020) <www.doingbusiness.org> accessed 25 April 2021. It is worth highlighting that after data irregularities on Doing Business 2018 and 2020 reported internally in June 2020, the World Bank management paused the subsequent Doing Business report and initiated a series of reviews and audits of the report and its methodology. See the World Bank's statement here: World Bank, 'World Bank Group to Discontinue Doing Business Report' (2021) <www.worldbank.org/en/news/statement/2021/09/16/world-bank-group-to-discontinue-doing-business-report> accessed 9 April 2022.
37 Unfortunately, Dubai was not independently assessed as an economy in the ranking.
38 World Bank, 'Resolving Insolvency Methodology' (2020) <www.doingbusiness.org/en/methodology/resolving-insolvency> accessed 25 April 2021.
39 ibid.
40 CEIC Date, 'Non Performing Loans Ratio' (2022) <www.ceicdata.com/en/indicator/non-performing-loans-ratio> accessed 9 April 2022.
41 Latham & Watkins, 'COVID-19: Managing Financial Difficulties in the United Arab Emirates' (2020) <www.lw.com/thoughtLeadership/COVID-19-Managing-Financial-Difficulties-in-the-United-Arab-Emirates> accessed 25 April 2021.
42 Zain Sharar and Michael Earley, 'Bankruptcy in Qatar' [2019] MENA Bus Law Rev Third Q 48–49.
43 Commercial Companies Law, ch 11.
44 Roger Phillips and Jo Rolls, 'An Overview of the Qatari Insolvency System' [2016] INSOL Wrld – Fir Q 6–7.
45 Buckingham and others (n 4) 16.
46 John Armour and others, *Principles of Financial Regulation* (OUP, 2016) 341.
47 One example is a bail-out which utilises state resources to keep the bank out of bankruptcy. Another example is a bail-in which consists of reorganising the failing bank through voluntary agreement among the banks' creditors and shareholders.
48 Buckingham and others (n 4) 13.
49 ibid 15.
50 CMS Law-Now, 'The New UAE Central Bank Law' (2019) <www.cms-lawnow.com/ealerts/2019/02/the-new-uae-central-bank-law> accessed 25 April 2021.

51 Amjad Ali Khan and Stuart Walker, 'United Arab Emirates' in Jan Putnis (ed), *The Banking Regulation Review* (2nd edn, Law Business Research, 2011) 584.
52 See in particular the Prudential – Investment, Insurance Intermediation and Banking Module (PIB) [VER38/04–21], and Recovery and Resolution Module (RAR) [VER1/04–21].
53 Clifford Chance, 'Qatar Publishes Revised Central Bank Law' (2013) <www.cliffordchance.com/content/dam/cliffordchance/briefings/2013/02/qatar-publishes-revised-central-bank-law.pdf> accessed 25 April 2021.
54 ibid.
55 Qatari Law No. 13 of 2012, art 180.
56 ibid art 176.
57 For a comprehensive review of these theories, see, Saleh Al-Barashdi and Horace Yeung, 'Varieties of Theoretical Approaches to Corporate Insolvency Law' (2018) 9 Sultan Qaboos Uni J Art Soc Sci 23.
58 Reinier Kraakman and others, *The Anatomy of Corporate Law* (3rd edn, OUP, 2017) 128–40.
59 Using the UK as an example, ss 213 & 214 of the Insolvency Act (IA) 1986 on wrongful and fraudulent trading may be relevant.
60 Again using the UK as an example, ss 238 & 239 of the IA 1986 on preferences and transactions at an undervalue are relevant.
61 In the UK, there are five main statutory procedures; four of these are provided for in the IA 1986, and the fifth provided by the Companies Act (CA) 2006. They are administration; administrative receivership; restructuring; statutory compromises, compositions and arrangements with creditors; and winding up (liquidation).
62 Vanessa Finch and David Milman, *Corporate Insolvency Law* (3rd edn, CUP, 2017) 21.
63 DIFC Insolvency Law, art 7.
64 Finch and Milman (n 63) 22.
65 See 11 U.S.C. § 1101.
66 Gerard McCormack, 'Control and Corporate Rescue: An Anglo-American Evaluation' (2007) 56 Intl Comp Law Q 515.
67 But this general view is subject to the CVA procedure, the new standalone moratorium (Part A1 IA 1986) and the facility of a 'light-touch' administration in the UK. These all have DIP features.
68 By the court on the application of the company, its directors, one or more of the company's creditors or a combination of these parties; out of court on the application of the holder of a qualifying floating charges; and out of court on the application of a company or a company's directors. Finch and Milman (n 63) 313.
69 DIFC Insolvency Law, art 32.
70 IA 1986, para 3 of Sch B1.
71 DIFC Insolvency Law, art 37.
72 Finch and Milman (n 63) 18–19. A more comprehensive appraisal can be seen in Kayode Akintola and David Milman, 'Rise, Fall and Rebirth of Receivership in UK Corporate Law' (2020) 20 J Corp Law Stud 99. They are of a more positive view that administrative receivership is far from 'dead.'
73 DIFC Insolvency Law, art 42.
74 Finch and Milman (n 63) 21.
75 IA 1986 ss 84 & 122.
76 Kristin van Zwieten, *Goode on Principles of Corporate Insolvency Law* (5th edn, Sweet & Maxwell, 2019) 190.
77 DIFC Insolvency Law, art 51.
78 Phillips and Rolls (n 45).
79 *Qatar Financial Centre Authority v Silver Leaf Capital Partners LLC* (QFC Civil and Commercial Court Case No: 0001/2009) paras 32–33.

80 QFC Insolvency Regulations 2005, pts 2–5.

81 Clifford Chance, 'New UAE Bankruptcy Law: Analysis and Highlights' (2020) <www.cliffordchance.com/content/dam/cliffordchance/briefings/2020/06/new-uae-bankruptcy-law-analysis-and-highlights.pdf> accessed 25 April 2021.

82 ibid.

83 Latham & Watkins (n 41).

84 ibid.

85 Qatari Law No. 11 of 2015.

86 ibid art 307.

87 Yet, as noted above, the Qatari banking law does allow the Central Bank to be the interim administrator of distressed financial institutions. See Qatari Law No. 13 of 2012, art 176.

88 Paula Boast and Jodie Martyndale-Howard, 'The Effect of Contractor Insolvency on Construction Projects in the Middle East' (2019) <www.charlesrussellspeechlys.com/en/news-and-insights/insights/constuction-engineering-and-projects/2019/the-effect-of-contractor-insolvency-on-construction-projects-in-the-middle-east/> accessed 25 April 2021. Note Kuwait has since then passed their long-awaited Insolvency Law (Kuwait Law No. 71/2020), leaving Qatar as the only country without a dedicated insolvency law in the region (but note the presence of such law in the QFC).

89 See e.g., CA 2006 s 170; and *Re Smith and Fawcett Ltd* [1942] Ch 304.

90 CA 2006 ss 171–77. The availability of a misfeasance action means that these general directors' duties remain relevant in liquidation because directors can still be made accountable for a breach of fiduciary or other duty in relation to the company by any creditor(s), or by the liquidator as the representative of the general creditors, and therefore made to contribute to the company's pool of assets. See IA 1986 s 212.

91 Kraakman and others (n 59) 128.

92 IA 1986 ss 213–14.

93 van Zwieten (n 77) 765–66.

94 DIFC Company Law, ss 69–76; cf ss 171–77 of CA 2006. A misfeasance action is also available in the DIFC to compel wrongdoing directors compensate the company in respect of any misfeasance or breach of any fiduciary or other duty in relation to the company. See DIFC Company Law s 115(b).

95 Sch 2 of DIFC Company Law; Sch 5 of DIFC Insolvency Law.

96 QFC Companies Regulations 2005, art 55(2)(A). A misfeasance action is also available in the QFC to make these general directors' duties enforceable. See QFC Companies Regulations 2005, art 105(2).

97 QFC Companies Regulations 2005, art 55(2)(B); cf ss 171 & 173 of CA 2006.

98 QFC Companies Regulations 2005, art 55(2)(C); cf s 174 of CA 2006.

99 QFC Companies Regulations 2005, art 55(2)(D) & (E); cf ss 175–77 CA 2006.

100 QFC Insolvency Regulations 2005, arts 102–3; the remedy is provided in art 105.

101 ibid art 193.

102 Clifford Chance (n 82).

103 UAE Insolvency Law, art 144.

104 Art 22 the UAE Commercial Companies Law. The full article reads, 'A person authorised to manage the company shall preserve its rights and extend such care as a diligent person. Such person shall do all such acts in agreement with the objective of the company and the powers granted to such person by virtue of an authorisation issued by the company in this respect.'

105 Joel Slawotsky and Jon Truby, 'The Director Duty of Care in Qatar' (2016) 26 Duke J Comp Intl Law 337.

106 Qatari Commercial Companies Law, arts 108–11.

107 ibid art 113.

108 Slawotsky and Truby (n 106) 371.

109 Qatari Commercial Companies Law, arts 334–35.
110 ibid art 298. The law requires that if the losses of a limited liability company reach half its capital, the management shall within 30 days of the loss reaching this amount suggest to the general assembly the matter of covering the capital or dissolving the company.
111 Paul Davies and Sarah Worthington, *Gower Principles of Modern Company Law* (10th edn, Sweet & Maxwell, 2016) 1164.
112 van Zwieten (n 77) 614.
113 A floating charge on the company's undertaking or property created at a relevant time is invalid. See IA 1986 s 245.
114 One example is a type of transaction called 'extortionate credit transactions', as per IA 1986 s 244.
115 IA 1986 ss 238–39.
116 van Zwieten (n 77) 616.
117 Norton Rose Fulbright, 'Middle East: Distressed Debt: Antecedent Transactions in the UAE' (2020) <www.nortonrosefulbright.com/en/knowledge/publications/f77f43a7/middle-east-distressed-debt> accessed 25 April 2021.
118 The list includes: 1. Donations, gifts or transactions without consideration, excluding small gifts which are normally given; 2. Any transactions in which the obligations of the Debtor significantly exceed the obligations of the counterparty, whether such obligations were in cash or in kind; 3. Early settlement of any debts, regardless of the method of payment; 4. Settlement of payable debts by any means other than the method agreed between the Debtor and a creditor or by any methods that are different from those usually followed for settlement of that type of debt; 5. Creating a new security of any type on the Debtor's Assets to secure payment of an earlier debt.
119 QFC Insolvency Regulations 2005, art 142.
120 ibid art 143.
121 ibid art 145.
122 ibid art 144.
123 Mahesh Uttamchandani, *'No Way Out': The Lack of Efficient Insolvency Regimes in the MENA Region* (World Bank Policy Research Working Paper 5609, 2011) 7 <https://openknowledge.worldbank.org/bitstream/handle/10986/3375/WPS5609.pdf?sequence=1&isAllowed=y> accessed 25 April 2021.
124 Art 337 of the Qatari Companies Law states that, 'Without prejudice to the right to claim indemnification when applicable, any act, transaction or decision issued in violation of the provisions of this law shall be void without prejudice to the rights of third parties acting in good faith.'
125 Uttamchandani (n 124) 4.
126 Cranston and others (n 3) 175–76.
127 Banking Act 2009, s 7.
128 ibid ss 11–13.
129 Cranston and others (n 3) 182.
130 Qatari Law No. 13 of 2012, arts 173, 176.
131 ibid. art 176.
132 UAE Federal Law No. 14 of 2018, art 116.
133 ibid art 119.
134 Linklaters, 'GCC Quarterly Review Q2 2021' (2021) <www.linklaters.com/en/knowledge/publications/alerts-newsletters-and-guides/2021/july/05/gcc-quarterly-review-q2-2021> accessed 10 April 2022.
135 Regulatory Law Amendment Law (DIFC Law No. 1 of 2021), Ch 3; forming Part 5A of the Regulatory Law (DIFC Law No. 1 of 2004).
136 ibid ch 4.
137 ibid art 84V.
138 Uttamchandani (n 124) 1.

139 For an appraisal for their former regime, refer to Saleh Al-Barashdi, 'A Critical View of the Current Bankruptcy Regime in Oman' (2016) 13 Intl Corp Rev 36. The new Omani law (Royal Decree 53/2019) came into effect on 7 July 2020.

140 Gilles Cuniberti, 'The International Market for Contracts: The Most Attractive Contract Laws' (2014) 34 Northwest J Intl Law Bus 455.

141 Melissa Hancock, 'Pace of Regional Rivalry Quickens' (*Financial Times*, 19 October 2012) <www.ft.com/content/bb9e38e6-187b-11e2-8705-00144feabdc0> accessed 25 April 2021.

142 Christopher Williams and others, 'New Insolvency Law for the Dubai International Financial Centre ("DIFC") Issued' (2019) 9 Natl Law Rev <www.natlawreview.com/article/new-insolvency-law-dubai-international-financial-centre-difc-issued> accessed 25 April 2021.

7 Cyprus After the 2013 Banking Crisis

The Journey Towards Recovery

Sofia Ellina

Introduction

The general proposition of this chapter is that "banks fail, and should be allowed to fail"[1] as long as it does not have a contagious effect.[2] To achieve this, however, a structured system and options for prompt resolution need to be in place. This is an important issue since banking crises can have a grave impact on economies.[3] In 2013, Cyprus had an unhealthy economy that affected the stability of the banking system and vice versa.[4]

As per the International Monetary Fund (IMF), up until 2001, Cyprus was included in the Middle East and Europe under Developing Countries but, since then, it has been considered as a developed country.[5] The events that led Cyprus into a crisis that endangered the solvency of the whole country, which could have resulted in turning it from a developed country back into a developing country. Although Cyprus may no longer be classed as a developing country, its economy has been plagued by severe crises that necessitated the initiation of unorthodox measures to deal with the crisis. As there was a "too-big-to-fail" perception in Cyprus, the seriousness of the situation was not realised on time which caused a further deterioration of the economy. Arguably, if Cyprus was not part of the European Union (EU), the events of 2013 would have resulted in a sovereign default.

This chapter considers how this problem was dealt in Cyprus which is important for determining the effectiveness of the bank resolution tools for resolving, and, possibly, precluding, bank insolvencies. Lessons that arise from the Cypriot banking crisis experience can be instrumental to both developed and developing countries as well as to regulators. Regulators should focus on creating a safe space for banking systems and allow systemic financial institutions to methodically fail.[6] Non-viable banks could obstruct the development of other banks therefore, such banks should have the option of liquidation, which could facilitate the creative destruction principle.[7] The creation of an effective framework is a difficult task for regulators as they need to ensure that effective tools – that can prevent and deal with a bank failure – are in place and simultaneously promote an innovative and a competitive banking system.

DOI: 10.4324/9781003173984-9

Simple insolvency procedures are not usually suitable to solve problems of financial institutions as their failure can have an irretrievable hit on a country's economy.[8] Circa 2012–2013, Cyprus needed immediate attention as the economy was on the edge of catastrophe. The only option of Cypriot banks at the time was the corporate liquidation procedure. The Cypriot insolvency law framework was not in effect at the time as it was initiated in 2015 through the Insolvency Law 2015 N. 65(I)/2015. During 2013, Basil III was in force that has as a purpose mitigating risks for banks[9] but, there was not an EU legislation that dealt specifically with the resolution of a banking crisis. There is a need to create an infrastructure for financial institutions that can circumvent loss of confidence. This is because deposit runs can lead to broad systemic risks that could cause the devastation of a nation's economy. As such, normal insolvency procedures are not capable of dealing with the contagion risks[10] since financial institutions need early intervention and speed, something that normal insolvency procedures will struggle to provide.[11]

Bail-out which is an option that was used in the past in countries like Greece was not favoured as it creates a moral hazard and burdens taxpayers. Bail-out is financial assistance that is traditionally given by the government of a country, which is borne by the taxpayers. Bailing out the distressed banks as a sole tool was not enough and will arguably never be enough. The tools that were included in the Bank Recovery and Resolution Directive (BRRD)[12] (that was at its drafting stages) became useful for dealing with the crisis. These tools were developed as a response to the 2007–2008 global financial crisis as there was a need for strategies and mechanisms capable of dealing with imminent crisis. Bail-in was the main innovative tool used in Cyprus and was also included in the BRRD. The use of bail-in impacted the decision of adopting it officially in the BRRD that became available right after the Cypriot banking crisis. A resolution authority will impose a bail-in on certain financial institutions and this aims at making it financially stable through recapitalising it and effectively dealing with the reasons that led to the failure. Bail-in converts uninsured deposits into equity or writes-off a part of the deposits on a going-concern basis to achieve the aforementioned. The Cypriot experience illustrates that a bail-out should be used as a method of last resort to avoid using public support that could drain the finances of that country or of the European Union. As such there could be an introduction of a new norm through the bail-in tool which is an alternative to government-funded rescues. There was a public outcry in Cyprus when the decision to use the bail-in tool was taken. Although the purpose of moving from bailouts to bail-ins is to minimise the burden on the public, the tools can be affected in different ways. The caution against bailouts can be seen from judicial decisions that have been taken right after bail-in came into play.[13]

The events that led to the banking crisis and the measures enforced to deal with the crisis can be used as a paradigm for imitation and possibly aversion. Non-performing loans (NPLs) that are often a result of poor banking regulation produces instability to the banking system and to the country's financial system as a whole. The corollary is to explore the bail-in tool and the other steps taken to minimise the risk of having an increased number of NPLs in Cyprus as well the measures that have been proposed by the EU that were introduced to avert a possible contagion. In more detail, this chapter will examine whether the bail-in tool of the Resolution of Credit Institutions and Investment Firms Law 22(I)/2016 (Resolution Law 2016), which transposed the BRRD, is capable of evading and/or dealing with an imminent banking crisis.

Section "Background: Economic History of Cyprus Until the Banking Crisis", which follows, is a pithy depiction of the historical economic background of Cyprus until the events that led the country to the verge of recession. Section "The Too-Big-to-Fail Concept" discusses the too-big-to-fail concept from the lens of Cyprus. Section "The NPL Menace in the Cypriot Banking System" examines the effect of NPLs in a banking system and how Cyprus dealt with this menace. Section "Developments in Cyprus After the Resolution Measures Were Imposed" analyses the resolution tools that were applied in the 2013 banking crisis of Cyprus as well as the importance of protecting secured depositors and the effect of capital controls. Section "BRRD and the Effects of Bail-in" scrutinises the BRRD with focus on the bail-in tools. Section "Conclusions: Lessons Learnt from Cyprus" concludes with identifying whether its application has worked for Cyprus.

Background: Economic History of Cyprus Until the Banking Crisis

After the independence of Cyprus in 1960,[14] there was steady economic progress. From focusing on the agricultural industry, Cyprus started dealing with real estate development, tourism and investments.[15] The war with Turkey in 1974 affected the upward development of Cyprus as it deteriorated the economy and left the country with unemployment rates that reached 30 per cent.[16] From 1977, with the trend of offshore companies – that is now abolished due to the entrance of Cyprus to the EU in 2004 – Cyprus managed to revive and its economy flourished again.[17]

The financial problems that followed in the subsequent years were, perhaps unintendedly, driven by the EU membership of Cyprus; it led to overconfidence, under-estimation of risks and reckless decisions.[18] Bad corporate governance decisions and operations generated most of the problems that led the banks in distress.[19] From a corporate law and governance perspective much of this at EU level is left to member states through the use of directives thus, perhaps Cypriot legislators should have done more. This is also closely aligned with the too-big-to-fail problem that is discussed further in the next section. Cyprus' new status as a member state of the EU was responsible for the foreign capital inflow that went into Cyprus' banks and the property market.[20] As a result of the rapid credit growth and the unmaintainable property bubble, the financial stability of the Cypriot economy became unbalanced.[21]

The worldwide economic crisis of 2008 minimally affected Cyprus and this continued during the 2009 recession. Although the impact on Cyprus was not direct, there was an indirect influence from the problems that the Greek economy was facing.[22] In June 2012, Cyprus applied for financial assistance from Europe and the IMF. Several events caused a delay in reaching an agreement and what followed was the financial turmoil of the two largest banks of Cyprus, which led to a sovereign debt crisis.

In March 2013, the Eurogroup[23] and the IMF made the decision that public funds were not capable of saving the banks as the public funds of Cyprus were already stretched.[24] This was a major problem for Cyprus given that the capital of €5.8 billion, which was the shortfall, had to be raised internally. This led to a discussion on the options that Cyprus had to cover this amount. An agreement was reached between the Eurogroup and the Cypriot government on 16 March 2013 on how to generate revenue to recapitalise the distressed banks. The agreement – that was subject to approval by the Cypriot Parliament – included a bank deposit levy of 9.9 per cent for deposits over €100.000 and of 6.75 per cent of deposits below €100.000 on all Cypriot banks. In the meantime, all of the banks remained closed, and restrictions were put on cash withdrawals through capital controls. The Parliament rejected this agreement after the vast outcry that was created both nationally and in the EU.

In the early hours of 25 March 2013, the discussions on how to raise the capital of €5.8 billion continued. Without an agreement the banks could not open as if they reopened without an agreement that would have been with a new currency, which would not have allowed Cyprus to remain in the EU. With the default of the sovereign the consequences could have been disastrous.[25] Hence, the European Commission, the European Central Bank and the IMF (Troika) finally agreed on an economic adjustment programme with Cyprus, which stopped the breakdown of the euro and the default of Cyprus. This consisted of an international bail-out of approximately €10 billion as long as several conditions were fulfilled.[26] These requirements included, *inter alia*, a bail-in of 47.5 per cent on deposits beyond €100.000 at the Bank of Cyprus (BoC)[27] and extinguishing deposits over €100.000 at the Cyprus Popular Bank (Laiki).[28] Laiki was liquidated with the good part of it being merged with the BoC. A security on deposits below €100.000 was triggered although in the initial negotiations there was an offer having a bail-in on all deposits.[29] Depositors were left unsettled throughout Europe (especially in Greece and Slovenia) due to the outcome of the negotiations between Cyprus and Troika.[30] The criticisms regarding bail-in and the near bail-in on secured deposits is a vital part of the discussions in this chapter.[31]

Following the memorandum of understanding between Cyprus and Troika, the incorporation of an effective insolvency regime in Cyprus prevailed to be necessary hence, the Insolvency Law 2015 N. 65(I)/2015 was enforced with examinership being introduced. The Troika officials argued that the inauguration of rescue culture within the Cypriot insolvency regime was inevitable. As a result, the examinership procedure was initiated and there were changes on the liquidation procedure, schemes of arrangement and receivership.

The resolution framework adopted by Cyprus in March 2013[32] was certainly "tested in fire."[33] Cyprus gradually started recovering as the economic adjustment program was exited in 2016.[34] This chapter examines whether the recovery of the Cypriot economy is attributable to the resolution tools used during the banking crisis.

The Too-Big-to-Fail Concept

Too-big-to-fail financial institutions tend to receive advantages that other smaller financial institutions do not receive. The largest banks of a country are usually perceived as too-big-to-fail as the stability of the economy is to a certain extent depending on them. The failure of a too-big-to-fail institution may have a domino effect and as a result cripple the country's economy therefore, the government will subsequently support the financial institution.[35] When the national economy is at stake the government's involvement in funding the financial institution is inevitable.[36] Too-big-to-fail is classified as a common problem in banking as the health of large banks is linked with the national economy. As such, large financial institutions receive the guarantee of a bail-out in times of distress. This expectation that the government will rescue these financial institutions incentivises them to expand their balance sheet through leverage and to take more risks including precarious assets.[37] These institutions can exploit the position to the maximum advantage, which is arguably what happened in Cyprus.

The banks in Cyprus before the 2013 banking crisis were thought to be too-big-to-fail, which created a moral hazard.[38] Often this happens to large banks and that was the case for the BoC and Laiki that were the two largest banks in Cyprus at the time. For a bank to be classed as systemic its balance sheet should exceed the 20–30 per cent of the country's Gross Domestic Product (GDP). BoC reached 211 per cent of Cyprus' GDP while Laiki reached 190 per cent.[39] Demetriades stated "When it is 200% of GDP, it is not just systemic. It is controlling. An entire society was completely captured."[40] Namely, the whole economy of Cyprus was dependent on these banks.

Financial instability is closely linked with the phenomenon of too-big-to-fail.[41] The Cypriot banks expected that they would have been bailed-out by the government therefore, they had taken excessive risks and wasted resources. The years 2004–2010 was the period that stigmatised these banks as during this period there was a dangerous rapid growth. This overconfidence led to branches spreading, mainly in Greece and East Europe. The failure of these banks is associated *inter alia*, with poor governance, the exposure to the Greek Government bonds, from giving high deposit rates and having lax lending standards that led to an excessive amount of NPLs.[42] Public authorities also did not do anything to stop the harm from spreading as they did not realise the danger that these banks had put themselves in.[43]

A massive risk that the Cypriot banks had taken was the investment in the Greek Government Bonds that amounted to almost €5.8 billion.[44] In 2011, a levy was imposed on the Greek Government Bonds, which generated a massive loss of 4.5 billion for Cypriot banks. This was the beginning of the end of Laiki as it was the bank that invested the most in the Greek Government Bonds. There was excessive risk taking and reckless decisions regarding the purchase of Greek

Government Bonds from Cypriot banks. For instance, in December 2009, the BoC sold Greek Government Bonds worth €1.7 billion (which left them with an exposure of only €0.1 billion), yet without wasting any time BoC began to purchase Greek Government Bonds worth approximately €2.4 billion by June 2010.[45] There is the counterargument that government bonds do not carry any risks according to requirements set by Basel.[46] The amount of the investment in Greek Government Bonds suggests otherwise as the amount lost equates to 25 per cent of the GDP of Cyprus.[47]

The moral hazard becomes a vaster problem when uninsured creditors are supported in an extensive grade. After the levy on Greek Government Bonds Laiki was in need of Emergency Liquidity Assistance (ELA).[48] The guarantee that Laiki provided were discounted assets. The crisis led Laiki in securing €2.5 billion of ELA in October 2011.[49] By January 2012, the ELA amount that Laiki received reached €3.7 billion, while the ELA amount increased to €5.7 billion by May 2012. The continuous injections of liquidity from ELA signalled the concerning state of Laiki. In June 2012, the amount that was injected by ELA totalled to €8 billion. It was obvious that Laiki was insolvent, but the liquidity injections continued as in July 2012 the total of ELA was at €9.6 billion. The ELA to Laiki went beyond €11 billion by the time Laiki was liquidated.[50] The economic problems that Laiki was facing were so vast which thus necessitated the bail-out injection by the government that reached €1.8 billion in mid-2012.[51]

There was the perception that whatever happened the default of the biggest bank would not have been allowed as public funds (i.e., ELA and the bail-out in 2012) would always support those banks. This made risk taking not that risky in the banks' perspectives as they believed that the government would not let them fail as that would have affected the national economy. This is the epitome of the too-big-to-fail problem, which is why the Eurogroup in March 2013 wanted to put an end to this. This was because the banks were not only too-big-to-fail but also too-big-to-save, as a taxpayer bail-out would have gotten the sovereign debt out of control, which could have resulted in the country's bankruptcy.[52] The amount that the banks needed to recapitalise the banks was €13.5 billion (this was the 80 per cent of Cyprus' GDP at the time). It was the fact that it was systemic that safeguarded the country from exiting the Eurozone.

As such, the harsh tool of bail-in was implemented with the hope of introducing a framework that would put an end to moral hazard and maybe eliminate the too-big-to-fail problem. The purpose was not only to eliminate the problem in Cyprus but to send the message to other Member States of the EU as well. That said, policymakers who are in favour of the bail-in tool are incentivised by the possibility of putting an end to the too-big-to-fail problem. This is a significant option for the banks to recapitalise and resolve the crisis themselves without putting the responsibility on the taxpayers, but on the investors, when the banks reach the point of non-viability.[53] The effects of the bail-in tool as well as to whether it reduces the risk of contagion is discussed further.

The NPL Menace in the Cypriot Banking System

Certain events led to liquidation of Laiki and the restructuring of BoC through the bail-in tool on bank deposits. As discussed earlier, in 2011 the excessive exposure to the Greek economy – as Cypriot banks overinvested in Greek Government Bonds – impacted the economic stability of Cyprus[54] and the first recession made its appearance.[55] The failure of a bank is closely connected with NPLs hence, NPLs of the banking system of Cyprus had a major impact on the banking crisis.[56] According to the European Banking Authority (EBA), Cyprus is currently still the second in Europe with most NPLs, with Greece being the first.[57] NPLs are an endogenous factor that makes banks susceptible to financial instability and possible failure; therefore, the increase of NPLs in 2013 impacted the banking crisis of 2013.

Statistics conducted by the European Banking Authority (EBA) regarding NPLs indicate that in 2013 the ratio was 38.5 per cent[58] which was disproportionate with the 2011 ratio that reached 9.9 per cent. EBA has logged in September 2019 that the average percentage of NPLs in the EU is 2.9 per cent and simultaneously in Cyprus the ratio reached 21.1 per cent.[59] Per the EBA statistics in December 2020, the NPLs ratio in Cyprus was at 11.5 per cent that is a significant drop since in March 2020 the ratio was at 20.1 per cent.[60]

Campbell emphasises that a key to an effective system is the decrease of NPLs, as excessive NPLs can be a profound menace to the banking infrastructure of Cyprus, and it can subsequently have macroeconomic reverberations.[61] The target of the policy makers and banks post-2013 was to introduce measures that would alleviate the NPL predicament in Cyprus. This could have the reflection of a control system and the efficacy of enforcement proceedings.[62] The options that banks can choose are the debt-to-asset swap (DTAS), cash payment, sale of business and/or assets and enforcement/insolvency proceedings. In Cyprus, as regards to the enforcement/insolvency procedure the most prevalent are liquidation, receivership, foreclosure and examinership. In August 2018, BoC announced the initiation of the Helix project with Apollo Global Management LLC in which €2.7 billion of NPLs were sold.[63] In June 2021, the completion of the Hellix Project 2 was announced by BoC that sold portfolios of loans of which €1,311 million were NPLs.[64] These agreements targeted the reduction of NPLs and the amelioration of the asset quality that are retained by banks.[65]

It is important to understand the reasons that led to a vast percentage of NPLs in order to circumvent that from happening again both in Cyprus and internationally. All start from the lax corporate governance of the Cyprus banks and the deficient lending practices that were facilitated from the legal and regulatory framework. Pre-2014 the practices were sufficiently different from the norms in other European countries.[66] There was a discrepancy of the definitions that Cyprus, other European and international countries had on NPLs. The Central Bank of Cyprus (CBC) defined NPLs as loans that are past due 90 days but excluded loans that were fully secured by tangible collaterals.[67] Another issue was that banks allowed loan modifications, which deemed problematic loans as performing. European and international norms define all loans that are 90 days delinquent as NPLs. By 2015 Cyprus also adopted this definition that EBA uses.[68] The balance sheet of the banks during the years of 2007–2011 was weakened as a consequence of their practices.

The years before the banking crisis there was a property bubble and an overinvestment in property and real estate construction that had its input on increased NPLs.[69] In particular, the 72.4 per cent of construction loans were NPLs.[70] An excessive credit growth had appeared as the value of collaterals was constantly rising. The banks had neglected the possible risks though and this is also because they overly relied on collaterals and guarantees rather than establishing a mechanism to determine whether the borrowers are able to repay their loans.[71] The fact that banks allowed collateral arrangements involving excessive cross-collateralisation worsened the situation. Another collateral arrangement that complicated matters was when a group of companies was concerned, which meant that this involved cross-shareholdings, cross-pledges, cross-guarantees and floating charges. The balance sheet of the banks was gravely affected after the declining value of real estate as this also had a major impact on the value of collaterals.

When the GDP of Cyprus dropped in 2012, the unemployment rates rose, and real estate prices dropped aggressively that had an impact on the increasing NPLs. This did not immediately alarm the borrowers as they were aware of the lax legal framework of foreclosure. During the time the foreclosure procedure was time-consuming[72] which disincentivised borrowers to repay their debts. The banks hesitated to use foreclosure due to the lengthy process and that led to unpropitious reverberations on recovery.

The procedure of foreclosure that allows private auctions was implemented in 2014 in Cyprus through the Immovable Property (Transfer and Mortgage) Law 142(I)/2014 following the Memorandum of Understanding with Troika. The reinvigorated foreclosure procedure targeted the reduction of NPLs. An evaluation expert is needed to estimate the open market value (OMV) of the assets before the commencement of foreclosure. At the first auction the 80 per cent of the OMV should be reserved, where the bank is forbidden from bidding.[73] If the result of the auction is unsuccessful, a second auction can occur in which the bids cannot be lower than the decreased value of 50 per cent of the OMV.[74] If six months have passed since the first auction with the assets not being sold, the bank will have the opportunity to credit the bid provided that it is at an OMV.[75]

Politicians described this tool as draconian and that it could cause grave consequences in society.[76] These new laws are to some degree oppressive to debtors as the sale of their assets is forced. Nevertheless, foreclosure is not the prevalent option since banks are in preference of using other alternatives first thus, this tool is merely utilised when the debtor has failed to fulfil his/her liabilities. In fact, this means that the assertions of politicians could be an exaggeration. This procedure is principally designed for defaulters who are not in agreement with any consensual arrangements that were previously offered to them by creditors.

Creditors tend to go for DTAS before they decide to use foreclosure but if the director is not in consent, this will no longer be an option. While directors can initially not be in acquiesce to a DTAS, they can be forced into it through foreclosure. Albeit a DTAS could have taken place without foreclosure, the fact that the director was not concurring with the creditor to have a DTAS had as an outcome a non-consensual DTAS through foreclosure. One could argue that a consensual solution could be more profitable for both sides since the foreclosure expenditures could have been avoided and the value of the assets could have been kept maximised.

The contrasting procedures of examinership[77] and foreclosure were recommendations of Troika hence, one could question the simultaneous implementation of both. On one hand foreclosure goes against the axiom rescue culture that Troika aimed to incorporate within the Cypriot jurisdiction. On the other hand, rescue culture and foreclosure are intertwined in the sense that foreclosure should exist for corporate rescue to have a sustainable development. With the hope of having some of their debt deducted, some debtors become strategically in default. The existence of foreclosure can possibly operate as a menace to those debtors provided that this tool generates an efficacious infrastructure to minimise NPLs.

Foreclosure has the purpose of being less time-consuming from other available enforcement processes and also to speed up the process of decreasing NPLs. However, the course of action of several cases is postponed owing to the legal challenges that are brought to the court by the directors. These delays defeat one of the main benefits of foreclosure; thus, it was decided by the Parliament that foreclosure necessitated an enhancement, which took place in 2018.

The 2018 amendments include the elucidation and the restriction of circumstances in which the directors can make objections against foreclosure to the court. The justification of introducing e-auctions is to make auction routes less burdensome to use. While the banks were able to bid within 12 months since the first auction, the time was lessened to six months. Even though this could be criticised as a creditor-oriented amendment it made the procedure more accessible and minimised the impediments that foreclosure previously comprised. The purpose of those amendments was to ease the access to foreclosure. The attempt to ameliorate foreclosure was legitimate however, it is still in the early stages of its implementation thus, the effect is still uncertain as statistical importance is not effectuated yet.

On another note Arsalidou and Kambia-Kapardis argue that the main cause of the banking crisis was the poor corporate governance that also extends to the cause of the increased NPLs.[78] They also highlight that:

> The interwoven relationships and strong connections that exist between politicians and businesses, the failure to control the phenomenon of the "revolving doors," as well as the expectation that banks will voluntarily comply with corporate governance codes in a culture where the prevailing attitude is that of the "old boys' network," are signs of corporate governance gone wrong.[79]

Due to those relationships the corporate governance of Cypriot banks did not convey the spirit of meritocracy, accountability and support. There was too much political interference in banks that were supposed to be private. Proof of the poor corporate governance and the lax lending practices that led to the catastrophe of the Cypriot banking system can be seen from some examples that were identified at the Investigative Committee of the Cypriot banking crisis.[80] The first is that a member of the BoC board and the remuneration committee obtained loans from the bank that amounted to 27 million and if that was not shocking enough, in the second example, the BoC's chairman obtained loans that reached approximately 319 million over a period of less than 20 years.[81]

Developments in Cyprus After the Resolution Measures Were Imposed

What Happened in Laiki and Bank of Cyprus After the Economic Adjustment Programme

The Resolution of Credit and Other Institutions Law 17(I)/2013 (2013 Resolution Law) was enacted to restructure, recapitalise and revive BoC and Laiki. There was no legislation that was dealing with the resolution of banks prior to this. The 2013 Resolution Law originates from an early draft of the BRRD that arose out of the global financial crisis of 2008.[82] This means that to a certain extent the Cypriot banking crisis informed the last version of the BRRD of 2014. The 2013 Resolution Law gave the power to the CBC to become a resolution authority which meant that they gained the ability to impose measures on credit, banking and cooperative institutions.

The agreement that was negotiated did not come without consequences since an unprecedented restructuring and resolution was expected that had to be conducted swiftly to circumvent the banks and the economy from facing further deterioration. The first action that was taken was to ring-fence the Cypriot banking system from the Greek banking system through selling the branches that Laiki and BoC had in Greece.[83] This had as a purpose the avoidance of a contagion to Greece, which could have impaired the Greece economy even further.

Part of the agreement in the Eurogroup and of the resolution plan of Cyprus was to divide Laiki into 'good' bank and 'bad' bank. The 'good' bank included NPLs, insured deposits and the ELA that Laiki borrowed from the CBC. The remaining assets like subsidiaries in other countries, uninsured deposits and other creditors were placed into the 'bad' bank, or in other words, the legacy bank.[84] Whatever remained from the legacy bank was finally liquidated while the 'good' bank was merged with the restructured BoC. The bailout of Troika as well as the bail-in on uninsured bank deposits recapitalised BoC. Uninsured amounts that exceeded €100.000 were converted into equity, which necessitated the increase of the share capital of BoC. In July 2017, it was decided that the 47.5 per cent of deposits beyond €100.000 was going to be bailed-in which generated media, citizen and political scrutiny. The 81 per cent of the share capital was being held by bailed-in depositors.[85] The deposits that were transferred from Laiki to BoC reached €4.5 billion.[86]

The essence of the bail-in at the BoC was that it converted the uninsured deposits into equity. Those bailed-in amounts were the internal funds that were used to recapitalise BoC. In this way the bank did not become a burden to the taxpayer directly. The rationale behind bail-ins is to not externalise the need for funds and to not rely on public subsidy.[87] It was believed that the taxpayers could not afford a bail-out that reached the amounts needed. The target of moving from bail-outs to bail-ins was to minimise the too-big-to-fail issue, reduce the impact that a bail-out could have had in a real economy and to accelerate recovery. Another reason the decisions led to a bail-in of uninsured depositors was because most of the large depositors were non-residents with the majority of them being Russians.[88] Christine Lagarde[89] stated that

> the authorities took bold steps to address the crisis, including the upfront resolution and restructuring of the two largest and insolvent banks at no fiscal cost, while protecting insured depositors. They also implemented ambitious fiscal consolidation measures. Nevertheless, challenges ahead are significant, including restoring credibility in the banking sector and reducing fiscal deficits and debt to sustainable levels.[90]

The resolutions measures that were taken were undoubtedly audacious and for that reason it gained global media attention. The bail-in though safeguarded a vast majority of the taxpayers and thus future generations since most of the uninsured deposits did not belong to Cypriots. Through protecting public finances, the most financially vulnerable citizens were also protected as the bail-in focused on affecting the wealthiest citizens.

Protecting Insured Depositors

The fact that the Eurogroup entertained the possibility of bailing-in insured deposits from all the banks in Cyprus – even those that did not require intervention – should not be neglected. This decision would have created a dangerous precedent that could have caused runs on big deposits in other EU countries, which could have affected the stability of more banks in the EU. This caused a vast outcry in Cyprus as all depositors were going to be affected, which influenced the Parliament to reject that agreement of 16 March 2013. Although the deposits of insured depositors were not bailed-in, the confidence of depositors was blurred.[91] Insured depositors need to feel the safety that in an insolvency outcome, they will be prioritised over uninsured depositors.

Insured deposits are in this situation amounts that do not exceed €100.000, which means that that amount is safe even if the bank collapses. This practice transmits confidence and trust in the banking system.[92] There is an analogous protection through the Financial Services Compensation Scheme that safeguards deposits up to £85.000.[93] The Cypriot government did not contemplate the breadth of implications that this proposal could have had as it would have gone against the Cypriot depositor protection scheme. This was in accordance with the European Union Deposit Guarantee Schemes Directives. Directive 94/19/EC that was amended by Directive 2009/14/EC. There was criticism all over the EU on disregarding the Directive and that the outcome of these negotiations undermined the whole banking market of the EU.[94] These developments had as a result the fear that there would be deposit runs[95] – especially by the large depositors who would want to find a safe space for their money[96] – hence, the corollary was the introduction of capital controls.

The Effect of Capital Controls

The measures taken to rescue the banks required intervention to avoid the runs on bank deposits that would further devastate them. This had as a result the initiation of several capital controls through The Enforcement of Restrictive Measures on Transactions in case of Emergency Law of 2013, Law 12(I) of 2013. These capital controls included amongst other things, the limit of withdrawing €300 cash per day, to not spend more than €2000 per day, the exportation of money abroad that had as a purpose an investment was restricted and the Central Bank of Cyprus had to grant their approval for transferring money beyond €5000.[97] Cyprus is the first Eurozone country that enforced capital controls, which was quite strict for a country that small.[98] The intentions were genuinely for safeguarding the banks but, this ultimately had some other consequences. Investments were vastly affected as the capital controls in Cyprus lasted for two years.

It is sensible to presume that anyone with large deposits would pursue to find a safe place for their money. If this had happened as a consequence of the measures that were taken to deal with the crisis, the injection of €10 billion to recapitalise the banking system would have been futile as without those deposits, the banking system would have collapsed in its totality. As such, capital controls were the necessary evil to keep BOC and the country going. These measures lasted for approximately two years that caused further implications to the Cypriot economy. Iceland was another country that applied capital controls in 2008 when the country was in distress. Danielson and Arnason described these measures as draconian as they violate civil rights and disturb national economic growth.[99]

These measures were introduced to avoid the destruction of the economy, but they do not come without consequences. Danielson shows his disapproval towards capital controls as he stated that capital controls are desperate measures that result from the loss of control of the national public authorities.[100] He also added that anyone who has massive bank deposits will find a way to take the money out of the country even if the route is not entirely legal.[101] The effects of capital controls include the deterioration of trust of national and international investors, increased risks regarding taking loans and investments and also the society loses its confidence in the system as they feel that their rights have been violated.[102] There have been debates on whether capital controls are legal.[103] There have been discussions of whether it comes into conflict with the fundamental principle of free movement of capital in the EU.[104] Article 65 clarifies that Member States of the EU are allowed "to take measures which are justified on grounds of public policy or public security." That said, Cyprus can enforce this to justify the legality of capital controls. As the trust on the banking system had almost vanished with the unorthodox bail-in tool, further safeguards for it to operate more effectively were necessary. This had as a result the disruption of the real economy,[105] which became more acute with their continuation for two years.

Judicial Actions that Followed the Initiation of the Bail-in Tool

Another consequence of the bail-in was the commencement of several national judicial actions as well as EU judiciary actions. These actions challenged the legality of bail-ins through arguing that it went against particular domestic and EU norms. None of the actions have been successful either for technical reasons or due to the fact that these measures were necessary to avert a sovereign default.

The domestic actions heard by the Supreme Court of Cyprus focused on requesting the annulment of Decrees 103 and 104 that triggered the resolution measures on both Laiki and BoC.[106] The cases argued that the decrees should be annulled for certain reasons that included the infringement of property rights[107] and that decrees impinge the principle of non-discrimination and equal treatment.[108] The Supreme Court held that this was not a public matter since the depositors that lost part of their deposits could not directly challenge those decrees. In other words, the decrees were directed at Laiki and BoC which meant that a judicial review claim could only be brought by the banks and not individuals. As such, the Supreme Court directed the applicants to bring an action under private law rather than public law as their application did not fall within the spectrum of judicial review.[109]

A group of depositors brought actions to the General Court (GC) of the EU. In *Mallis v European Commission*,[110] the action targeted the annulment of the Eurogroup's decision on 25 March 2013 and in *Ledra Advertising Ltd v European Commission*,[111] it was argued that some provisions regarding the bail-in in the Memorandum of Understanding (MoU) should be annulled.[112] They also claimed compensation for the losses that the depositors faced, which were caused by the bail-in. The applicants of *Ledra* requested compensation that equalled their losses from the bail-in. As the applicants believed that there was a breach of primary EU Law, they tried to rely on Articles 263, 268 and 340, TFEU. Breach of the right of property was one of the main arguments used. In *Mallis* the applicants argued that the decision of the Eurogroup was in reality of the Commission's and the European Central Bank's (ECB). The GC held that the Commission and the ECB were not allowed to enforce their decisions at the Eurogroup. As a result, the *Mallis* case was dismissed.

The GC clarified that the MoU was incorporated by the European Stability Mechanism (ESM) and Cyprus and not by the Commission. The MoU was signed by the president of the Commission but on behalf of the ESM and not of the Commission. The action of Ledra to the GC was based on the lawfulness of the

MoU, which meant that they did not have the jurisdiction to annul any of its provisions since the ESM or Cyprus were not an institution, body, office or agency in accordance with Article 263(1), TFEU. They also added that it was the decrees that triggered the bail-in and not the MoU, which are subject to domestic law and not EU law.[113]

Both *Mallis* and *Ledra* went to the Court of Justice of the European Union (CJEU). In *Mallis* the applicants adhered to their argument about the admissibility of the Eurogroup. The CJEU agreed with the GC by stating that the role of Commission and ECB at the Eurogroup was merely informative. The applicants further argued that the Eurogroup's decision was ultra vires and that it infringed the right of property. The CJEU rejected this since the Eurogroup was not within the definition of an EU body under Article 263, TFEU and they also clarified that the Eurogroup and the Council of Ministers were completely separate.[114] In *Ledra* the applicants were not just restricted under a judicial review under Article 263, TFEU as they sought damages from the Commission and ECB under Articles 268 and 340, TFEU. To answer whether damages should be given under Article 340, TFEU, the CJEU had to conclude whether the bail-in was lawful. The GC rejected the claim under Article 340 TFEU, but the CJEU dealt with it differently.

The CJEU accepted that the bail-in breached the applicants' right of property. These issues invariably infringe property rights, and this would be permissible as long as they are proportionate or justifiable in the sense that there were no alternative measures to achieve the intended policy objective. The rules of the game change when in a distressed scenario could be in itself a justification.[115] The most important part of the decision was the following:

> In view of the objective of ensuring the stability of the banking system in the euro area, and having regard to the imminent risk of financial losses to which depositors with the two banks concerned would have been exposed if the latter had failed, such measures do not constitute a disproportionate and intolerable interference impairing the very substance of the appellants' right to property. Consequently, they cannot be regarded as unjustified restrictions on that right.[116]

The CJEU indicates that even though the bail-in breaches some fundamental rights provided by the EU legislation, it is justifiable as it safeguards the public through preserving the stability of banks. The assumption that the depositors would have been in a worse position if both banks were liquidated is questionable though as the 'no creditor worse off' has not substantially been explored by the case.[117] However, in practice it could have been problematic to predict the consequences for creditors in a hypothetical scenario. As the only option at the time was the normal liquidation procedure, the CJEU would have to evaluate the outcome for creditors if that route was followed. This might have not been appropriate for the CJEU to address as the conclusions would largely be based on mathematical and economic scenarios that are normally not within the expertise of the judiciary.[118]

BRRD and the Effects of Bail-in

As there was a crisis in several EU Member States, the introduction of harmonised bank resolution tools was going to help with addressing the flaws of previous regimes. The purpose of the BRRD was to circumvent spill-overs all over the EU, to enhance market discipline, reduce the need for governmental bailouts and to decrease moral hazard.[119] Early intervention and resolution are key aspects behind the initiation of the BRRD toolkit. The toolkit does not only facilitate the continuance of the financial institution as a going concern but also ensures that the institution is liquidated in a methodical manner.[120] To initiate any of the resolution tools, there should be a public interest concern.[121] If the financial institution is not systemic, normal insolvency procedures will apply instead of the resolution tools.[122] A key consideration is that shareholders and creditors should be in a better position under a resolution rather than in a direct liquidation or another insolvency procedure.

The resolution authority – which is CBC in Cyprus – is required to evaluate whether the financial institution is in a non-viability state. An independent evaluator is appointed to aid the resolution authority, who needs to consider the following important points: (1) establish when it is best to intervene to facilitate the reduction of possible losses; (2) ensure that creditors will be in a better position than in liquidation; (3) consider the priority claims;[123] (4) make sure that the financial institution value is maintained.

The resolution toolkit is (a) the sale of business tool; (b) the bridge institution tool; (c) the asset separation tool; and (d) the bail-in tool. The first three were traditionally used in the past even though the BRRD was not in force. For the resolution of the Cypriot banks all the aforementioned tools were used with the true innovation being the bail-in tool, which is the reason that this section is focusing on the bail-in tool. To gain some context on the resolution tool, the first three tools are briefly discussed.

For the sale of business tool, there is a transfer of ownership, assets and liabilities of the financial institutions to a purchaser.[124] The sale consists of a valuation and a conduct of a marketing process that includes the assets, rights and liabilities of the institution. The consent of shareholders is not required, which makes the process quicker. At the same time, the interests of the shareholders need to be considered. Through a bridge institution tool, a bridge bank absorbs the critical functions of the distressed financial institution.[125] The resolution authority bears the responsibility of deciding whether a bridge bank should be formed without the necessity of having shareholder consent. The bridge bank will consequently be merged with another bank through the usage of the sale of business tool. Therefore, the bridge bank vanishes after the sale is formulated. From the perspective of Cyprus, the bridge bank was the 'good' bank of Laiki that ceased to exist after it was merged with BoC. The asset separation tool has the power of dividing assets, rights or liabilities of the institution to either resolution or bridge bank or to other asset management vehicles.[126] This means that this tool separates non-viable assets and liabilities from the viable ones. Again, an equivalent tool was used in

Cyprus to divide Laiki into a 'good' and 'bad' bank. These three tools have been in place for a long time, and they do not carry any controversial features like the bail-in tool.

Having already discussed aspects of the bail-in tool throughout this chapter, this section focuses on criticising further this tool. To recap some of its main components, the way to achieve its purpose is through recapitalising the financial institution internally. The bail-in tool and the BRRD more generally, target to ensure financial stability and to gain confidence in the banking sector through considering the possible effects on the society when a banking crisis emerges.[127] Huertas characterised bail-in as "a heart transplant" because it is equivalent to putting a new heart in a body where its heart is shutting down.[128] This will carry the possibility of rejecting the transplant, which means that even if everything is correctly applied there is still a chance of failure.

Bail-in allows the write-down of equity and debt instruments as well as the conversion of debt instruments into equity.[129] The legislation prohibits the bail-in of deposits protected under the Deposit Guarantee Scheme.[130] A further criticism on the resolution of banks in Cyprus was that pension scheme accounts were either wiped-out if they belonged to Laiki or bailed-in if they were in BoC. Consequently, the population's trust and confidence in the banking system was further disintegrated. The BRRD attempts to deal with this through giving the discretion to the resolution authorities to decide the type of deposits that they would allow to be bailed-in.[131]

The thinking behind the bail-in was to circumvent a contagion and they also argued that depositors received a better outcome than if the banks were directly liquidated. The BRRD conveys that the BRRD tools are prioritised over governmental assistance, which should be a measure of last resort. As such, bail-in and the other resolution tools are capable of dealing with the moral hazard that has been caused by the perception of too-big-to-fail.[132] The tools aid the bank to liquidate without the need for a bail-out. If bail-out was the first line of defence, the taxpayer would have paid the price through further austerity measures.

Early intervention is key to applying bail-in effectively as a lesser amount will need to be bailed-in to recapitalise the bank. As such, as the exposure of depositors and other creditors will not be extensive, a knock-on effect is averted. With early intervention, the value of the assets of the bank are retained to an extent, which signals that the no creditor worse off principle is sufficiently applied and not breached, since when a bank is extensively deteriorated its value is reduced even further.[133] There will be an outcry when applying such a tool very early, but if the application is structured and methodical, contagion risks may be reduced. This is where the Cypriot case departs from this as early intervention was not the case when contemplating that Cyprus asked for financial assistance in mid-2012. By the time Cyprus requested that, the banks were already in a deteriorating state. There was procrastination involved and a moral hazard, which delayed a resolution. The BRRD and subsequently the Resolution Law 2016, dealt with this through officially incorporating an article that has as a requirement of early intervention.[134] Early intervention is also essential for reducing the costs of the resolution or liquidation. There could be a drawback to this as the resolution could be accessed too early therefore, the resolution authority should be cautious about this. This is the thinking behind the temporary appointment of an administrator to determine whether a resolution is compatible with the circumstances.[135]

Conclusions: Lessons Learnt from Cyprus

The number of NPLs – that went out of control a few years before the bank resolution occurred – had an input towards the further deterioration of the banks as they were a burden to the banks' balance sheet. It is important to create a system in which NPLs are restricted from increasing. The authorisation of loans in Cyprus used to be very flexible as simple guarantees or assets that were already collateralised were enough. Currently the regulations regarding the obtaining of loans are stringent, which is disincentivizing investment that could have a negative impact on the economy. The ideal would be to identify the golden mean as too flexible or too strict are both not desirable. Introducing procedures that are working effectively can also motivate debtors to keep up with their repayments.

As a result of the bail-in tool in Cyprus, the lack of confidence was widespread throughout Europe. Investments were gravely affected after the shock of the bail-in tool, and there was the near collapse of the Euro currency in Cyprus, which could have led to the exit from the EU and there were capital controls in place for approximately two years.[136] There were other factors that affected the trust of depositors with the bail-in being the strongest one.

Bail-in should not be treated as a panacea since its role is to deal with financial institutions after distress had occurred rather than avert it. The purpose of the existence of the bail-in tool and the other resolution tools cannot be neglected as the too-big-to-fail perception is a main factor for the distress of most systemic banks. As a result, the resolution tools can restore the balance of the market since it motivates creditors to initiate a monitoring function.[137] The reduction of the need for state aid was spread in the Eurozone after the Cypriot crisis as well as the initiation of the BRRD. A caveat is that bail-ins do not completely evaporate the need for a bail-out.

Lessons learnt from the CJEU decisions is that the implementation of the bail-in tool needs to be proportional as it breaches property and equality rights. This means that the bail-in should only be available if it is in the interests of the public. The alternative would be to use the normal insolvency procedures rather than the resolution tools. Therefore, the resolution tools cannot be extended as it would be in breach with property rights.[138] Schillig argues that the resolution tools should not be *ultima ratio* by stating: "if the default option is likely to be unsuccessful – in other words, less effective for achieving the legitimate aim of protecting depositors – why retain it at all?" Schillig further suggests that through removing the need for public interest, investment will be encouraged, prices will be fixed and there will be more certainty to the system in which creditors would benefit from.

The hardest part would be to convince the public that the effects of the bail-in can have positive effects and not to make them lose trust in the system. Evidence has been produced that under certain circumstances the bail-in can work and it is also producing optimistic results only through its existence. There was a chaotic implementation of the bail-in tool in Cyprus but, against all odds it did aid BoC to overcome its difficulties. If it was applied earlier, then the position of both Laiki and BoC could have been more favourable. The important issue is to keep the banking system credible and effective thus, be cautious about the extension of the resolution tools in general.

Notes

1 Tobias Asser, *Legal Aspects of Regulatory Treatment of Banks in Distress* (IMF, 2001) 15.
2 The contagion risk is often described as systemic risk. See more about this: Rosa Maria Lastra, 'Systemic Risk, SIFIs and Financial Stability' (2011) 6(2) Cap Mark Law J 97–213.
3 John Boyd, Sungkyu Kwak and Bruce Smith, 'The Real Output Losses Associated with Modern Banking Crises' (2005) 37(6) J Mon Cre Bank 977–99; Valerie Cerra and Sweta Chaman Saxena, 'Growth Dynamics: The Myth of Economic Recovery' (2008) 98(1) Am Econ Rev 439–57.
4 This was also seen in the 1997 Asian crisis, where a banking crisis was affected by exogenous economic circumstances; Asser (n 5).
5 IMF (n 1).
6 Thomas Philippon and Aude Salord, 'New ICMB/CEPR Report: Bail-ins and Bank Resolution in Europe' (August 2017) <https://voxeu.org/article/new-icmbcepr-report-bail-ins-and-bank-resolution-europe> accessed 11 April 2022.
7 James White, 'Death and Resurrection of Secured Credit' (2004) 12 Am Bank Ins Law Rev 139, 151.
8 Ross Cranston and others, *Principles of Banking Law* (3rd edn, OUP, 2018) 171.
9 This can be for example the maintenance of leverage ratios and to upheld particular capital levels. This could have helped to avert failure but not to address a banking crisis.
10 Contagion risks describe a situation where the financial distress of one institution could spread to another causing a knock-on effect.
11 European Commission, 'Proposal for a Directive of the European Parliament and of the Council Establishing a Framework for the Recovery and Resolution of Credit Institutions and Investment Firms' 2012/0150' (6 June 2012) 5 <https://eur-lex.europa.eu/LexUriServ/%20LexUriServ.do?uri=COM:2012:0280:FIN:EN:PDF> accessed 11 April 2022.
12 Now Directive 2014/54/EU that was amended by Directive 2017/1132.
13 Nationally: Supreme Court of Cyprus 07/06/2013, Case No. 553/2013: *Myrto Christodoulou and Others v Kentriki Trapeza Kyprou and Others a.o.*; Supreme Court of Cyprus 09/10/2014, Case No. 1034/2013: *Vias Dimitriou and Others v Kentrikis Trapezas Kyprou and Others)*; EU: *Mallis v European Commission* (C-105/15 P) EU:C:2016:702; [2017] 1 C.M.L.R. 36; *Ledra Advertising Ltd v European Commission* (C-8/15 P) EU:C:2016:701; [2017] 1 C.M.L.R. 35.
14 Treaty Concerning the Establishment of the Republic of Cyprus, No. 5476 (16 August 1960) <https://peacemaker.un.org/sites/peacemaker.un.org/files/CY_600816_TreatyNicosia.pdf> accessed 24 April 2022.
15 Costas Stamatiou, 'Cyprus's Bank Resolution Framework: Tested in the Fire' (2015) 30 J Intl Bank Law Rev 171.
16 Republic of Cyprus, *About Cyprus* (Press and Information Office, 2001) 151.

17 Elias Neocleous, 'Cyprus: The Offshore Regime And Cyprus' Accession To The European Union – The Offshore Regime of Cyprus' (3 December 1997) <www.mondaq.com/cyprus/x/3199/Environmental+Law/The+Offshore+Regime+And+Cyprus+Accession+To+The+European+Union+The+Offshore+Regime+of+Cyprus> accessed 24 April 2022.
18 Panicos Demetriades, 'Political Economy of a Euro Area Banking Crisis' (2017) 41 Cam J Econ 1249–64, 1257.
19 Demetra Arsalidou and Maria Krambia-Kapardis, 'Weak Corporate Governance Can Lead to a Country's Financial Catastrophe: The Case of Cyprus' (2015) 4 J Bib Lit 361–82, 363.
20 Demetriades, 'Political Economy of a Euro Area Banking Crisis' (n 22).
21 The hypothesis of financial instability in similar circumstances was first laid down by Minsky: HP Minsky, *The Financial Instability Hypothesis* (Levy Economics Institute of Bard College, Working Paper No. 74, 1992).
22 David Lascelles and others, 'Independent Commission on the Future of the Cyprus Banking Sector: Final Report' (31 October 2013) 23 <www.centralbank.cy/images/media/pdf/LSE_ICFCBS_Final_Report_10_13.pdf> accessed 24 April 2022 (ICFCBS Report).
23 Group comprised by Ministers of Finance in Member States that have the Euro as their currency.
24 Panicos Demetriades, *A Diary of the Euro Crisis in Cyprus: Lessons for Bank Recovery and Resolution* (Palgrave Macmillan, 2017) 84.
25 Demetriades, 'Political Economy of a Euro Area Banking Crisis' (n 22) 1257.
26 Costas Xiouros, 'Handling of the Emergency Liquidity Assistance of Laiki Bank in the Bailout Package of Cyprus' (21 April 2013) <https://papers.ssrn.com/sol3/papers.cfm?abstract_id=2254499< accessed 24 April 2022.
27 The largest bank of Cyprus in 2013. Initiated through the Regulatory Administrative Act No 103, EE, Annex III(I), No 4645, 769–80, 29 March 2013 (Decree 103) that was adopted by Resolution of Credit and Other Institutions Law 17(I)/2013.
28 The second largest bank of Cyprus in 2013. Initiated through Regulatory Administrative Act No 104, EE, Annex III(I), No 4645, 781–88, 29 March 2013 (Decree 104) that was adopted by Resolution of Credit and Other Institutions Law 17(I)/2013.
29 Andrew Campbell and Paula Moffatt, 'Protecting Bank Depositors after Cyprus' (2013) 1 NIBLeJ 4.
30 Demetriades, 'Political Economy of a Euro Area Banking Crisis' (n 22) 1249.
31 Sections 5 and 6 of this chapter.
32 Resolution of Credit and Other Institutions Law 17(I)/2013.
33 Stamatiou (n 19) 171.
34 A post-surveillance program was activated until 2029 provided that the 75% of all debt is repaid: 'Post-Programme Surveillance Report Cyprus' (Autumn 2018) <https://ec.europa.eu/info/sites/info/files/economy-finance/ip092_en.pdf> accessed 24 April 2022.
35 Peter Lim Felton, 'Too Big to Manage: A Case for Stricter Bank Merger Regulation' (2012) 52 Santa Clara Law Rev 1081.
36 Cranston and others (n 12) 11.
37 Gara Afonso, Joao Santos, James Traina, 'Do 'Too Big To Fail Banks Take On More Risk?' (2014) 20 Fed Res Bank New York, Econ Pol Rev, Special Issue: Large and Complex Banks 1–18, 1.
38 Excessive risk-taking without considering the adverse consequences as there is a feeling that a safety net is in place.
39 Demetriades, *A Diary of the Euro Crisis in Cyprus* (n 28) 54.
40 ibid 55.
41 ICFCBS Report (n 26).
42 ibid.

43 ibid.
44 PIMCO, 'Independent Due Diligence of the Banking System of Cyprus' (March 2013) <http://ftalphaville.ft.com/files/2013/04/reportasws.pdf.pdf> accessed 24 April 2022.
45 Alvarez & Marsal, 'Investigation Report, Bank of Cyprus – Holdings of Greek Government Bonds' (26 March 2013) <www.news.cyprus-property-buyers.com/wp-content/uploads/2013/04/April04_2013_AM.pdf> accessed 12 April 2022.
46 Alexander Michaelides, 'Cyprus: From Boom to Bail-In' (2014) 29(80) Econ Pol 639–89, 670.
47 ibid.
48 The Central Bank of Cyprus grants liquidity to the bank through ELA only if the bank is solvent.
49 Antonis Antoniou, 'Λαϊκή: Καταστροφή εξ Ελλάδος' (15 April 2013) <www.sigmalive.com/inbusiness/news/business/40289/laiki-katastrofi-eks-ellados> accessed 24 April 2022.
50 ICFCBS Report (n 26) 23.
51 ibid.
52 Demetriades, *A Diary of the Euro Crisis in Cyprus* (n 28) 197.
53 Thomas Huertas, 'Will Bust Banks Be Born Again by Bail-In?' (2019) 4 JIBFL 224.
54 Daniel Stavárek, *Lessons Learned from the 2013 Banking Crisis in Cyprus* (Proceedings of the 10th International Scientific Conference, 10–11 June 2013).
55 Elias Neocleous and Maria Kyriacou, 'Cyprus: A Colonial Inheritance' (11 March 2013) <www.mondaq.com/cyprus/x/226084/offshore+financial+centres/A+Colonial+Inheritance> accessed 24 April 2022.
56 Leslie Teo and others (eds), *Financial Sector Crisis and Restructuring Lessons from Asia* (International Monetary Fund, Occasional Paper No. 188, 2000).
57 EBA (n 2).
58 The World Bank, 'Bank Nonperforming Loans to Total Gross Loans (%) – Cyprus' <https://data.worldbank.org/indicator/FB.AST.NPER.ZS?locations=CY> accessed 24 April 2022.
59 European Banking Authority, 'Risk Dashboard-Data as of Q4 2020' <www.eba.europa.eu/sites/default/documents/files/document_library/Risk%20Analysis%20and%20Data/Risk%20dashboard/Q4%202020/972092/EBA%20Dashboard%20-%20Q4%202020.pdf> accessed 24 April 2022.
60 ibid.
61 Andrew Campbell, 'Bank Insolvency and the Problem of Non-Performing Loans' (2007) 9(1) J Bank Reg 28.
62 ibid.
63 Bank of Cyprus, 'Agreement for Sale of a Portfolio of Non-Performing Loans' (28 August 2018) <www.bankofcyprus.com/globalassets/investor-relations/press-releases/eng/20180828-helixannouncement_eng_final.pdf> accessed 24 April 2022.
64 Bank of Cyprus, 'Completion of Project Helix 2 (Portfolios A and B) – Sale of Non-Performing Loans' (28 June 2021) <https://bankofcyprus.com/globalassets/investor-relations/press-releases/eng/20210628-helix-2_completion_announcement_eng_final.pdf> accessed 24 April 2022.
65 Cat Rutter Pooley and Robert Smith, 'Bank of Cyprus Sells €2.7bn Bad Loans to Apollo' (*Financial Times*, 28 August 2018) <www.ft.com/content/25cb5846-aa8b-11e8-89a1-e5de165fa619> accessed 24 April 2022.
66 PIMCO (n 48) 12.
67 Demetriades, *A Diary of the Euro Crisis in Cyprus* (n 28) 188.
68 IMF, 'Cyprus' (November 2018) <www.imf.org/~/media/Files/Publications/CR/2018/cr18338.ashx> accessed 11April 2022.
69 Sofronis Clerides, 'The Collapse of the Cypriot Banking System: A Bird's Eye View' (2014) 8(2) Cyp Econ Pol Rev 3–35, 25.
70 ibid.

71 Demetriades, *A Diary of the Euro Crisis in Cyprus* (n 28) 188–89.
72 Scott Brown, Demetra Demetriou and Panayiotis Theodossiou, 'Banking Crisis in Cyprus: Causes, Consequences and Recent Developments' (2018) 22(1–2) Multi Fin J 63–118, 99.
73 Immovable Property (Transfer and Mortgage) Law 1965 (9/1965) Part VIA, s 44E (1).
74 ibid Part VIA, s 44E (4).
75 ibid Part VIA, s 44D (1), s 44IA (1).
76 Maria Kyriacou, 'Supreme Court's Role in Reviewing Proposed Legislation' (2014) Intl Law Off <www.neocleous.com/publications/reviewing-proposed-legislation-pdf> accessed 24 April 2022.
77 Examinership is the first procedure that was introduced in Cyprus that has as a purpose the corporate rescue. The initiation of an insolvency law framework and of the rescue option for distressed companies was in the requirements of Troika in 2013.
78 Arsalidou and Krambia-Kapardis (n 23) 361–82.
79 ibid.
80 G Pikis, A Kramvis and E Nicolaou, 'Three-Member Investigative Committee on the Banking and Finance of the Republic of Cyprus' (28 September 2013) <www.stockwatch.com.cy/media/announce_pdf/Report_Committee_Ypourgiko_3.10.2013.pdf> accessed 24 April 2022.
81 ibid.
82 Christian Duve and Philip Wimalasena, 'Who Decides Whether Bail-In Is Legal? What Comes After Cyprus and Greece?' (2015) 9(3) Law Fin Mark Rev 177–86.
83 Gikas Hardouvelisa and Ioannis Gkionis, 'A Decade Long Economic Crisis: Cyprus Versus Greece' (2016) 10(2) Cyp Econ Pol Rev 3–40, 16; Demetriades, *A Diary of the Euro Crisis in Cyprus* (n 28).
84 Demetriades, 'Political Economy of a Euro Area Banking Crisis' (n 22) 1260.
85 Bank of Cyprus, 'Recapitalisation through Bail-in and Resolution Exit Bank of Cyprus Announcement' <www.bankofcyprus.com/en-GB/Start/News_Archive/Recapitalisation-through-Bail-in-and-Resolution-Exit-Bank-of-Cyprus-Announcement/> accessed 24 April 2022.
86 Brown, Demetriou and Theodossiou (n 76) 85.
87 Thomas Huertas, 'The Case for Bail-Ins' in A Dombret and P Kenadjian (eds), *The Bank Recovery and Resolution Directive* (De Gruyter, 2013) 4.
88 Maurice Mendelson and Martins Paparinskis, 'Bail-Ins and the International Investment Law of Expropriation: In and Beyond Cyprus' (2013) 28 J Intl Bank Fin Law 475–79, 475.
89 Managing Director and Chair of the Board of the IMF.
90 IMF, 'Press Release: IMF Executive Board Approves €1 Billion Arrangement Under Extended Fund Facility for Cyprus' (15 May 2013) <www.imf.org/en/News/Articles/2015/09/14/01/49/pr13175> accessed 24 April 2022.
91 Ian Jack and Tom Cassels, 'Cyprus: An Analysis of the Impact of the Resolution Methodology on Stakeholders' Claims Including the Emergency Liquidity Assistance' (2013) 8(4) Cap Mark Law J 450–63, 453.
92 Campbell and Moffatt (n 33).
93 Bank of England, 'Financial Services Compensation Scheme' <www.bankofengland.co.uk/prudential-regulation/authorisations/financial-services-compensation-scheme#:~:text=Amounts%20of%20compensation%3A%20deposits,-Customer%20deposits%20held&text=The%20deposit%20protection%20limit%20applies,to%20two%20times%20%C2%A385%2C000.> accessed 24 April 2022.
94 Niall Lenihan, 'How Has the EU Protected Depositors in the Financial Crisis?' (2014) 16 Cam Yearbook Euro Leg Stud 289–312, 304.
95 Andrew Campbell and Peter Cartwright, *Banks in Crisis* (Ashgate, 2001) 193.

96 ibid.
97 Brown, Demetriou and Theodossiou (n 76) 8.
98 ibid; Matthew Klein, 'How Did Cypriots Respond to the 2013 Banking Crisis?' (20 March 2018) <www.ft.com/content/6c337371-0c34-38f4-9330-2ac88c0b7ce2> accessed 24 April 2022.
99 Jon Danielsson and Ragnar Arnason, 'Capital Controls Are Exactly Wrong for Iceland' (14 November 2011) <https://voxeu.org/article/iceland-and-imf-why-capital-controls-are-entirely-wrong> accessed 24 April 2022.
100 Jon Danielsson, 'The Capital Controls in Cyprus and the Icelandic Experience' 28 March 2013 <https://voxeu.org/article/capital-controls-cyprus-and-icelandic-experience> accessed 12 April 2022.
101 ibid.
102 ibid.
103 Frances Coppola, 'Capital Controls in the Eurozone: Restricting International Trade to Preserve It' (24 June 2019) <www.americanexpress.com/en-gb/business/trends-and-insights/articles/capital-controls-in-the-eurozone/> accessed 12 April 2022.
104 Treaty on the Functioning of the European Union (TFEU), Article 63; Martin Sandbu, 'Legal Debate Over Cyprus Capital Controls' (25 March 2013) <www.ft.com/content/a723d6e4-955a-11e2-a151-00144feabdc0> accessed 12 April 2022.
105 Alexander Apostolides, 'Beware of German Gifts Near Elections: How Cyprus Got Here and Why It Is Currently More Out Than in the Eurozone' (2013) 8(3) Cap Mark Law J 300–18.
106 Supreme Court of Cyprus 07/06/2013, Case No. 553/2013: *Myrto Christodoulou and Others v Kentriki Trapeza Kyprou and Others a.o.*; Supreme Court of Cyprus 09/10/2014, Case No. 1034/2013: *Vias Dimitriou and Others v Kentrikis Trapezas Kyprou and Others).*
107 Constitution of Cyprus, Article 23.
108 Constitution of Cyprus, Article 28.
109 For a criticism of the Supreme Court's decision see: Jenny Giotaki, 'The Cypriot "Bail-In Litigation": A First Assessment of the Ruling of the Supreme Court of Cyprus' (2013) 8 JIBFL 485.
110 (C-105/15 P) EU:C:2016:702; [2017] 1 C.M.L.R. 36.
111 (C-8/15 P) EU:C:2016:701; [2017] 1 C.M.L.R. 35.
112 ibid para 24.
113 ibid paras 57–58.
114 In their decision they applied the logic from the *Thomas Pringle v Government of Ireland and Others* (C-370/12) ECLI:EU:C:2012:756.
115 Charter of Fundamental Rights of the European Union (2010/ C 83/02) OJ EU 30.3.2010 C83/389, Article 52.
116 *Ledra*, para 74.
117 Mikaella Yiatrou, 'The Myth of Cypriot Bank Resolution "Success": A Plea for a More Holistic and Less Costly Supervision & Resolution Approach' (2017) 18(3) Euro Bus Org Law Rev 503–33.
118 Napoleon Xanthoulis, 'ESM, Union Institutions and EU Treaties: A Symbiotic Relation' (2017) 1 Int J for Fin Ser 21–33.
119 Michael Schillig, *Resolution and Insolvency of Banks and Financial Institutions* (OUP, 2016) 54–55.
120 BRRD, Recitals 5–14.
121 BRRD, Article 32(1)(c); Resolution Law 2016, Article 42(1)(c).
122 BRRD, Articles 31, 32(5); Single Resolution Mechanism Regulation, Article 18(5); Resolution Law 2016, Article 42(3).
123 BRRD, Article 36(8); Resolution Law 2016, Article 47(8)(a).
124 BRRD, Article 38(1); Resolution Law 2016, Article 48.

125 BRRD, Article 40; Resolution Law 2016, Article 50.
126 BRRD, Article 42; Resolution Law 2016, Article 52.
127 Andromachi Georgosouli, 'The Transnational Governance of Bank Resolution and the Treatment of National Regulatory Variation in the E' (2021) 80(1) C Law J 74–100, 75.
128 Thomas Huertas, 'Necessary but Not Sufficient: Stay Upon Resolution via Bail-In' (2020) 4 JIBFL 235.
129 BRRD 43(2)(a) and (b); Resolution Law 2016, Article 53(1)(a) and (b).
130 BRRD 44(2)(a)-(g); Resolution Law 2016, Article 54(2)(a)-(g).
131 BRRD 44(3); Resolution Law 2016, Article 54(6).
132 Emilios Avgouleas and Charles Goodhart, 'Critical Reflections on Bank Bail-ins' (2015) 1 J Fin Reg 3–29.
133 This is further supported in Regulation 806/2014 Article 15(1)(g); See also the following: J. Doyne Farmer, Charles Goodhart and Alissa Kleinnijenhuis, 'The Current Bail-InDesignDoesNotResolvetheToo-Big-To-FailProblem'(1October2021)<https://voxeu.org/article/current-bail-design-does-not-resolve-too-big-fail-problem> accessed 12 April 2022.
134 BRRD, Article 27; Resolution Law 2016, Articles 23–29.
135 BRRD, Article 29; Resolution Law 2016, Articles 46 (called special administrator by this legislation).
136 Brown, Demetriou and Theodossiou (n 76).
137 Avgouleas and Goodhart (n 136).
138 Michael Schillig, 'EU Bank Insolvency Law Harmonisation: What Next?' [2021] Intl Insol Rev 1–28, 13–15.

8 Bank Insolvencies and the UNCITRAL Model Law

Clara de Sousa Alves and Pedro Ferreirinha

Introduction

The proliferation of cross-border insolvencies in the last decade suggests that international insolvency law, despite recent efforts of policy makers, needs to keep pace with the reasons and outcomes associated with these insolvencies. While transnational insolvencies increased dramatically as a result of globalisation and increased international trade, the 2008 global financial crisis also accentuated the need to properly manage these insolvency proceedings. Of course, we could not overstate the impact of the Covid-19 pandemic on the stability of the world economic system.

With the increase in incidences of cross-border insolvencies, the UNCITRAL Model Law[1] has become an important instrument for harmonising the rules on cross-border insolvency proceedings. However, the development of the Model Law was brought about as existing domestic legal regimes could not deal with the increasing number of cross-border insolvencies and the corresponding legal complexities.

With this and many other questions in mind, we divided our paper into three parts. Firstly, we examine why banks[2] need a different legal regime from that which applies to non-financial institutions; we also examine what issues arise from cross-border insolvencies and how this feeds into the optimal legal framework for regulating distressed multinational banks. Secondly, we analyse how the UNCITRAL Model Law's principles could be taken into account in the matter of bank insolvencies. In that regard, we scrutinise the nature, organisation, advantages and challenges of this framework as well as its key implications for banks. Third, we dedicate the final aspect of our paper to post-pandemic insolvencies, where we explore a set of possible reforms that could alleviate insolvency problems in future economic crises.

A Special Regime for Banks

Banking is, by default, an inherently risky business. Banks are highly leveraged credit institutions that accept unsecured deposits from the public at large and extend loans to individuals and businesses. These institutions also raise debt to invest in risky assets. Adding to this risk is "the maturity and liquidity

DOI: 10.4324/9781003173984-10

transformation that banks tend to engage in: their assets tend to be longer-term and less liquid than their liabilities".[3] Being exposed to risk, means being potentially exposed to failure, and, ultimately, to insolvency. Whereas in general insolvency law, 'insolvency' can traditionally be defined as the "failure to pay obligations as they fall due (equitable/cash-flow insolvency)", or "the condition when liabilities exceed assets (balance sheet insolvency)",[4] in relation to banks, the determination of regulatory insolvency is "generally based on a process of risk evaluation and capital measurement".[5] This means that it is the banking supervisory authority that determines when there is a ground for intervention and, therefore, when a bank is insolvent.[6]

So, why should banks be accorded a special insolvency treatment in comparison with other industries? Why is a special regulatory regime for insolvent banks needed, rather than a corporate insolvency law? The simple answer is that banks play a special role in a country's economy. There is a close linkage between the health of the real economy and the financial stability, meaning that "collectively, their functions are so important as to constitute a sort of public service".[7] In order to justify any special policy treatment of banks, reference is commonly made to the systemic effects of bank failures, the public interest, the level of public confidence and the need for a discreet resolution mechanism. There are three characteristic functions of banks that should be highlighted in this matter.[8] First, banks typically hold highly liquid liabilities in the form of customer deposits; while such funds might legally be owned by the bank,[9] they are, nevertheless, repayable to the customer on demand. On the asset side, however, a bank generally holds assets in the form of loans. This creates future liquidity when, according to the loan contracts, the bank's counter parties reimburse the bank.[10] Secondly, banks perform financial services that are essential to the functioning of an economy, due to their role in facilitating the free-flow of credit, taking deposits and processing payments. In this regard, the emergence of capital markets in the credit intermediation process and their capacity to mobilise capital does not dislodge the role and value of banks.[11] Third, banks constitute "the means of transmission for monetary policy, that is, the link between the monetary policy process and the economy".[12]

That being said, it is vital to ask another question: Can banks go bankrupt as any other non-financial institution? "Banks that are no longer viable, should be allowed to fail".[13] However, there is an understanding that some banks are so important that they should receive financial assistance to the necessary extent to keep them from failing: a commonly known doctrine referred to as "too-big-to-fail". Recently, one could point that there are more banks that would be considered "too-big-to-fail". There are three big reasons that are behind this premise. First is the consolidation process within the banking sector; the banking sector is one controlled by financial conglomerates. Second is linked to technological advances, which require big banks to play a more significant role in payment systems and rely on uninsured wholesale funding. Lastly, the activities of major banks are increasing in complexity and, perhaps, one might suggest that these banks have now become "too complex to fail".[14]

In the event that a core bank is in distress, governments and central banks take the first actions to cover creditors' losses (except for shareholders and bondholders) and, ultimately, organise a bailout.[15] It must be noted that the banking legislation of most countries does not envisage the emergency actions to be taken in case a bank runs into a crisis. This approach arises from a prudential principle, known as "constructive ambiguity", intentionally done so that banks do not predict a government's response.[16] Following the prudential principle, the main goal of a bank resolution regime should be to protect financial stability. Therefore, the resolution framework must be designed in a way that permits early intervention in order to preserve the bank's value, its viability or, where the latter is impossible, to ensure that the bank is liquidated in a proper manner (so that its liquidation has as little impact as possible).[17] Priority should be given to "minimise the economic impact of bank failures through ensuring the continuous smooth function of payment and settlements systems, protecting the depositing public and preserving banks important credit intermediation function".[18] Furthermore, the regulatory framework must deal not only with the problems of how to prevent banks from falling, but also with falling banks that are on the way to fail, since bank failures happen notwithstanding the best efforts of prudential regulation, supervision and oversight.[19] On the other hand, bank insolvency rules are designed not only to secure the stability of the financial system, but also to protect the interests of the depositor, as well as general economic interests. These measures serve two main objectives: to rescue a bank and preclude liquidation, as well as to protect the rights of the bank's creditors and its assets in the course of resolving its pecuniary problems.

In conclusion, as demonstrated by the recent financial crisis, there is an urgent need for special resolution regimes, designed for banks, outside the general corporate insolvency framework. The concept of insolvency, as planned under the general insolvency law is inappropriate for these institutions. Bank insolvencies are plainly different to general company insolvencies as exemplified by the desire for governments to intervene. Consequently, different rules should be considered, with a different scope, objective and nature. The extent to which such rules are needed may vary from country to country. It depends on the "flexibility of the judicial system and the relationship between banking and insolvency law".[20]

Aspects on Cross-Border Insolvencies

Having analysed why banks need special treatment, it is time to ask the following questions: what should be the ethos of the legal framework for regulating multinational banks in distress? Moreover, what issues arise and what rules are applied during cross-border insolvencies?

First, banking is a business without borders. One can point to four key factors that are responsible for the globalization of financial services:

> financial liberalisation, where countries allow the operation of foreign financial institutions; risk diversification, where financial institutions have

the opportunity to diversify their risk and look for new business opportunities in overseas markets; servicing key corporate clients, where banks support corporations expanded abroad and profit from their expansion plans; and lastly, brand value concerning emerging markets, where a brand is internationally recognized and has a local presence in foreign markets.[21]

Secondly, taking these factors into account, banks have organised themselves in multinational structures, thus creating a global financial network with a centralised funding. These entities are generally composed of a head office with attached branches in multiple countries, rather than as a corporate group with subsidiaries.

Third, when dealing with insolvencies of multinational banks, the importance of harmonised policies, synchronised actions and the application of coordinated resolution systems is widely recognised. It is important to state that "a resolution system cannot be effective unless the framework applicable on a cross-border basis is developed".[22] In fact, although national corporate and bank insolvency laws are fundamental when addressing cross-border insolvencies, they are not, *per se*, enough to fully protect the legal interests at stake. Indeed, in the absence of an international regime, the resolution of cross-border institutions is subject to different national laws which require multi-jurisdictional cooperation; this is not always available.[23]

Finally, there are standard international rules governing the failure of financial companies and banks, which can be grouped into: multilateral agreements (such as Convention on Private International Law and Convention Regarding Bankruptcy – Nordic Bankruptcy Convention); private international norms (such as the Principles of Cooperation in Transnational Insolvency Cases, or the Cross-Border Insolvency Concordat), the European Union's insolvency measures (such as the EC Regulation on Insolvency Proceedings); and the UNCITRAL Model Law. Even though all of these regimes are very different, they are all designed to harmonise separate national insolvency proceedings which involve an internationally active debtor. Following the scope of this article, we will not analyse all these international measures, but we will focus and dedicate our research to the UNCITRAL Model Law and its principles in the following chapters.

The UNCITRAL Model Law on Cross-Border Insolvencies

The Need for an International Agreement

When hearing about this topic (unknown to some countries), there are some questions that immediately arise. Why is it so important to talk about cross-border insolvencies in a banking context? What does the United Nations and its commission on international trade law have to do with this subject? Is UNCITRAL Model Law a potential solution for the coordination of international insolvencies? If so, what step is missing? Why was this convention not widely adopted by states?[24]

Well, as we saw in the previous section, there is a symbiotic relationship between viable banks and the stability of the financial system, and that is why banks need special treatment in comparison with other financial companies. The purpose for the application of special rules during bank insolvency cases is allied with public interest in financial stability and with the systemic effects bank failures may cause. Therefore, the existence of a legal framework for bank insolvency is extremely important. But the difficulty with most insolvency cases these days is that they are not contained within one jurisdiction. The phenomenal growth in international trade and investments has increased the incidence of corporate entities having businesses, assets, debtors and creditors in more than one country.[25] Actually, there are multinational empires[26] like "real corporate archipelagos", stretching across the globe.[27]

One disadvantage of such a global marketplace is that it brings about a corresponding risk of cross-border insolvencies since the risk of business failure is no longer geographically limited.[28] In truth, with the increasing globalization of businesses with assets in several countries, there is a need for a common set of insolvency rules across nations.[29] As an example, we can point out the widely recognised "Maxwell Communications Corporation, the Bank of Credit and Commerce International" and the "Lehman Brothers" cases.[30] As a result, the need to create a stable environment for international trade to be able to operate required the design of specific rules regarding cross-border insolvency.

In short, cross-border insolvency is a term used to describe the circumstances in which an insolvent debtor has assets and/or creditors in more than one country.[31] UNCITRAL, through its influence in international trade and commerce, is in a unique position to raise the level of awareness among nations of the problems and difficulties and to encourage the development and common application of basic attitudes towards recognition and assistance.[32] Before moving on to the analysis of the UNCITRAL Model Law on cross-border insolvency, it is important to address, briefly and in first line, the problems that govern cross-border insolvency which this convention aims to solve. Some of these issues consist of inefficiency, lack of speed and high costs.[33] These problems are easily explained because insolvency rules are in different languages, in different countries, with different traditions and under different legal systems. Put differently, there are no universal and uniform rules, and each country has its own laws for resolving the insolvency scenario.

Another complication related to cross-border insolvencies is the emergence of conflicts of laws. These issues are bound to arise especially in relation to the recognition of court decisions and regulations of foreign jurisdictions, judicial recognition and enforcement of foreign judicial proceedings, recognition of the claims of foreign creditors, and the differences in the applicable laws regarding the disposal of assets.[34] We ought also to point out that, while transnational insolvencies increased dramatically as a result of globalization and increased international trade, the global financial crisis caused a global focus-shift to the management of these proceedings in ordinary corporate and banking contexts.[35] Moreover, the widespread nature of cases associated with the global financial crisis highlighted the need for a robust, cooperative and harmonised regulation in transnational insolvency cases. The Model Law has enabled the introduction of this type of regulation, and, arguably, in the countries where it has been adopted disputes have been resolved more efficiently and with adherence to published rules.[36]

Is the UNCITRAL Model Law a Potential Solution on Cross-Border Bank Insolvencies Issues?

Historically, 1994 marks the year that UNCITRAL together with INSOL International (an international association of restructuring, insolvency, and bankruptcy professionals) held the first of two preliminary international colloquia specifically planned to discuss international insolvencies issues. One year after, following the success of the first event, UNCITRAL and INSOL International co-hosted the second colloquium that culminated later that year, in the beginning of a project to draft a Model Law on cross-border insolvency by the United Nations Commission on International Trade Law.[37] On 15 December 1997, the working group responsible for this project achieved a consensus (in a remarkably short period of time) and immediately after, the United Nations recommended the adoption of the Model Law on Cross-border Insolvency by Member States as part of domestic legislation. In that year, the General Assembly of the United Nations passed a resolution (*inter alia*) recommending that all States review their legislation on cross-border aspects of insolvency to determine whether the legislation met the objectives of a modern and efficient insolvency system.[38] The resolution went on to ask that States give favourable consideration to enacting the Model Law on Cross-Border Insolvency which had been developed by the Working Group on Insolvency Law and adopted by UNCITRAL, "bearing in mind the need for an internationally harmonised legislation governing instances of cross-border insolvency".[39]

In fact, the Model Law was a unilateral legislative framework for cross-border insolvencies, focusing upon what is required to facilitate the management of cross-border insolvency cases and providing an interface between jurisdictions. The Model Law was designed to "assist States to equip their insolvency laws with a modern, harmonised and fair framework to address more effectively instances of cross-border insolvency ".[40] Hence, the Model Law does not attempt to unify the substantive insolvency laws of different countries, but rather focuses on encouraging cooperation and coordination between jurisdictions.[41]

The text covers foreign proceedings relating to insolvency where the purpose of the proceeding is reorganisation or liquidation of the debtor if the proceeding is "collective" and assets and affairs of the debtor are subject to court control or supervision.[42] Exclusions are contemplated by the Model Law and banking and insurance intuitions are a common example; exclusions for financial and investment institutions, clearing houses and commodity brokers have also been introduced in some enacting legislation.[43] In general terms, the purpose of the Model Law is to provide effective mechanisms in dealing with cross-border insolvency cases through a simplified regime.[44] In sum, the Model Law is a short document consisting of only thirty-two articles and accompanied by an explanatory Guide to Enactment.

The UNCITRAL Model Law on cross-border insolvency is based on four principles of "access" by a foreign representative to the courts of the enacting State, "recognition" by the state of the foreign proceedings, "relief" which ensures the granting of interim reliefs pending recognition and "co-operation" and "co-ordination" which require courts and insolvency administrators in various states to communicate and cooperate for maximization of assets for the benefit of all creditors. Moreover, we can say that the "access principle" establishes the circumstances in which a foreign insolvency representative has rights of access to the receiving court in the enacting State from which recognition and relief are sought. The "recognition principle" permits the receiving court to make an order recognising the foreign insolvency proceedings (either as a foreign main or non-main proceeding). The "relief principle" applies to three distinct situations. Interim relief may be granted to protect assets within the jurisdiction of the receiving court where an application for recognition is pending. Automatic relief applies if a receiving court recognises the foreign proceedings as a main proceeding. Finally, discretionary relief is available, in addition to automatic relief, in respect of main proceedings as well as recognised non-main proceedings. The "cooperation and coordination principle" places obligations on both courts and insolvency representatives in different jurisdictions to communicate and cooperate to the maximum extent possible, to ensure that a debtor's insolvent estate is administered fairly and efficiently, with a view to maximizing benefits to creditors.[45]

Finally, we can conclude that the Model Law has well-defined parameters. First, the Model Law applies to insolvency proceedings where a foreign representative or foreign creditor requests assistance, or otherwise wishes to commence or participate in a proceeding, in a local court. Second, the Model Law applies when a local court requests assistance from a foreign representative or foreign court. Third, the Model Law governs concurrent, domestic, and foreign insolvency proceedings pending simultaneously. It is therefore evident from our discussion on the contemporary nature of banks that, bar the Model Law's obvious exclusion of banking institutions, the Model Law's ethos would fit the organisational and other cross-border issues associated with bank insolvencies.

Nature and Organisation

The Model Law on cross-border insolvency, unlike a multilateral convention, merely provides a legislative guide for States to modify their laws in order to ensure the consistency of insolvency laws and practices between different countries. Thus, it confers a State the freedom to decide how it wishes to incorporate the Model Law into its domestic legislation.[46] Moreover, it has well-defined parameters and also provides clear definitions for key terms used through its text. This means that the Model Law on Cross-Border Insolvency provides clear definitive guidelines on how to handle interpretation issues and conflicts of laws.

Regarding the division, the Model Law is divided into five chapters, each dealing with a different aspect of cross-border insolvency.[47] Chapter I lays down the scope of application of the law, certain definitions and other preliminary provisions.

Chapter II provides for the access of foreign representatives and creditors in insolvency proceedings having a trans-boundary nature. Chapter III provides for the recognition of foreign proceedings and associated relief. Chapter IV is concerned upon cooperation between courts in different jurisdictions and the insolvency representatives themselves. Chapter V addresses the confusing issue of commencing and coordinating simultaneous local and foreign insolvency proceedings. Chapter V is broken down into five articles, three of which directly address the problems involved in concurrent and multiple proceedings.[48]

In view of its advantages, there have been many incentives for the application of this Model Law on cross-border insolvency. Since the creation of the Model Law in May 1997, UNCITRAL has also vigorously pushed for the adoption of the Model Law by States. For example, UNCITRAL provided a useful Guide to the Enactment of the Model Law 1997. It apparently considered that the Model Law would be more effectively used by legislators if the Guide could give a "background and explanatory information". In 2004, UNCITRAL produced a Legislative Guide on Insolvency Law for the use of States when enacting new or reviewing existing insolvency laws. In 2009, UNCITRAL published the Practice Guide on Cross-Border Insolvency Cooperation. This document provides information for insolvency practitioners and judges on cooperation and communication in cross-border insolvency cases.

In addition, UNCITRAL provides technical assistance to promote its work and "the use and adoption of the legislative and non-legislative texts it has developed to further the progressive harmonization and unification of private law". UNCITRAL's technical assistance is readily available to States considering adopting the Model Law as part of their domestic insolvency legislation.[49] Efforts to implement this Model Law are visible and an example of this is the fact that several global institutions have recommended the adoption of the Model Law. The International Monetary Fund in 1999 recommended the adoption of the Model Law as an "effective means" of encouraging judiciary and regulators of different nations to recognise foreign proceedings as well as to enhance their cooperation and coordination in cross-border insolvencies.

Advantages

The Model Law on Cross-Border Insolvency essentially has two main objectives. The first is to implement a more coherent and efficient international insolvency legal system. In pursuing this goal, the Model Law requires cooperation between the courts, provides for fair and efficient proceedings, and protects the interests of all parties including foreign and domestic creditors. The second goal of the Model Law is derivative of the first. Through the creation of a more structured international insolvency legal framework, the Model Law seeks to further the interests of the economic community.[50]

At first the Model Law on Cross-Border Insolvency permits and requires courts and administrators to cooperate with one another to the maximum extent possible. Second, the Model Law on cross-border insolvency enables a foreign insolvency administrator or representative to have standing in a local proceeding and to obtain relief in an efficient manner. Third, it requires a base level of equal treatment of foreign and local claims.[51] In a general sense, the adoption of the Model Law supports the rule of law by promoting an ordered approach to cross-border insolvencies. Where jurisdictions with which the debtor has relevant connections have adopted the Model Law, this can assist with harmonising the approach taken by insolvency representatives in those jurisdictions to effect a reorganization or liquidation. This in turn can maximise the value of the debtor's assets in the process. Further, the Model Law provides harmonisation both in access to the courts and in recognition and relief by those courts. Indeed, the concept of equality of treatment between local and foreign creditors can be found throughout the text of the Model Law.

Problems

The success of the Model Law "is heavily dependent upon whether, and in what manner, countries choose to enact it".[52] Fact shows that until May 2022 49 countries adopted the Model Law on cross-border insolvency into their national law. This raises the question: why have so many countries not yet adopted the Model Law on cross-border insolvency into their national law? It is arguable, and probably self-evident, that the more an international law instrument is adopted, the more it would be easier to achieve its designated objectives. The answer is that it is not a treaty or a convention but a recommended legislative text which does not compel adoption or implementation. Nonetheless, a favourable point is that, currently, there are few international law instruments that directly regulate cross-border insolvency. Furthermore, we must take into account that the Model Law is an instrument of soft law, and therefore, with limited binding power.[53] As an example of a successful soft law (in the same mould of the Model Law), we point to the UNIDROIT Principles of International Commercial Contracts, which is also light-touch and non-binding in its principles. Similar to other model laws, the Model Law is arranged in order to become a source law with the aim of uniting the diversity of national laws. Nevertheless, it is still fully dependent on the legislators and courts (judicial and arbitral) to decide how far the Model Law could be adapted to support their insolvency problems. In order to encourage the adoption of the Model Law by States, the UNCITRAL promoted workshops, organised colloquia, incited discussions and public consultations which involved judges, government officials, insolvency experts and practitioners.[54] Despite all these efforts by the UNCITRAL, the Model Law on Cross-Border Insolvency has a low level of adoption. There are several causes that may explain why the Model Law on Cross-Border Insolvency is not widely adopted.

Firstly, the Model Law on Cross-Border Insolvency is not an international binding agreement. As stated before, it is a "recommendation" for a legislative text, therefore, it does not force a country to adopt or implement it. Secondly, even if a State decides to implement the Model Law, there is still an enormous freedom to decide how and to what extent include these principles into their domestic legislation. Thirdly, there is the classical issue regarding the need of maintaining a State sovereignty and enforcing their law, specifically with regard to assets in their own territory, so that it can be handled in accordance with the State's own law.[55] Fourth, several countries are focused on pursuing their own national interests. There is no branch of law that has formed more than the consideration of national economic policies and commercial philosophies.[56] Fifth, the international cooperation which is recommended by the Model Law is not always the main interest, other endemic interests may be at stake, especially in case of cross-border insolvencies subject to the local media and public oversight. Sixth, multiple countries are bound by international agreements on cross-border insolvency in their national legislation and/or other regional instruments that are considered more relevant than Model Law on Cross-Border Insolvency. The adoption of the Model Law could create legal problems for countries which are already bound by a convention or an international agreement on cross-border insolvency.

Finally, while the problem of independent insolvency is not, itself, a new problem, the truth is that, as we have seen, the resolution of the problem itself faces many obstacles with regard to differences in existing legal systems. However, nowadays, there has been an increasing volume of rules and regulations, directives, conventions, treaties, practice standards and guidelines on best practices about cross-border insolvency since the Model Law came into force.

Implications for Banks

In most jurisdictions, there are no specific rules to address the failure of a bank with foreign branches. As mentioned earlier, the UNCITRAL Model Law on Cross-Border Insolvency exempts banks from its scope. Therefore, one may ask: does this mean that the absence of special rules for dealing with banks that have established themselves in foreign jurisdictions is a sign that such rules are not necessary? Several failures of multinational banks and multiple international reports suggest exactly the contrary.

Banks are mentioned as examples of entities that a State might decide to exclude from the scope of the Model Law. The reason for the exclusion would typically be that the insolvency of such entities gives rise to a particular need to protect vital interests of a large number of individuals or that the insolvency of those entities usually requires particularly prompt and circumspect action in order to preserve wider goals, such as to avoid massive withdrawals of deposits. Nevertheless, policy considerations underlying special insolvencies regimes for those entities like banks call for special solutions in cross-border insolvency cases.[57]

In relation to our study, there are two elements of approach developed by UNCITRAL that we can point out as potentially relevant for banks and that should be taken into account in case of cross-border insolvencies. First, the UNCITRAL Model Law specifies the mechanisms for coordination between cross-border insolvency cases and judicial courts.[58] While the Model Law requires a court to recognise the existence of insolvency proceedings in other jurisdictions, it enables such a court to maintain broad discretion on the extent to which it would defer to the decisions and requests made by the courts and insolvency officials in other jurisdictions, particularly where local public considerations are involved. This means that coordination is aimed at reducing the potential for competing and inconsistent decisions on the assets and liabilities of the debtor.[59] Second, UNCITRAL addresses a number of specific procedural issues that could be inauspicious to coordination. However, it is important to reiterate that the UNCITRAL Model Law does not impose the substantive law which would be applicable to key transactions or assets. These issues are left to individual national laws. Lastly, the Model Law has the potential to facilitate unification and centralisation in insolvency proceedings. These principles suggest a close cooperation of countries and provide means by which foreign insolvency representatives (liquidators, administrators) may have access to courts in another jurisdiction.

Post-Pandemic Insolvencies: A Cursory Thought

Without doubt, the recent COVID-19 pandemic has had a negative impact on the global economy. Mostly, the impact of a global pandemic. Across the world, companies, regardless of their size, are experiencing harsh economic realities and facing contractions in production. Moreover, the COVID-19 pandemic has generated liquidity pressures for businesses, accelerated dynamic (and sometimes costly) changes to business models, while increasing the volume of viable businesses that could fall into insolvency (once all Government support is withdrawn). Apart from the economic disruption, the pandemic has also caused a liquidity shortfall for both businesses and individuals, weakening their ability to meet debt payment obligations which, ultimately, results in a in a wave of post-pandemic insolvencies. Given the scale and consequences of the current crisis we understand that a fundamental reform of insolvency law is urgently needed. In fact, post-pandemic insolvencies should not be seen as fatal, but as an opportunity to evolve. We support a set of possible reforms that could alleviate insolvency problems in future crises.

First, a potential measure would be to improve in-court insolvency procedures. Some insolvency cases are often resolved out-of-court which results in several negative consequences. For instance, out-of-court workouts often favour banks over other creditors, which, in turn, limits capital market development. Out-of-court restructuring is also less efficient when dealing with deeply distressed firms or complex capital structures that banks typically have. This is accentuated by the lack of transparency in out-of-court proceedings. Second, measures should be taken to facilitate and promote in-court restructuring/rescue as opposed to liquidation. Liquidation is not the optimum procedure for preserving viable-but-distressed banks (and indeed any other commercial entity). On the other hand, in-court restructuring also facilitates liquidity provision during the restructuring phase due, at least in part, to the confidence stakeholders will have in the proceedings due to the court's oversight. Third, it is important to make good use of pre-insolvency procedures or early intervention mechanisms in a timely fashion in order to avoid overlaps with existing in-court procedures triggered by insolvency.

To conclude, governments must confront this upcoming increase in insolvencies by strengthening insolvency regimes as well as developing agile preventative mechanisms and effective judicial processes. Taking these actions could generate considerable gains in the ability to mitigate future adverse shocks and build a more resilient insolvency international law.

Conclusion

We conclude this paper with a summary of our thoughts on the need of a bespoke cross-border insolvency framework for banks.

A Banks need special legal treatment in comparison with other non-financial companies. This special treatment is the result of a public interest in preserving and protecting the stability of the financial system. To achieve this common goal, banks are subject to special rules.

B In relation to our subject, bank insolvency laws address several issues, such as, legal measures for the management of a bank insolvency, principles concerning the cross-border bank insolvency, cross-border resolution framework, bank insolvency supervision/oversight, etc.

C Today, the financial services sector is widespread, and cross-border banking has expanded exponentially. Therefore, it is more important than ever to carefully regulate the insolvency of multinational banks on a transnational level.

D Although the number of cross-border insolvency cases has increased in line with the volume of cross-border commerce, the adoption of national or international legal regimes equipped to address the issues raised by those cases has not kept pace. The lack of such regimes has often resulted in inadequate and uncoordinated approaches to cross-border insolvency that are not only unpredictable and time-consuming in their application, but also lack transparency as well as tools that are optimal to address the disparities and, in some cases, conflicts that may occur between national laws and insolvency regimes. These factors have impeded the protection of the value of the assets of financially troubled businesses and hampered their rescue.

E With the aim of helping States to equip their insolvency laws with a modern legal framework to more effectively address cross-border insolvency proceedings concerning debtors experiencing severe financial distress or insolvency, the United Nations Commission on International Trade Law elaborated a Model Law on cross-border insolvency.

F This legal instrument focuses on authorising and encouraging cooperation and coordination between jurisdictions, rather than attempting the unification of substantive insolvency law, and respects the differences among national procedural laws.

G We can also say that the Model Law changed the way it reacted to a cross-border insolvency, promoting simple and efficient procedures and providing clear and intelligible guidelines to determine what type of relief can be expected and granted. The Model Law also contributed to the equal treatment of all national and foreign creditors. But, more importantly, the Model Law lifts the cloud of legal uncertainty surrounding international insolvency issues. By increasing predictability, the Model Law could foment economic efficiency and, in the end, the entire international community will benefit. Put pithily, the Model Law is a good procedural framework for the efficient administration of cross-border insolvencies.

H While disparity in municipal legislation, public policy, commercial and socio-legal issues might account for why several countries tend to reject the Model Law, we suggest that its principles along with those of its associated frameworks, could bring some value to cross-border bank insolvencies for a number of reasons. These include the fact that it offers a lot of flexibility in its adoption by the various countries (which enables a State to maintain its sovereignty in order to enforce its laws and give priority to what is best for their national interests); the focus on international cooperation/coordination, including encouraging participation in planning proceedings despite the default exclusion of banks from the purview of the regime; and the fact some states in developed and developing regions have already adopted the Model Law or other instruments on cross-border insolvency, can only be a net-positive in bank insolvency contexts as, following the application of special bank insolvency rules, the proceedings could revert to a framework that still prioritises cooperation, coordination and systemic interests.

Notes

1 'UNCITRAL Model Law on Cross-Border Insolvency' (1997) <https://uncitral.un.org/en/texts/insolvency/modellaw/cross-border_insolvency> accessed 21 January 2022.
2 This investigation focuses on clearing banks as opposed to investment banks. Investment banks have unique economic issues, which are generally beyond the scope of this article.
3 Wouter Bossu Wim Fonteyne and others, 'Crisis Management and Resolution for a European Banking System' International Monetary Fund <https://citeseerx.ist.psu.edu/viewdoc/download?doi=10.1.1.609.1872&rep=rep1&type=pdf> accessed 1 June 2022.
4 A useful discussion of these tests of insolvency would be seen in the United Kingdom's Supreme Court decision in *BNY Corporate Trustees Services Ltd v Eurosail-UK 2007–3BL plc* [2013] UKSC 28.
5 Eva HG Hüpkes, *The Legal Aspects of Bank Insolvency: A comparative Analysis of Western Europe, the United States and Canada* (Kluwer Law International, 2000).
6 Mariam Ioseliani, *Aspects of Bank Insolvency* (Erasmus Universiteit Rotterdam. Faculteit der Rechtsgeleerdheid ed, Erasmus Universiteit, 2011).
7 Hüpkes, *The Legal Aspects of Bank Insolvency* (n 5) 3.
8 Eva HG Hüpkes, 'Insolvency – Why a Special Regime for Banks?' in *Curriculam Development Monetary Finance Law* (vol 3, International Monetary Fund, Forthcoming) accessed 20 October 2020.
9 Otherwise, banks might not be able to lend those monies out and, therefore, lack the ability to generate assets. On the legal position in common law jurisdictions on the relationship between banks and customer deposits in bank accounts, a useful-long-standing

would be found in the United Kingdom's House of Lords decision in *Foley v Hill* (1848) 2 HLC 28, 9 ER 1002.

10 Bob Wessels, *Current Topics of International Insolvency Law* (Kluwer, 2004) 177.

11 Hüpkes, 'Insolvency – Why A Special Regime for Banks?' (n 8).

12 ibid.

13 David G Mayes, *An Approach to Bank Insolvency in Transition and Emerging Economies* (Bank of Finland Discussion Papers, Paper No. 4) <https://papers.ssrn.com/sol3/papers.cfm?abstract_id=504922> accessed 31 January 2022.

14 For a general sentiment on this point, see again, Ioseliani, *The Legal Aspects of Bank Insolvency* (n 5) 3.

15 ibid.

16 For criticism of this approach in the context of the failure of Northern Rock, see Bank of England, 'Ten Years On: Lessons from Northern Rock' (Single Resolution Board Annual Congress, Brussel (29 September 2017) <www.bankofengland.co.uk/-/media/boe/files/speech/2017/ten-years-on-lessons-from-northern-rock.pdf> accessed 1 June 2022.

17 Ross Leckow and Ceyla Pazarbasioglu, *Resolution of Cross-Border Banks: A Proposed Framework for Enhanced Coordination* (International Monetary Fund, 2012) ch 6.

18 International Monetary Fund, 'An EU Framework for Cross-Border Crisis Management in the Banking Sector' European Commission Consultation <https://www.imf.org/external/np/eur/2010/pdf/012910.pdf>.

19 Hüpkes (n 5) 3.

20 Hüpkes (n 5) 3.

21 See, generally, Ioseliani, *The Legal Aspects of Bank Insolvency* (n 5).

22 International Monetary Fund, 'Resolution of Cross-Border Banks – A Proposed Framework for Enhanced Coordination' (Prepared by the Legal and Monetary and Capital Markets Departments) <www.imf.org/external/np/pp/eng/2010/061110.pdf > accessed 21 May 2020.

23 ibid.

24 The UNCITRAL Model Law has been adopted by 49 countries. United Nations, *Overview of the Status of UNCITRAL Conventions and Model Laws* (United Nations, 2022).

25 Rosalind Mason, 'Cross-Border Insolvency Law: Where Private International Law and Insolvency Law Meet' (2008) 28 Intl Insol Law.

26 As a matter of fact, domestic systems, and not only those in developing regimes, may lack sufficient tools to address the more complex and sophisticated business structures (known to date or that may emerge in the future), such as multinational enterprises. For further developments, *vide* I Mevorach, *Insolvency within Multinational Enterprise Groups* (OUP, 2009); I Mevorach, *The Future of Cross-Border Insolvency. Overcoming Biases and Closing Gaps* (OUP, 2018).

27 James HM Sprayregen and Gordon W Johnson, 'Social Protection: Pensions and Priorities. Weaving the Safety Net for an Aging Workforce in the New World of Globalisation (Comparative Lessons And Experience)' (Sixth Annual International Insolvency Conference) <https://www.iiiglobal.org/events/annual-conferences/>.

28 Kent Anderson, 'The Cross-Border Insolvency Paradigm: A Defense of the Modified Universal Approach Considering the Japanese Experience' (2000) 21 Uni Pa J Intl Law.

29 S Chandra Mohan, 'Cross-Border Insolvency Problems: Is the UNCITRAL Model Law the Answer?' (2012) 21 Intl Insol Rev 199.

30 Jamie Altman, 'A Test Case in International Bankruptcy Protocols: The Lehman Brothers Insolvency' (2011) 12 San Diego Intl Law J 463.

31 Corporate Law Economic Reform Program Proposals for Reform: Paper No. 8, *Cross-Border Insolvency: Promoting International Cooperation and Coordination* (Commonwealth of Australia, 2002).

32 Ron Harmer, 'Session II: What Has Been Done and What Is Proposed: Australia' (1995) 4 Intl Insol Rev 36.
33 Mohan (n 29).
34 Ian F Fletcher, *The Law of Insolvency* (4th edn, Sweet & Maxwell Ltd, 2009).
35 Jay Lawrence Westbrook, 'An Empirical Study of the Implementation in the United States of the Model Law on Cross Border Insolvency'' (2013) 87 Am Bank Law J.
36 Felicity Deane and Rosalind Mason, 'The UNCITRAL Model Law on Cross-border Insolvency and the Rule of Law: Cross Border Insolvency and the Rule of Law' (2016) 25 Intl Insol Rev.
37 Mohan (n 29).
38 United Nations Commission on International Trade Law, *UNCITRAL Model Law on Cross-Border Insolvency with Guide to Enactment and Interpretation* (United Nations Publication, 13 January 2021).
39 JA Barrett, 'Various Legislative Attempts with Respect to Bankruptcies Involving More Than One Country: IV, UNCITRAL' (1998) 3(3) Tx Intl Law J 561.
40 United Nations Commission On International Trade Law, *UNCITRAL Model Law on Cross-Border Insolvency with Guide to Enactment and Interpretation* <https://uncitral.un.org/sites/uncitral.un.org/files/media-documents/uncitral/en/1997-model-law-insol-2013-guide-enactment-e.pdf> accessed 13 January 2021.
41 United Nations Commission On International Trade Law, *UNCITRAL Model Law on Cross-Border Insolvency with Guide to Enactment* (United Nations Publication, 12 November 2020).
42 In accordance with Article 2 of UNCITRAL Model Law of Cross-Border Insolvency. United Nations Commission on International Trade Law, *UNCITRAL Model Law on Cross-Border Insolvency with Guide to Enactment and Interpretation* (United Nations Publication, 14 May 2022).
43 According to Article 1, Paragraph 2 of UNCITRAL Model Law of Cross-Border Insolvency. United Nations Commission on International Trade Law (n 42).
44 United Nations Commission on International Trade Law, 'UNCITRAL Model Law on Cross-Border Insolvency: The Judicial Perspective' (July 2011) <https://uncitral.un.org/en/texts/insolvency/explanatorytexts/cross-border_insolvency/judicial_perspective> accessed 4 January 2021.
45 Barrett (n 39) 561.
46 Bob Wessels, *International Cooperation in Bankruptcy and Insolvency Matters* (OUP, 2009).
47 Claudia Tobler, 'Managing Failure in the New Global Economy: The U.N.C.I.T.R.A.L. Model Law on Cross-Border Insolvency' (1999) 96 Tx Law Rev 383.
48 Ronald J Silverman, 'Advances in Cross-Border Insolvency Cooperation: The UNCITRAL Model Law On Cross-Border Insolvency' (2015) 6 ILSA J Intl Comp Law 266.
49 Rami Borai, *Cross-Border Corporate Insolvency: A Modest Proposal for an Enhanced International Approach* (Queen Mary-University of London, 2009).
50 Paul H Zumbro, 'Cross-Border Insolvencies and International Protocols – an Imperfect but Effective Tool' (2010) 11 Bus Law Intl 158.
51 ibid.
52 Wessels, *International Cooperation in Bankruptcy and Insolvency Matters* (n 46).
53 Sefriani, 'Ineffectiveness of the Law on Cross Insolvensi Uncitral Model' (2017) 8 Yustisia Jurnal Hukum – Indonesia Islamic University 38.
54 Jenny Clift, *Cross-Border Insolvency: A Commentary on the UNCITRAL Model Law* (Global Business Publishing, 2006).
55 Steven J Arsenault, 'Leaping Over the Great Wall: Examining Cross-Border Insolvency in China Under the Chinese Corporate Bankruptcy Law' (2011) 2 Intl Comp L Rev 1.

56 Peter Millet, ‘Cross-Border Insolvency: The Judicial Approach’ (1997) 6 Intl Insol Rev 99.

57 Although banks might be excluded from this scope, there is opportunity to get them to participate in a planning proceeding, see Article 18 of the UNCITRAL Model Law on Enterprise Group Insolvency (MLEGI). See also para 37 of the Guide to enactment on the MLEGI.

58 United Nations Commission on International Trade Law (n 42).

59 Michael Krimminger, *Deposit Insurance and Bank Insolvency in a Changing World: Synergies & Challenges* (International Monetary Fund Conference, 2004) <www.imf.org/external/np/leg/sem/2004/cdmfl/eng/mk.pdf> accessed 14 May 2022.

Postscript: (Re-)Balancing the Priorities of Bank Insolvency Law in Developing Economies

This closing segment of the book is mercifully brief. It is a further reflection on the priorities and principles of bank insolvency law in developing economies. At the risk of stating the obvious, the outcomes of bank insolvency proceedings (and, by extension, the effectiveness or confidence of stakeholders in bank insolvency law) will turn on the construction of these priorities and principles. It is useful to recall some of the key objectives of bank resolution regimes highlighted throughout this book, and to juxtapose it with the question of divergent priorities of stakeholder interests identified in the prologue to this text. While the objectives of bank resolution regimes include rescue or restoration of the insolvent bank – through or outside early intervention mechanisms, orderly winding-up (or 'wind-down') of the bank, and effective cross-border cooperation and coordination in cross-border insolvencies, questions of priority of interest in the enactment of the resolution or insolvency procedure might include: prioritisation of creditor interest; rescue or rehabilitation of the distressed bank; and protection of the financial ecosystem.

A useful starting point for regulators and enactors of the bank insolvency regime in these jurisdictions is that these priorities are not necessarily mutually exclusive – at least not when they are considered on a case-by-case basis. For example, by promoting rescue or rehabilitation of the distressed bank, the regime could also achieve protections of systemic stability and, possibly, safeguarding of the interests of creditors who may be able to recoup their debt following a typical debt composition arrangement. Similarly, prioritisation of creditor interests, such as those of depositor-creditors,[1] might protect the financial ecosystem and aid a rescue of the whole or part of the ailing bank by precluding a run on the banks. Thus, rather than electing between these priorities, the prudent course for policy-makers in enacting bank insolvency law may be to equip regulators or officeholders with a robust resolution toolkit that could be deployed in the exercise of their best commercial judgement to achieve the optimum outcome or priority as the case and wider economic circumstances demand.

A further point is that experience has shown that the order of these priorities may evolve. This book has already discussed a paradigm shift in the legal regime governing bank insolvency from the satisfaction of creditors' interests or individual resolution to a more collective regime centred on public interest considerations.[2] This is hardly unique to bank insolvency law. For in ordinary corporate insolvency law, we have also seen a transmutation in ideology from a creditor-centred regime to one that is now fixated on the rescue ideology as is evidenced by the number of rescue regimes in insolvency legislation that are available to distressed business in different jurisdictions.[3] Such transitions in legislative priority are often driven by change in macroeconomic conditions and the response of market participants to such change. Thus, an effective bank insolvency law in developing economies should be flexible enough to assimilate a *volte face* in the ordering of these priorities. In this context, it is also useful to point out that, without prejudice to the well-founded concerns of systemic stability and rescue, there is no reason to discard or neglect the role of winding-up or liquidation (which is largely titled towards collective realisation of individual creditor claims) in the effective resolution of bank insolvencies. In appropriate cases, particularly where the bank is insolvent and without a viable business, liquidations possess creative-destructive value that could protect economic stability via an orderly and efficient exit of the distressed entity from the market and recycling of assets back into the economy by way of distribution of available assets to creditors.[4]

A final point here concerns rescue or rehabilitation of distressed banks. We have already seen that, through the use of early intervention mechanisms, there is marked preference for the bank resolution regime to be deployed timely, at an early stage and before the bank is actually insolvent.[5] Again, a parallel may be drawn in this respect with the introduction of preventive restructuring tools in ordinary insolvency proceedings in other jurisdictions.[6] Timing is critical to the effectiveness of the tools in corporate and bank insolvency contexts. If the question is whether to rescue banks outside of insolvency (early intervention) or to rescue within insolvency (for example, via bank administration proceedings), the vote ought to go to orchestrating a resolution of the bank's financial position outside of formal insolvency proceedings and before it is commercially insolvent. The reasons for this choice include the fact that, despite the global embrace of the rescue ideology in insolvency proceedings, many market players are still rational and apathetic enough to distrust insolvent entities or engage with them economically in a meaningful manner. Thus, value maximisation, which is critical to rescue, might be difficult to achieve in formal insolvency proceedings. Moreover, timely pre-insolvency intervention might preclude the bank from breaching covenants in events of default clauses in their commercial agreements that may be connected with the occurrence of an insolvency event or commencement of insolvency proceedings. This could reduce the bank's liabilities and cost of resolution process while enhancing the prospects of rescue or financial outcomes of other creditors. After all, *a stitch in time saves nine . . . and more than a dime.*

Kayode Akintola

Notes

1 A palpable concern of the bank resolution regime as seen in varied deposit insurance/protection schemes examined in this book and the FSB, 'Key Attributes of Effective Resolution Regimes for Financial Institutions' (15 October 2014) <www.fsb.org/wp-content/uploads/r_141015.pdf> accessed 30 April 2022.

2 See the discussions on Bank Insolvency Law in Kenya in ch 5 above. See also B Wessels and M Haentjens, 'Three Paradigm Shifts in Recent Bank Insolvency Law' (2016) 31 J Int Bus Law Rev 396–400.

3 For a discussion of this point in English Law, see *Powdrill v Watson & Anor (Paramount Airways Ltd)* [1995] 2 AC 394 at 441–42 and 445C-D (Lord Browne-Wilkinson); *Re Carluccio's Limited* [2020] EWHC 886 (Ch). See also, K Akintola, 'Pro-Commerce Outlooks: The Bane of English Corporate Insolvency Law?' (2021) 34 Insol Intl 6–9.

4 On the subject of 'creative-destruction', see, generally, JA Schumpeter, *Capitalism, Socialism and Democracy* (Harper & Brothers, 1942) 81–86, ch VII; CW Frost, 'Bankruptcy Redistributive Policies and the Limits of the Judicial Process' (1995) 74 NCLR 75–139. Liquidation may also promote business (not 'corporate') rescue through business and/asset sales.

5 FSB (n 1) Key Attribute 4.1.

6 For examples in English and EU Law, see Insolvency Act 1986, Part A1; Companies Act 2006, Part 26A; The European Restructuring Directive – Directive (EU) 2019/1023. See also G McCormack, *The European Restructuring Directive* (Edward Elgar, 2021).

Index

Note: Page numbers in **bold** indicate a table on the corresponding page. Page numbers followed by "n" indicate a note.

For Product Safety Concerns and Information please contact our EU
representative GPSR@taylorandfrancis.com
Taylor & Francis Verlag GmbH, Kaufingerstraße 24, 80331 München, Germany

www.ingramcontent.com/pod-product-compliance
Ingram Content Group UK Ltd.
Pitfield, Milton Keynes, MK11 3LW, UK
UKHW020140200926
475702UK00005B/830

* 9 7 8 0 3 6 7 7 1 1 8 6 3 *